The Faith
of the
Pilgrims

Other Books by the Author

The Pilgrim Way
Pilgrim House by the Sea
Thanksgiving Day
They Stand Invincible: Men Who Are Reshaping
   Our World
With One Voice: Prayers from Around the World
Sky Pioneer: The Story of Igor I. Sikorsky
They Dared to Live
They Did Something About It
They Work for Tomorrow
They Dare to Believe
Discovery, A Guidebook in Living
A Boy's Book of Prayers
The Ascending Trail
Christian Conquests
Builders of a New World
The Great Empire of Silence
The Fifth Race

The Faith
of the
Pilgrims

)(°)(°)(°)(°)(° *An American Heritage*

Robert M. Bartlett

A PILGRIM BOOK
from
UNITED CHURCH PRESS
New York/Philadelphia

Library of Congress Cataloging in Publication Data

Bartlett, Robert Merrill, 1898-
　　The faith of the Pilgrims.

　　(A Pilgrim book)
　　Includes bibliographical references and index.
　　1.　Pilgrims (New Plymouth Colony)　2.　Puritans.
3.　Massachusetts—History—New Plymouth, 1620-1691.
I.　Title.
F68.B26　　　974.4'82　　　77-16308
ISBN 0-8298-0337-8

United Church Press, 287 Park Avenue South
New York, New York 10010

To
my wife,
Sue Nuckols Bartlett

Contents

List of Illustrations   9
Preface   11
Introduction   13

List of Illustrations

The following illustrations appear in a group between pages 192–93:

Preface

This book is the result of research by one who has lived with the Pilgrim Story for forty years. I have studied the original writings of the Pilgrims as well as relevant works by leading historians and have done research in England, Holland, and America.

I have watched the seasons come and go from a gambrel-roof house built by Pilgrim Robert Bartlett in 1660. When winter drives the winged creatures from the beaches and a northeaster foams the sea, I think of the shallop maneuvering the first passengers from the *Mayflower* onto the Rock, as a somber landscape presented "a weatherbeaten face." When the shadbushes blossom and the herring run upstream to spawn, I envision the fifty-one survivors gathering about Town Brook to wash their clothes and feast their eyes on the budding trees after that first fearful winter that claimed one half of their company.

I can feel their presence near at hand on warm summer days, when they would reap their barley, oats, and flax. When the swamp maples turn red and bayberries are gathered, and ducks and geese call from the sky, I recall their plantation village, the shocked corn stored within the stockade, pumpkins and squash piled close by, beans and onions hung up to dry—the setting for their harvest thanksgiving.

I feel that I have received some insight into their faith and the abiding influence of their religion. I have sensed it in town meeting as citizens spoke their minds as free people, and after debate took a vote and made a decision. I have been conscious of the survival of their ideals as I worshiped in meetinghouses established by their children that not only provide charm for the landscape but also give proof of the eternal need of humanity for divine guidance. In colleges across this vast land I have been reminded of these Pilgrims who honored the Bible, books, and learning. When I stand on Burial Hill, looking out over Plymouth harbor and the events of 358 years, when I watch the unending line of millions of people year after year who pause reverently by Plymouth Rock, I sense something more than I find in court and church records, in inventories and letters. These first settlers emerge before me as living people who have a story to tell, if we will let them speak for themselves. I am using their own words from primary documents as much as possible.

The epic of what these "little people" achieved on their own, with the help of their God, has not been surpassed in the history of this country.

Robert M. Bartlett
Plymouth, Massachusetts

Introduction

I charge you before God and his blessed angels that
you follow me no further than you have seen me
follow Christ. If God reveal anything to you by any
other instrument of his, be as ready to receive it as
ever you were to receive any truth from my ministry.
For I am confident the Lord has more truth and light
yet to break forth out of his Holy Word.

The Lutherans cannot be drawn to go beyond
what Luther saw, for whatever part of God's will he
had further imparted and revealed to Calvin, they
[the Lutherans] will rather die than embrace it. And
so you see the Calvinists stick fast where he left them.
This is a misery much to be lamented; for though
these men were precious shining lights in their times,
yet God had not revealed his whole will to them. And
were they now living, they would be as ready and
willing to embrace further light as that they had
received.

—John Robinson[1]

The Pilgrims were a unique group in the Puritan movement which sought to reform the Established Church. The
Puritans spearheaded the Reformation in England. Henry
VIII (1509-47) has been credited with making the break
with the Church of Rome. However, he was interested
only in political control of the church, not in its reform.

The pope had given him the title of "Defender of the Faith" because of his stand against Luther. The king persuaded Parliament to make him "Supreme Lord of the Church of England." He then raided the monasteries and appropriated their wealth.[2] People reasoned, "Better the king than the pope." Unwittingly, Henry encouraged progress in religion by publishing the Great Bible in the native tongue and by inviting Erasmus from Holland to Cambridge University, where Erasmus promoted study of the New Testament in Greek and a new approach to Christian scholarship. These steps helped lay the foundations of a new ecclesiastical order which could be harmonized only with the Protestant outlook.[3]

Under Edward VI (1547-53), the ten-year-old son of Henry VIII and Jane Seymour, Archbishop Cranmer made efforts to upgrade the lamentably inadequate education of the clergy. The *Book of Common Prayer* was revised. Martin Bucer of Strasbourg was brought to Cambridge to lecture in theology, and Paulus Fagius came to teach Hebrew.

"Bloody" Mary Tudor (1553-58), the daughter of Henry VIII and Catherine of Aragon, followed the ten-day reign of Lady Jane Grey. She married Philip II of Spain and set out to restore Roman Catholicism. Her persecution of the Puritans drove her people from loyalty to Rome. She determined to exterminate the reformers, and executed nearly three hundred of the foremost men in the country. Many scholars fled to Europe, forming close ties with Reformation leaders in Holland, Switzerland, Germany, and France, which eventually strengthened reform in the homeland.

Under Elizabeth I (1558-1603) the Puritans regained some favor, but this daughter of Henry VIII and Anne Boleyn, like her father, loved pomp and power more than the Christian faith. The church was made a department of state. "There should be no conventicles and chapels, to be nurseries of sedition."[4] Elizabeth disliked the Roman Catholics, who considered her a bastard, and the Puritans, who demanded an independent church. She had herself named "Supreme Governor of the Church." Puritans pushed for reforms in Parliament as well as in religion. A royal commission was set up to handle ecclesiastical affairs, and Elizabeth continued to restrain liberals and to appoint uneducated and unworthy men to church livings.

A basic concern of the Puritans was reform of the ministry. Church livings were passed out by the crown and the bishops with little or no regard for intellectual or spiritual qualifications. *A Parte of a Register* and *Seconde Parte of a Register*, issued in the reign of Elizabeth, pointed out the distressing fact that there were many incompetent clergy in the parishes. "Lewd," "of scandalous life," "a drunkard," "a grievous swearer," "a bad liver," "a gamester," "a pot companion," "a common ale-house haunter and gamester," "his conversation is mostly in hounds," "a very careless person, he had a childe by a maid since he was instituted and inducted"—these were some of the descriptions of the clergy at the time.[5]

The queen and her archbishop resisted efforts of reformers to worship on their own. George Cotton was cast into prison without trial for twenty-seven months because he listened to a reading from the Bible by the Puritan John Greenwood in the home of a friend. A law was passed in 1593 that any person who tried to dissuade anyone from attending the parish church, either by speech or by pen, should be committed to prison until he submitted.[6]

Intellectuals John Greenwood and Henry Barrowe, who dared to separate from the Established Church, were hunted down and locked up for years until they were finally hanged on April 6, 1593. John Penry, another Separatist, had been a classmate of William Brewster, who was later to become elder of the Pilgrim church, when they studied at Peterhouse College, Cambridge. Penry was arrested by Archbishop Whitgift for his agitation in Wales and his recantation was demanded. He replied, "Truth, being found, hold it we must, defend it we must." A few days after the execution of Barrowe and Greenwood, Penry was hanged, drawn, and quartered.

It was in such an atmosphere of discontent with the state of the ministry, the totalitarianism of the church hierarchy, and the efforts to control religious expression and assembly that the early secret meetings of the Pilgrims came into being in a few small hamlets in East Anglia, where Nottinghamshire, Yorkshire, and Lincolnshire converge.

Efforts to organize these freedom-seekers continued under James I (1603-25). The Pilgrims were hopeful that an era of tolerance might dawn under this young king who came out of "the Scotch mist," where he had been tutored by Presbyterians. Petitions and appeals led to the Hampton Court Conference of 1604. After parading his knowledge, James ended hope of conciliation with these words: "If this be all your party hath to say, I will make them conform themselves, or else I will harry them out of the land, or else do worse."[7]

During the period under Elizabeth and James, clandestine gatherings were held in East Anglia villages. Attending the meetings were independent-minded farmers, artisans, merchants, and a few Cambridge intellectuals who sought freedom to discuss the Christian religion and the right to worship according to conscience.

This area had become a center of liberal thought. Three Cambridge-trained ministers emerged as leaders: John Smyth of Gainsborough, Richard Clyfton of Babworth, and John Robinson of Sturton le Steeple. They carried the reform concepts of Cambridge University to these country parishes to the north and criticized the hierarchy of the church, the rule by bishops and priests under the dominance of the royal family, the incompetence of untrained and undedicated clergy, and the neglect of parishioners in not teaching them the Bible and the principles of Christianity.

Early meetings were held in Old Hall in Gainsborough under the protection of William Heckman and his wife, Rose, daughter of Sir William Lodge, with the support of John Smyth, the local vicar, "a man of able gifts and a good preacher." Smyth had been deposed as "a factious man" from his church in nearby Lincoln in 1602, due to his Separatist leanings.[8] In his new parish of Gainsborough he was soon in trouble again, and he decided to flee to Holland with a few of his followers.

During this period reform-minded people journeyed to All Saints' Church in Babworth to hear Richard Clyfton, an able preacher who was reprimanded by his bishop and deprived of his living in 1605. One of his admirers was William Brewster, leading citizen of Scrooby, five miles away, who had studied at Cambridge, served under Queen Elizabeth in the foreign service, and lived in the London court. Brewster was postmaster, bailiff, and manager of the estate of the archbishop of York and he opened the great manor house to Pilgrim meetings. William Bradford recorded that the reformers "ordinarily met at his [Brewster's] house on ye Lord's day . . . and with great love he entertained them when they came, making provision for them to his great charge."[9]

Brewster invited the homeless Clyfton to come with his family to Scrooby, live in the manor house, and preach to the company of seekers. Brewster also knew John Robinson, born in nearby Sturton le Steeple in 1576, the son of a prosperous yeoman family. He was familiar with Robinson's career as a student and teacher at Corpus

Christi College in Cambridge. Robinson had married Bridget White, who came from a respected Nottinghamshire household, in 1603. At that time he lost his post as fellow and dean of Corpus Christi and took a position at St. Andrew's Church in Norwich. Here he decided to follow his Separatist leanings and made an open break with the Established Church, which led to his dismissal and his return to Sturton le Steeple. Brewster brought him and his family to Scrooby, where he worked with Clyfton with the growing congregation.

There were initially two groups of Pilgrims, one in Scrooby and one in Gainsborough, but travel was tedious and royal spies checked continually on their movements. In 1606 the Scrooby congregation was formed. After consenting to the covenant, the members chose Clyfton as pastor, Robinson as teacher, and Brewster as elder. A number of men and women who later proved leaders in Holland and America were part of this band. William Bradford joined as a teenager. John Carver, a well-to-do businessman, was to serve as a deacon in Leyden and as the first governor of Plymouth Colony.

The ecclesiastical authorities launched a vigorous effort to wipe out the Scrooby radicals in 1607. A number were threatened with arrest. Brewster paid a $3,000 fine to protect friends. He was branded "a very dangerous schismatical Separatist, Brownist, and an irreligious subject." Brewster and his associates realized they would soon be imprisoned and so planned to follow their friend John Smyth to Holland.[10]

William Bradford later recorded that about sixty citizens had been arrested for their religious beliefs, "allowing them neither meat, drink, fire or lodging, nor suffering any whose hearts the Lord would stir up for their relief, to have any access to them, so as they complained that no felons, traitors, nor murderers in the land were thus dealt with."[11] Spies were employed by the crown to engage them in conversation in an effort to trick them into saying something that could be used as evidence against them.

> After these things they could not long continue in any peaceable condition, but were hunted and persecuted on every side, so as their former afflictions were but as flea-bitings in comparison of these which now came upon them. For some were taken and clapped in prison, others had their houses beset and watched day and night, and hardly escaped their hands; and the most were fain to flee and leave their homes and habitations, and the means of their livelihood.[12]

The first effort to escape from the port of Boston in 1607 failed, and their leaders were locked up in the Guild Hall there for over a month. Their second attempt in 1608, from the Humber River in the north, succeeded, and on various ships their company landed at length in Amsterdam. They accepted no aid from the Dutch, as did some of the English refugees, insisting that they would support themselves with whatever jobs they could find. They made friendly contact with the Ancient Brethren, a Separatist church led by Francis Johnson, a fiery reformer, but they were disappointed by the controversy in his flock. Unhappy over the theological discord, they loaded their scant possessions on barges and moved on to Leyden, where they were welcomed by the magistrates of that city.

Richard Clyfton chose to remain in Amsterdam along with John Smyth. John Robinson had by this time emerged as the spiritual leader of the group. His followers built a meetinghouse and a colony of cottages called the Green Gate across the narrow Kloksteeg street from St. Peter's Dutch Reformed Church and some three blocks from the leading Protestant university in Europe. A faculty of distinguished scholars had been gathered at the new institution, founded in 1575 as a reward to the citizens of Leyden for their resistance during the long war with Spain. Robinson lectured at the university and Brewster tutored students in English.

The Pilgrims had moved into a tolerant atmosphere supported by the university and the civic leaders. In 1581 the Leyden magistrates had declared: "Liberty has always consisted in uttering our sentiments freely; and the contrary has always been considered the characteristic of tyranny. Reason, which is the adversary of all tyrants, teaches us that truth can be as little restrained as light."[13] Other freedom-seekers had preceded the Pilgrims to Leyden from Spain, Portugal, and France. It was a welcome liberation for those who had been considered criminal outcasts.

Their twelve years of exposure to the broad religious views, the popular education, and the political democracy of the Dutch stretched the outlook of the Pilgrims. As they learned Dutch and French and mingled with continental Protestants, Roman Catholics, Jews, and freethinkers, they grew beyond provincial Church of England attitudes and found themselves practicing intercommunion with other Christians, like the Huguenots, Walloons, and Dutch Reformed, who had been aliens to them but now were friendly neighbors. They embarked on a new course toward universal thinking, led by John Robinson, who was a pioneer in religious fellowship.

As a Cambridge professor and the author of significant books, Robinson enjoyed friendship with a number of Dutch intellectuals. He entertained English scholars like Ames, Parker, and Jacobs, who were recognized at the university. He was friendly with John Polyander, the theologian; Francis Junius, regent of the university; John Hornbeck, theologian; Antonius Walaeus, translator of the

Bible and an authority on Aristotle; and Festus Hommius, rector of the theological college.

The encounter of the Pilgrims with James I, who spied on them while they were in Holland, minimized chances of favorable consideration of their plan to move to the New World. Their king had formed a firm dislike for these rebels.

Independent of outside support and sustained by their own labors in an alien country, the Pilgrims proved that they were capable of facing hardship and surviving. Holland was a school of preparation for the still greater adventure of removal to the New World and the founding of the first self-supporting colony there. Upheld by their religious faith, they were emboldened to venture farther and settle in New England.

They were pleased with the friendship of the Dutch, who praised them for their diligence and honesty, and as happy in Holland as people could be in an adopted land. But they wanted a place of their own, where they could preserve their native tongue, culture, and beliefs. Their future in Leyden was fraught with uncertainties. The antagonistic policies of James I made it impossible for them to return home. The Thirty Years' War threatened to embroil all Europe. The Twelve-Year Truce between the Netherlands and Spain would end in 1621. They endeavored to think of "a timely remedy."

There was some talk of moving to Guiana in South America, but that did not appear feasible. Dutch friends suggested that they might settle along the Hudson River in New Amsterdam, but the government could give them no financial support. Their own king looked upon them as heretics and they could expect no sanction or subsidy from the homeland such as had been extended to the Virginia Colony. The Pilgrims therefore set out to find their own backers. After extensive negotiations, a group called the London Merchant Adventurers offered funds at high interest and stiff terms that required settlers to work on a communal, nonprofit basis for seven years until they had paid their debt. They protested against the harsh contract, but could not secure more humane treatment.[14]

The first expedition would be in the charge of Elder Brewster, and certain chosen people would accompany him. Robinson and the others would come later. It was agreed that "those who went should be an absolute church of themselves, as well as those that stayed, seeing in such a dangerous voyage, and a removal to such a distance, it might come to pass they should (for the body of them) never meet again in this world." It was also planned that those who remained would cross over "as soon as they could."[15]

Through private enterprise they bought the *Speedwell*, and the first advance contingent set sail on July 22, 1620 from Delfshaven, the seaport near Leyden. This small vessel was to join the larger *Mayflower*, which they rented, and the two ships were to sail together from Southampton. The *Speedwell* proved unseaworthy and, after an extensive delay, was eliminated. Some had to return to Leyden and to villages in England. The rest of the *Speedwell* passengers crowded aboard the ninety-foot square-rigger, the ancient wine ship called the *Mayflower*. The fact that the little craft carried 102 passengers and a crew of 25 to 30 forms a record as spectacular as the fact that she survived the rough seas on a voyage of sixty-six days with seasickness and scurvy raging and no one sure of their destination. Only one Pilgrim, William Butten, a youthful servant of Dr. Samuel Fuller, died, but Oceanus Hopkins was born to replace him. One hundred and two made it to Plymouth.

When the Pilgrims crept into the harbor of Provincetown on November 20, seeking a haven from another storm, they were without a clear-cut patent for a New England settlement and did not know where they were. They hoped that they were north of the boundaries of Virginia, so they might be free from the dominance of James I. They were exhausted, undernourished, and near panic. There was unrest among some of the passengers and "mutinous speeches" were heard, so the wiser heads drew up the Mayflower Compact before they landed. It was signed by forty-one male settlers and indentured workers as the political basis for their settlement. They then elected Deacon John Carver as their governor for a one-year term. He died in the spring, and William Bradford was elected in his place.

After exploring Cape Cod for a month, they decided to go ashore at Plymouth. On December 21 they anchored the *Mayflower* in the harbor and the shallop carried an advance company to the Rock on the sand near Town Brook. On Christmas Day they cut down the first tree to make the first planks to frame the first cottage at Plymouth Plantation. So moves the Pilgrim epic which has held the admiration of Americans through the centuries.[16]

CHAPTER 1

People of Providence

All great and honourable actions are accompanied with great difficulties, and must be both enterprised and overcome with answerable courage. It was granted the dangers were great, but not desperate; the difficulties were many, but not invincible . . . and all of them, through the help of God, by fortitude and patience, might either be borne or overcome.

—William Bradford[1]

The Pilgrims were motivated by a sense of Divine Providence that sustained them in times of testing and adversity. Bradford explained the agony of decision in planning their secret move from England to Holland:

Being thus constrained to leave their native soil and country, their lands and livings, and all their friends and familiar acquaintance, it was much; and thought marvelous by many. But to go into a country they knew not but by hearsay, where they must learn a new language and get their livings they knew not

how, it being a dear place and subject to the miseries
of war, it was by many thought an adventure almost
desperate; a case intolerable and a misery worse than
death. Especially seeing they were not acquainted
with trades nor traffic (by which that country doth
subsist) but had only been used to a plain country
life and the innocent trade of husbandry. But those
things did not dismay them, though they did sometimes trouble them; for their desires were set on the
ways of God and to enjoy His ordinances; but they
rested on His providence, and knew Whom they had
believed.[2]

Some ten years later John Robinson and William
Brewster wrote from Holland in 1617 to Sir Edwin Sandys
in England, in their effort to find backers for their vision-
ary project—their journey to the New World:

1 We verily believe and trust the Lord is with us,
   unto whom and whose service we have given ourselves in many trials, and that He will graciously
   prosper our endeavours according to the simplicity
   of our hearts therein.

2 We are well weaned from the delicate milk of our
   mother-country, and inured to the difficulties of a
   strange and hard land, which yet in a great part we
   have by patience overcome.

3 The people are, for the body of them, industrious
   and frugal, we think we may safely say, as any company or people in the world.

4 We are knit together as a body in a most strict and
   sacred bond and covenant of the Lord, of the viola-
   tion whereof we make great conscience, and by
   virtue whereof we do hold ourselves straitly tied to
   all care of each other's goods and of the whole by
   every one and so mutually.

5 Lastly, it is not with us as with other men, whom small things can discourage, or small discontentments cause to wish themselves at home again. We know our entertainment in England and Holland. We shall much prejudice both our arts and means by removal; who, if we should be driven to return, we should not hope to recover our present helps and comforts, neither indeed look ever, for ourselves, to attain unto the like in any other place during our lives, which are drawing toward their periods.[3]

Before the departure of the *Speedwell* from Delfshaven in the summer of 1620, "they had a day of solemn humiliation." Pastor Robinson preached on the story of the exile Ezra, who had led a contingent of Jews back to Jerusalem from the land of Persia. Ezra 8:21, RSV: "Then I proclaimed a fast there, at the river Ahava, that we might humble ourselves before our God, to seek from him a straight way for ourselves, our children, and all our goods." The pastor charged them to begin their enterprise in God's presence, to journey with him, seeking divine guidance rather than dependence upon physical force or violence. Following this message "the rest of the time was spent in pouring out prayers to the Lord with great fervency, mixed with abundance of tears."[4]

William Bradford wrote of the bold plan to depart from Holland for the wilderness of the New World:

It was answered, that all great and honourable actions are accompanied with great difficulties, and must be both enterprised and overcome with answerable courage. It was granted the dangers were great, but not desperate; the difficulties were many, but not invincible. For though these were many of them likely, yet they were not certain. It might be sundry of the things feared might never befall, others by provident care and the use of good means might in a great measure be prevented; and all of them, through the help of God, by fortitude and patience, might either be borne or overcome.[5]

Bradford mentions the religious impetus which was part of the motivation that turned their minds to the New World:

Lastly (and which was not least), a great hope and inward zeal they had of laying some good foundation, or at least to make some way thereunto, for the propagating and advancing the gospel of the kingdom of Christ in those remote parts of the world; yea, though they should be but stepping stones unto others for the performing of so great a work.[6]

Other factors, in addition to religious motivation, entered into decisions to set out for the New World. There were economic, political, and social limitations and frustrations in the homeland that stirred discontent. Restlessness and anxiety crept over England during the latter days of Elizabeth's reign, increasing under the Stuart kings James I and Charles I. There was disaffection with the church, and poverty, unemployment, and food shortages. The Stuarts brought increased burdens on the people due to their extravagance and unwise military moves. There were grievances that troubled the English and impelled them to consider the venture to America. This unrest encouraged colonizing from 1607 to 1660.[7]

Deacon Robert Cushman, in his address at Plymouth Plantation on December 12, 1621, emphasized the religious core of the enterprise: "And you, my loving friends, the adventurers to this Plantation, as your care has been, first to settle religion here, before either profit or popularity, so I pray you, go on to do it much more."[8]

Following the General Sickness of the first winter in Plymouth, when 51 of the 102 Pilgrims died, Bradford wrote:

> The spring now approaching, it pleased God the mortality began to cease amongst them, and the sick and lame recovered apace, which put as [it] were new life into them, though they had borne their sad affliction with much patience as I think any people could do. But it was the Lord who upheld them, and had beforehand prepared them; many having long borne the yoke, yea from their youth.[9]

He testified frequently to the spiritual support that the Pilgrims received in their tribulations:

> What could sustain them but the Spirit of God and His grace? May not and ought not the children of these fathers rightly say: "Our fathers were Englishmen which came over this great ocean, and were ready to perish in the wilderness; but they cried unto the Lord, and He heard their voice and looked on their adversity." Let them therefore praise the Lord because He is good: and His mercies endure forever.[10]

When word was received in Plymouth that Pastor John Robinson had died suddenly on March 1, 1625, as plans were underway to bring him from Leyden to Plymouth, Bradford wrote of the grief and perplexity that hung like a dark cloud over the colony:

> It is a marvel it did not wholly discourage them and sink them. But they gathered up their spirits, and the Lord so helped them, whose work they had in hand, as now when they were at lowest [ebb] they began to rise again, and being stripped in a manner of all human helps and hopes. He brought things about otherwise,

in His divine providence as they were not only upheld and sustained, but their proceedings both honoured and imitated by others.[11]

Captain Edward Johnson, in his *Wonder Working Providence*, spoke of the divine guidance that accompanied Plymouth and the beginnings of New England in the task of building "the most glorious edifice of Mount Sion in a Wilderness."[12]

Nathaniel Morton, Bradford's nephew, wrote his generation's interpretation of God's interest in the Pilgrim Story: *New Englands Memoriall: Or a Brief Relation of the Most Memorable and Remarkable Passages of the Providence of God, with Special Reference to the First Colony Thereof, Called New Plymouth* (1669). The college press in Cambridge printed the book for a fee of twenty pounds of corn and a barrel of beef.

The concept of the New World as a wilderness which awaited development by the Pilgrims is expanded by Peter N. Carroll, who explains the sense of commission they believed they had received from God. They had been called to settle uncultivated areas and build and plant a new community. This faith in mission helped to sustain them during their sacrifices and hardships.[13] The adventure of crossing the ocean with its perilous voyage and precarious landing brought the little band together in the feeling that they were a special company as they faced the unknown. They were bound together in a compact with God and with one another, as Israel was with Jehovah.

As Bradford retold the harrowing story of the struggle to fell the trees, hew the logs, adze beams, split shingles, frame the cottages, sow the grain, hunt, fish, battle disease, endure hunger, pay their debts, and keep praying, he wrote: "that their children may see with what difficulties their fathers wrestled, on going through these things, in the first beginnings: and how God brought them along, notwithstanding all their weaknesses and infirmities."[14]

The Pilgrims were lonely in the New World. During those twelve years in the Netherlands their hearts often ached with homesickness for the shores of England, for homesteads enlivened by the presence of kith and kin, for ancestral cottages and gardens, for fields and streams that once ministered to their happiness. They had to exert stoical control to resist the temptation to flee the Low Countries with their strange tongues and customs and the drudgery of menial labor and low wages, all for the sake of the right to defend the truth as they saw it, to worship their God in peace, and to be free from the control of despots. John Robinson gave voice to this acute heartache that he and his company suffered in Holland:

> Those who truly fear thee, and work righteousness, although constrained to live by leave in a foreign land, exiled from country, spoiled of goods, destitute of friends, few in number, and mean in condition, are for all that unto thee (O gracious God) nothing the less acceptable. Thou numberest all their wanderings, and puttest their tears into thy bottles. Are they not written in thy book? Towards thee, O Lord, are our eyes; confirm our hearts, and bend thine ear, and suffer not our feet to slip, or our face to be ashamed, O thou both just and merciful God.[15]

On the edge of the wilderness in Plymouth the traumatic shock of transportation to a new and more hostile environment caused the Pilgrims to look back with longing to the comforts of England. Even Holland, with its stern demands for self-support, was a land of luxury compared with the uncultivated wilds about them.

> Being thus passed the vast ocean, and a sea of troubles before in their preparation, they had now no friends

to welcome them nor inns to entertain or refresh their weatherbeaten bodies; no houses or much less towns to repair to, to seek for succour. . . . And for the season it was winter, and they that know the winters of that country know them to be sharp and violent, and subject to cruel and fierce storms, dangerous to travel to known places, much more to search out an unknown coast. Besides, what could they see but a hideous and desolate wilderness, full of wild beasts and wild men—and what multitudes there might be of them they knew not.[16]

Fear of the unknown, starvation, scurvy, Indians, and the cold would make the bravest of people homesick for the world they had left behind them. Bradford wrote:

For summer being done, all things stand upon them with a weatherbeaten face, and the whole country, full of woods and thickets represented a wild and savage hue. If they looked behind them, there was the mighty ocean, which they had passed and was now as a main bar and gulf to separate them from all the civil parts of the world. . . . What could now sustain them but the Spirit of God and His grace?[17]

Many a time in the blackness of the long nights, when hunger gnawed in their stomachs, when sickness was rampant, when fear clutched at their flickering hopes of success, how they must have longed for a bit of roast beef and Yorkshire pudding and the warmth of family and friends. Their God sustained them.

The months passed by as the settlers scratched the rocky soil to raise another harvest, built their fishing shallops and sailed them out to sea, and launched into fur-trading with their Indian neighbors. With more food and security, Bradford was able to write: "Meanwhile it pleased the Lord to give the Plantation peace and health and contented minds; and so to bless their labours as they had corn sufficient, and some to spare to others, with other food; neither ever had they any supply of food but what they first brought with them."[18] In 1623 he wrote to Robert Cushman, who was in England on a mission, that the Pilgrims "never felt the sweetness of the country till this year."[19]

They survived the "Great Hurricane" of August 1635. Isaac Allerton's pinnace was wrecked on the rocks off Cape Ann. The Rev. Peter Thatcher and the Rev. Jonathan Avery were on board with their families and were drowned with many others.[20]

In June 1638 a "great and fearful earthquake" shook the plantation

> with that violence as caused platters, dishes and such like things as stood upon shelves, to clatter and fall down. Yea, persons were afraid of the houses themselves. It so fell out that at the same time divers of the chief of this town were met together at one house, conferring with some friends that were upon their removal from the place, as if the Lord would hereby show the signs of His displeasure, in their shaking a-pieces and removals one from another.

The governor did not express his views on the theological implications of this near calamity, but he did quote from the Old Testament: "So powerful is the mighty hand of the Lord, as to make both the earth and sea to shake, and the mountains to tremble before him, when He pleases. And who can stay His hand?"[21] Bradford wrote:

> I cannot but here take occasion not only to mention but greatly to admire the marvelous providence of God. That not withstanding the many changes and hardships that these people went through, and the many enemies they had and difficulties they met

withal, that so many of them should live to very old age! It was not only this reverend man's [William Brewster] but many more of them did the like, some dying about and before this time and many still living, who attained to sixty years of age, and to sixty-five, divers to seventy and above, and some near eighty as he [Brewster] did. . . .[22]

What was it that upheld them? It was God's visitation that preserved their spirits, "they were persecuted, but not forsaken, cast down, but perished not . . ."[23]

Man lives not by bread alone. It is not by good and dainty fare, by peace and rest and heart's ease in enjoying the contentments and good things of this world only that preserves health and prolongs life.[24]

During the eventful decades, as he made entries in his journal, William Bradford maintained steadfast belief in Divine Providence. He lived in what Roger Williams called "wonderful, disputing and dissenting times." In addition to his encounter with this turmoil of ideas, he battled firsthand with the perils and pains of the struggle to survive in the American wilderness.

The faith that motivated Bradford to ally himself as a teenager with the unpopular Separatist congregation in Scrooby, under the rebuke of his relatives who threatened to disinherit him, survived through this momentous epoch until he was laid to rest with dignity and honor on Burial Hill in Plymouth. He was able to affirm for himself and his people: "But these things did not dismay them though they did sometimes trouble them; for their desires were set on the ways of God and to enjoy His ordinances; but they rested on His providence, and knew Whom they had believed."[25]

Thinking of the meetinghouse, where he had often

prayed and found strength, Bradford wrote prophetically: "Thus out of small beginnings greater things have been produced by God's hand who made all things of nothing, and gives being to all things that are; and, as one small candle may light a thousand, so the light here kindled hath shone unto many, yea in some sort to our whole nation."[26]

CHAPTER 2

An Intellectual Faith

Religion is the best thing, and the corruption of it the worst; neither hath greater mischief ever been found amongst men, Jews, Gentiles, or Christians, than that which hath marched under the flag of religion, either intended by the seduced, or pretended by the hypocrites.

—John Robinson[1]

William Bradford made it clear from the beginning of his journal, *Of Plymouth Plantation*, that he was presenting the record of a religion that was built on intellectual foundations. He sought

to have the right worship of God and discipline of Christ established in the church, according to the simplicity of the gospel, without the mixture of men's inventions; and to have and to be ruled by the laws of God's Word, dispensed in those officers, and by those officers of Pastors, Teachers and Elders, etc. according to the Scriptures.[2]

The nucleus of the Pilgrim congregation in England was a band of seekers who struggled to break through the hierarchy of organization, the maze of ritual and dogma, and the pretension of Christian piety that enmeshed the Church of England. They were radicals in the true sense of the word, probing to the roots to find the essentials amid the tangentials.

Their intellectual leaders were Cambridge scholars like John Smyth of Gainsborough, Richard Clyfton of Babworth, John Robinson of Cambridge, and William Brewster of Scrooby. They were fortunate to have men in their company like William Brewster, John Carver, William Bradford, Edward Winslow, Robert Cushman, Thomas Cushman, Samuel Fuller, Francis Jessop, Roger White, Nathaniel Morton, Thomas Willet, William Paddy, John Atwood, and Timothy Hatherly.

Bradford was a scholar. Although he never attended Cambridge, he had the earmarks of a university man. John Robinson and Elder Brewster saw the potential of this young orphan from a prominent family in nearby Austerfield and coached him in Latin, Greek, and Hebrew. He later turned to the study of Hebrew on his own, determined to read the Old Testament in the original. Judging by his journal, he must have also been tutored in religion and history, for he was familiar with the Bible and events of church history. He quoted Calvin, Zwingli, Beza, Farel, Whitgift, Pareus, Peter Martyr, Ridley, Bullinger, Naziansens, Henry Jacob, John Cotton, and Robert Baylie, and had a grasp on the significance of the Reformation in England and on the Continent.

Bradford was deeply religious and broad in outlook for his era, and he handled theological hot chestnuts with common sense. He was a practical person who, as governor, dealt daily with fur-trading, planting, harvesting, fishing, shipping, sessions of the Board of Assistants, the court, and the congregation. As a pupil of Professor Robinson, he seemed to be a kindred spirit, for he grasped and upheld his pastor's liberal outlook. It was from Robinson that Bradford absorbed a respect for learning and the open mind, accepting his precept expounded in Leyden: "I profess myself always one of them, who still desire to learn further, or better, what the good will of God is."[3]

The Pilgrim group had been brought into being in England through their common intellectual attack on the superstitions of the church. They repudiated accretions in ritual that had no justification in the Bible, ornamentations that had been introduced over the centuries that were extraneous, like bending the knee before taking communion, employing the sign of the cross before preaching a sermon, making the sign of the cross on the forehead of a baby before christening, using the ring in marriage, wearing vestments and surplices.[4] They insisted that these were malpractices that had collected like barnacles in Christian tradition.

Marriage, which had been exploited by the church, was removed from the manipulation of the clergy and handled by the magistrates. John Robinson told his Leyden flock that marriage should not be the responsibility of the church, subject to the control of the priests, but rather it should be handled by the state and civic officials.[5]

The Pilgrims took over the Dutch practice of marriage by civil authority and continued it in Plymouth until 1692, the year they were absorbed into the Massachusetts Bay Colony. This secularization of the marriage rite brought Edward Winslow before Archbishop Laud, when he returned to England in 1635 on a mission for the colony. He was charged with preaching as a layman and marrying people as a magistrate. The Plymouth ambassador stood his ground, admitting that sometime (wanting a minister) he did exercise his gift to help the edification of his brethren when they wanted better means (for a preacher), which was not often. Then about marriage, which he also confessed that having been called to the place of magistry, he had sometimes married some. And further told their Lordships that marriage was a civil thing and he found nowhere in the Word of God that it was tied to ministry. . . . Besides it was no new thing for he had been so married himself in Holland by the magistrates in their Statt-house.[6]

Edward Winslow was a second amanuensis of Robinson, who like Bradford responded to enlightened religion based on reason and study of the Bible. His books reflect admiration for the learned minister, the church as a fellowship of informed people, and a theology and polity that were on a level above the battleground of current contention. His writings recall with nostalgia the days in Leyden when as a young student fresh from the Kings School in Worcestershire he entered enthusiastically in the Pilgrim quest for reform and the recapture of essential truths. He used his talents setting type at the Pilgrim Press in order to publish books that would introduce the fresh air of truth into the chambers of duplicity in the palaces of the bishops and the king.

The Pilgrims eliminated holy water, relics, adoration of the cross, references to purgatory, and prayers for the dead "to avoid superstition." The church had been corrupted by usages that made capital of the grief and terror that preyed on people when loved ones passed away. The true church should be stripped of opportunities to exploit parishioners in such critical situations.

No ritual was used at funerals. Friends gathered around the minister and walked to the grave. They stood reverently without speaking while earth was lowered onto the coffin. They bowed in stoical dignity as they shut themselves off from efforts to wield control over life beyond death and to alleviate one another's grief with false promises. It was a demonstration of intellectual religion.

The Pilgrims also removed from their worship the pagan background of Lent, Easter, and Christmas rites that had become an agglomeration of non-Christian customs not justified by scripture but taken over by the church from pagan sources. These people were not joy-killers, who wanted to extinguish customs that had grown dear to their culture, but they were convinced that these features had led to suppression of the historical content and the spiritual meaning of the church year. Intent on accurate meanings, they pursued commonly accepted rituals to the kernel of truth that lay in their origins, affirming that they would stick with the actual facts as they found them recorded in the Bible.

The Pilgrims opposed the corrupt practices of the church: "To the destruction of how many thousand souls for whom Christ died, either by starving them through ignorance, or poisoning them by profane example."[7] The Church of England abounded in abuses and abominable practices: the dictatorial authority of the bishops, the selling of indulgences and favors, censorship and excommunication, the treatment of parish appointments or "livings" as political plums, and the selection of incompetent men as parish ministers. Intellectual integrity demanded an end to these infamies.

The original leaders of the Pilgrim congregation set a pattern of intellectual inquiry. John Smyth, Richard Clyfton, and John Robinson were preachers of ability who launched their followers on the path of questioning and investigation. The Scrooby church was formed out of these three nuclei.

After crossing over to Holland, John Robinson emerged as the intellectual and spiritual leader. After the move to Leyden, liberal-thinking exiles tended to augment Robinson's Green Gate congregation. The former Cambridge University dean gave three "lectures" a week for his people. He preached each Sunday morning and spoke at the Sunday afternoon service, in which lay members participated, and also at a weeknight gathering. We know from his book of essays, which are extracts from his sermons, that he was a scholarly preacher with wide-ranging quotations from the Bible, the church fathers, Reformation leaders, and contemporary theologians. We sense that the spiritual diet of the Leyden Pilgrims was of the quality of the Cambridge tradition. Robinson's presentations did not avoid encounters with the profundities of the faith but grappled with the deepest problems and issues of Christian theology. His books make clear that he was not bigoted, but tended to embrace ecumenical concepts.

The broader aspects of faith that Robinson championed were reflected in the attitudes and conduct of his followers in the New World: Brewster, Bradford, Winslow, Carver, Fuller, Cushman, Morton, Southworth, Blossom, Masterson, and Willet.

There were three eminent Puritan scholars who came to Leyden to engage in conferences with John Robinson, which indicates the esteem in which he was held. Bradford records that the Leyden congregation "knew Mr. Parker, Doctor Ames and Mr. Jacob in Holland, when they sojourned for a time in Leyden, and all three boarded together and had their victuals dressed by some of our acquaintances, and then they lived comfortable, and there they were provided for as became their persons."[8]

All three of these reformers were being hunted by James I. Their appearance in Leyden must have provoked excitement among the Pilgrims and increased their esteem for Robinson. No doubt these divines preached and lectured at the Green Gate, so parishioners were familiar with their views and books and were introduced to the foremost exponents of Puritanism. Not one of these visitors had dared to go as far as Robinson and separate with the mother church, but they all agreed on the evils that demanded reformation and the necessity for action. During their dialogues together, Robinson stood his ground. To him a break with the Established Church was imperative. Only severance would cause a stir sufficient to move the seemingly immovable hierarchy. Although he was a Separatist, Robinson's irenic nature caused him to champion Christian unity and endeavor to work in harmony with others.

William Ames, the leading theologian of the era, must have given the Green Gate people some insight into his profound thought and his role in the English Reformation. His work *The Marrow of Sacred Divinity* was widely read in England and on the Continent, and it was to become one of the chief textbooks at Harvard College for many years.

Robert Parker stirred some excitement at the Green Gate when he had made his escape from England, pursued by the archbishop because of his book *The Signe of the Cross*. He condemned use of the cross as a superstitious symbol. While in Holland he published a work against the teaching of the Apostles' Creed regarding Christ's descent into hell. Robinson took over a book Parker was unable to finish, *The Ecclesiastical Polity of Christ and the Opposed Hierarchial Polity*, wrote the foreword, and published it. The Leyden Pilgrims heard this reformer speak and learned something of his liberal opinions.

The third scholar, Henry Jacob, spent six or seven years in Leyden, was a member of the Green Gate congregation, and must have spoken frequently to the people. He had been arrested by the bishop of London for his books on reform of the church and forced to flee to Holland. Impressed by the success of the Leyden church, he returned to London in 1616 to form a similar congregation. Several of his followers moved his church to Scituate in 1634 and to Barnstable on Cape Cod in 1639.

John Robinson was able to maintain in Leyden the learning of Cambridge University through the quality of his preaching and his association with erudite Puritans. The proximity of Leyden University and its distinguished faculty stimulated him and his associates to engage in intellectual pursuits. Leyden was tolerant of all religious sects. It was the book-publishing center of Europe where the newcomers started their own Pilgrim Press. Several of their volumes offended authorities in England. *The Perth Assembly*, a Presbyterian blast from Scotland by David Calderwood, threw James I into a rage. He ordered his ambassador in the Netherlands to break up the press and arrest Brewster and his accomplices. There was a cloak-and-dagger chase, but the Dutch hid Brewster. His friends at the university tried to prevent the king's raid on the secret press but failed; in 1619 the Pilgrim Press was dismantled.

Thomas Brewer, an admirer of Robinson and Brewster, had served as a financial backer of the enterprise. He was arrested by James I and questioned for over two months. Returning to Holland, he soon left again for the homeland following the death of Robinson in 1625. Arrested in 1626 for his Separatist writings, Brewer was imprisoned for fourteen years. Released from the King's Bench Prison after paying a fine of £1,000, he died soon after as one of the unsung heroes of the Pilgrim Story.

Robinson had been trained for eleven years, while a student and teacher in Corpus Christi College, Cambridge, as a disciple of William Perkins, the eminent English Calvinist. Although Robinson accepted the basic tenets of Geneva, tempered from the rigidities of Calvin by Zwingli,

Beza, and the Dutch and English reformers, he leaned sufficiently toward humanism to avoid bigotry. The Pilgrim
Way was marked by the effort to employ reason. Robinson
wrote:

> Reason is that wherein man goes before all other
> earthly creatures and comes after God only, and the
> angels in heaven. For whereas God and nature hath
> furnished other creatures, some with hoofs, others
> with other instruments, and weapons both defensive
> and offensive, man is left naked, and destitute of all
> these, but may comfort himself in that one endow-
> ment of reason, and providence, whereby he is enabled
> to govern them all.[9]

Pinning their faith on the scriptures and on reason, the
Pilgrims dared to grapple with the profundities of faith and
controversial concepts like the sovereignty of God, predestination, salvation, escatology, biblical exegesis, the nature of the church, and the limits of civil authority.

This respect for learning, exemplified in regard for
Robinson, Ames, Parker, and Jacob, was reflected by the
Pilgrims in their esteem of Henry Ainsworth, whom they
met during their year in Amsterdam. This Hebrew scholar
translated the Pentateuch and wrote the *Book of Psalmes:
Englished both in Prose and Metre* in 1612, which became
the beloved hymnbook of the Pilgrims for many years.
During the quarrels among the Separatists in Amsterdam,
Ainsworth preserved a dignity and balance. He taught well
"without tossing and turning his book." In the midst of
the disputations in Amsterdam, the Leyden Pilgrims kept
their respect for Ainsworth.

The distinguished scholar John Pory of the Virginia
Colony enjoyed his visit at Plymouth in 1622 and praised
the settlers for their hospitality. When he departed on his
return voyage to England, Brewster and Bradford loaned

him some books from their libraries. Pory wrote on August 28, 1622 to Bradford:

To yourself and Mr. Brewster, I must acknowledge myself in many ways indebted; whose books I would have you think very well bestowed on him, who esteemeth them such jewels. My haste would not suffer me to remember, much less to beg, Mr. Ainsworth's elaborate work upon the five books of Moses. Both his and Mr. Robinson's do highly commend the authors as being most conversant in the Scriptures, of all others. And what good (who knows) it may please God to work by them, through my hands (though most unworthy), who finds such high content in them.[10]

This was quite a compliment from a member of Parliament and the Church of England to these two Separatist writers and to the interest in books he found evident at Plymouth.

The number of volumes possessed by settlers in the colony was remarkable, considering the size of the community, the high price of books, and the scarcity of personally owned books in this era. Although admittedly some of these were heavy theology and beyond the grasp of the average colonist, their presence nevertheless indicated a veneration of learning and the fact that their religion was related to the best Protestant thought of the day. The general distribution of the Bible and the Ainsworth psalter proves that the majority did read and had a vital interest in their religion.

Wills show that some in the colony signed with an X, indicating that they were ill versed in Elizabethan English. This is not surprising since illiteracy was widespread in England. Some may have used the sign for convenience even though they could read and write. Letters have been preserved from Carver, Cushman, Allerton, Fuller, Winslow, Bradford, Brewster, Blossom, and Masterson, all of whom handled the language well. Bradford and Winslow were versatile and gifted writers.

College-bred men were a rarity in the early seventeenth century in England and on the Continent, and likewise in Plymouth. William Brewster had studied at Cambridge. John Robinson's Cambridge learning permeated the early days of the colony. The first pastor, Ralph Smith, had been trained at Christ's College, Cambridge; John Rayner, the second, was from Emmanuel College, Cambridge. Roger Williams, a graduate of Pembroke College, Cambridge, was the celebrated teacher of the congregation; John Norton, another teacher, was a graduate of Peterhouse, Cambridge. The learned Charles Chauncy, the Hebrew scholar, was trained at Trinity in Cambridge. These ministers brought the tradition of learning from Cambridge and influenced the people of Plymouth, who looked up to them as their intellectual and spiritual guides.

The books listed in the inventories during the early years of the colony indicate that learning was held in high esteem. There was evidently a genuine interest in discussing the fundamentals of Christianity.

Plymouth Colony residents were required to prepare a last will and testament. After death, an inventory of possessions was prepared and registered. These inventories offer insight into home life: the furniture, clothing, bedding, linen, pewter, pottery, utensils, equipment, tools, animals, and books. The plantation had a fair supply of the last item.

William Brewster owned 393 books, 62 in Latin and the balance in English. An analysis of his library classified 98 books as expository, 63 as doctrinal, 69 as practical religion, 24 as historical, 38 as ecclesiastical, 6 as philosophical, 14 as poetical, and 54 as miscellaneous. Four books were by John Robinson. Eleven had been printed in Leyden by the Pilgrim Press.[11]

William Bradford also had at least four hundred volumes including works by Robinson, Calvin, Luther, Peter Martyr, Cartwright, Cotton, and Ainsworth, and several works in Dutch.[12]

Dr. Samuel Fuller owned three Bibles, a psalm book, a concordance, a catechism, titles by Robinson and Ainsworth, dictionaries, works on the Bible, and sermons, along with his "Physicke bookes" and "a Surgions chest with the things belonging to it."[13]

Captain Myles Standish had a surprising collection, in addition to titles of military science and history. He had three old Bibles, a New Testament, a psalm book, works of Calvin, Preston, Dod, Davenport, and Cotton, along with Homer's *Iliad*.[14]

Thomas Prence owned two Great Bibles, a Great Old Psalme Book, a collection of psalm books, works by Ainsworth, sermons, and biblical studies.[15]

John Atwood, who left a large estate and an extensive inventory, had eleven French Bibles, a concordance, works by Calvin, biblical treatises, sermons, and religious histories.[16]

William Bassett left books by Robinson and Ainsworth, a concordance, commentaries, sermons, and expository works.[17]

The inventories list religious books held by most of the settlers:

John Howland: one Great Bible, works by Tyndale, Williams, Ainsworth
Thomas Rogers: Rhemish New Testament
Nicholas Snow: one psalm book
Thomas Howes: two Bibles and other books
John Jenny: one Bible, Cartwright on the Rhemish Testament, etc.
Stephen Hopkins: diverse books

Godbert Godbertson: a Great Bible, Dod, Communion
of Sts. in French
John Thorp: a psalm book, a Bible
John Hazell: a Bible, works by Perkins, Ainsworth,
Cartwright, Josephus
John Forbes: three Bibles, two psalm books
John Walker: three Bibles
Thomas Blossom, Jr.: two old Bibles
William Thomas: books valued at £8.5.0
John Dunham: one Great Bible, a psalm book
Will Wright: one Great Bible, one little Bible, a psalm
book
John Brown: one Bible
Richard Lauchford: Ainsworth on Exodus
Francis Cooke: one great Bible
Sarah Jenney: a great Bible, a small Bible, psalm book,
Ainsworth, Cartwright
Mary Ring: one Bible, psalm book, Dod, *Troubler of the
Church of Amsterdam*
Stephen Dean: one Bible and other books
Joseph Tilden: books worth £8.16.0
Samuel Newman: a library worth £18
Alice Bradford: two Bibles
Josiah Cooke: two Bibles
Edward Foster: three Bibles and other books
James Lindale: one Bible, one commentary and other
books
Judith Smith: Bibles
Joseph Peck: three Bibles, other books worth £3
Richard Sares: one great Bible and other books
John Barker: two old Bibles and other books
John Faunce: one old Bible
John Lothrop: books worth £5
Ann Atwood: a French New Testament, a book of Dr.
Downhams, fifty-four small books[18]

Some insight into the intellectual background of the Pilgrim clergy is given by the library inventory of the Rev. Ralph Partridge, who came in 1636 and served as minister to Plymouth's closest neighbor, Duxbury. He owned Bibles, grammars, and lexicons in Hebrew, Greek, and Latin; works by Calvin, Beza, Cartwright, Perkins, Pareus, Chrysostom, Ambrose, Aquinas, Clement of Alexandria, Jerome, Junius, and Fulgentius; Bible commentaries; Reformation writers; and Puritan sermons.[19] Partridge was invited to the mother church in Plymouth to debate with Charles Chauncy, who championed baptism by immersion as the proper form for this sacrament. The Duxbury neighbor made an eloquent defense of sprinkling and won the approval of the congregation, but the intrepid Chauncy refused to budge.[20] Cotton Mather wrote that Partridge "had the loftiness of an eagle in the great soar of his intellectual abilities."

The Pilgrims respected the human endowment of reason and agreed with John Cotton, who said, "There is an essential wisdom in us, namely our reason which is natural." Like the Puritans, the Pilgrims honored education. What Miller and Johnson wrote of the people of the Bay applies to those of the first colony:

The greatness of the Puritans is not so much that they conquered a wilderness, or that they carried a religion into it, but that they carried a religion which, narrow and starved though it may have been in some respects, deficient in sensuous richness or brilliant color, was nevertheless indissolubly bound up with an ideal of culture and learning. In contrast to all other pioneers, they made no concessions to the forest, but in the midst of frontier conditions, in the very throes of clearing the land and erecting shelters, they maintained schools and a college, a standard of scholarship and competent writing, a class of men devoted entirely to the life of the mind and of the soul.[21]

CHAPTER 3

People of the Book

Reason, which is the adversary of all tyrants, teaches us that truth can be as little restrained as light.

—The Magistrates of Leyden (1581)[1]

Pilgrim religion was rooted in the basic principle of the Reformation—conformity to the word of God. The worship of the church and the government of the church were to be modeled upon the Bible. The Old and New Testaments were the revealed word of the Divine and directives for every phase of ecclesiastical and human conduct. The scriptures were sufficient to meet the needs of human beings even though the human beings were the product of original sin.

Church worship should be restored to the pattern of the primitive church, purified of its corruptions, simplified from its complex practices, freed from worldliness and commercialism, and replaced by spiritual qualities.

Nothing was a fundamental prerequisite in Christian belief unless it was justified by the scriptures. The unscriptural was considered false, and therefore was eliminated.

The Pilgrims criticized the *Book of Common Prayer* and the standardized forms of the mother church and sought to restore the primitive purity of the apostolic church.

Resistance to the prayer book was not caused by opposition to prepared prayers. The Pilgrims themselves sought to pray in beautiful language, with dignity and eloquence. What they resisted was the formal prayers of the establishment because they were standardized and therefore perfunctory. They were ordered read at every service and could not be altered in any part. The Pilgrims resented the singsong rendering of these stylized petitions by "dumb dog" curates and vicars who were insensitive to their meaning and spiritual content. The prayer book became a voice of empty form to thoughtful people.

"The holy Scriptures," taught Robinson, "are that Divine instrument, and means, by which we are taught to believe what we ought, touching God, and ourselves, and all creatures, and how to please God in all things, unto eternal life."[2] Robinson and the Pilgrims believed that they were in some way a small part of God's plan as outlined in the Bible, that God was speaking to them as well as to the characters in the book, and that God would continue to lead the Pilgrims as the Israelites had been led.

Deacon Robert Cushman said in Plymouth in December 1621: "But now the ordinary examples and precepts of the Scriptures, reasonably and rightly understood and applied, must be the voice and work that must call us, press us and direct us in every action."[3]

Henry Jacob, who was a member of the Leyden Pilgrim congregation, wrote of the word of God as the basic criterion for the church: "We are in conscience persuaded, that God's most holy word in the New Testament is absolutely perfect, for delivering the whole manner of God's worship."[4]

In reviewing the Reformation, William Bradford wrote:

The one side [the Reformers] laboured to have the right worship of God and discipline of Christ established in the church, according to the simplicity of the gospel, without the mixture of men's inventions; and to have and to be ruled by the law of God's Word, dispensed in those offices, and by those officers of Pastors, Teachers and Elders, according to the Scriptures.[5]

Edward Winslow also said of the Pilgrim church:

Our practice being, for aught we know, wholly grounded on the written word, without any addition or human invention known to us, taking our pattern from the primitive churches, as they were regulated by the blessed Apostles in their own days, who were taught and instructed by the Lord Jesus Christ, and had the unerring and all-knowing spirit of God to bring to their remembrance the things they had heard.[6]

Underlying the concern over the organization of the church and their criticisms of the establishment, there was a "passionate desire to recover the inner life of New Testament Christianity."[7] Hence the continual turning to the scripture and the testing of ecclesiastical practices by what was written in its pages.

The essays and theological writings of John Robinson are full of biblical references which impede the modern reader, who asks, Why this continual turning for sanction to the scriptures? This was the Pilgrim Way—constant perusal of the truths of holy writ, pondering its pages in decision-making, and using its truths as the ultimate test of validity.

The Pilgrims referred matters of judgment to the Bible. They were literalists like most of their peers. Robinson taught that only the "most sound and unresistible convictions of conscience by the word of God" could satisfy him as he made decisions. "It is unto me a matter of great scruple and conscience, to depart one hair-breadth from their [the apostles'] practice and institution, in anything ecclesiastical, touching the government of the church."[8]

This appeal to the Bible formed a supreme court in the realm of morality. In this era there was no conception of higher criticism. Many and varied meanings could be read into texts. There was some effort on the part of the Pilgrims to apply reason and common sense. Robinson wrote: "The words are to be understood according to the subject matter: the words of law and gospel according to the different nature of law and gospel, the words of history [to be weighed] historically; of a sacrament sacramentally and mystically."[9]

The ministers the Pilgrims knew—Robinson, Smyth, Clyfton, Ainsworth, Ames, Parker, Jacob, Williams, and Chauncy—had been trained in Hebrew, Greek, and Latin and were familiar with the Bible to some extent in the original and in the translations of Tyndale, the Genevan exiles, and the King James commission. They agreed that the main mission of the minister was to study and interpret this book to the people. These scholars had not been trained in the historical study of the Bible that came into being in the nineteenth century. Sometimes they indulged in typology, searching for Old Testament parallels to illustrate New Testament events in order to provide justification for the faith and practice of the church. They were prone to pull verses out of context in the effort to secure Bible-based proofs.

While ignorant of biblical interpretation in the modern sense, the Pilgrims tried to follow Robinson's emphasis on reason. He said that God made "two lights for the eye of the mind, the one, the scriptures, for her supernatural light; and the other, reason, for her natural light. . . .

Reason is that wherein man goes before all other earthly creatures and comes after God only."[10] The gift of reason was to be applied in examining the various sections of sacred writing: Were they intended to be history, law, poetry, or prophecy, and what was their purpose?

Pilgrim interpretation of scripture was literal and it often degenerated into an unscholarly reverence for texts. Yet their Bible diet did afford them a way of self-discipline and high standards for conduct. Their emphasis on private reading of the scriptures tended to promote literacy and give significance to individual believers, a thrust toward questioning the trappings of established religion and an outreach toward genuine meanings.

The Pilgrims hoped they could establish a culture in the wilderness that would be free from the corruptions of the Old World. The Bible was "the perfect rule of faith," the daily source of moral guidance and spiritual support. They felt they were combating the forces of Satan as Israel did in the Old Testament. England was their oppressor, like Egypt. King James was their pharaoh, and the Atlantic Ocean was their Red Sea. New England was to be their Canaan, they hoped and prayed.[11]

William Bradford was well qualified to outline the background of the Pilgrim church. He sensed that he had been an eyewitness to most of the major steps in the record from 1606 to 1648, so he set down in his *Dialogue* for the guidance of the new generation in Plymouth what he recalled as a first-generation Pilgrim. Bradford had been present at some of the earliest secret gatherings in Scrooby, Gainsborough, and Babworth. He knew John Smyth of Gainsborough, who preceded the Pilgrims to Amsterdam, and Richard Clyfton of Babworth, who helped John Robinson gather the Scrooby congregation in 1606, and was close to William Brewster, who had been a leader in bringing this company of seekers together. He knew the stormy elder statesmen of Separatism, Francis Johnson in Amsterdam and Henry Ainsworth, the learned translator and hymn-writer. He had been a confidant of John Robinson, who had served as his pastor for nearly fifteen years.

In his *Dialogue* the young men asked questions of their elders about the beginnings of their movement in England and Holland. Bradford tried to give them the background facts that formed the foundation events of the past fifty-five years. The young men asked if Robert Browne, a bold, early Separatist, was "the first inventor and beginner of this way." Governor Bradford answered that there had been reformers before Browne for a generation or more:

> No verily . . . the prophets, apostles and evangelists have in their authentic writings laid down the ground thereof and upon that ground is their [the Separatists'] building reared up and surely settled: moreover many of the Martyrs both former and latter have maintained as is to be seen in the acts and monuments of the Church; also in the days of Queen Elizabeth there was a Separated Church whereof Mr. Fitz was pastor; and another before that in the time of Queen Mary of which Mr. Rough was pastor or teacher and Cudbert Simson a deacon, who exercised amongst themselves, as other ordinances, so [such] Church censures, as excommunication, etc., and professed and practised that cause before Mr. Browne wrote it.[12]

Bradford made it clear that Pilgrim separatism was not a novelty of the English Reformation, but rather was built on precepts enunciated in the New Testament. This endeavor to revive the early church predated Robert Browne. Such an effort had been made during the reign of Queen Mary, when a secret Congregational church was gathered in London. Bradford appealed to the record of the martyrs, who long before had sacrificed for truth and freedom.[13]

The Pilgrims enjoyed hearing the Bible read and expounded. For them it was no dull exercise but a newly opened book. Hitherto it had been available only in Hebrew, Greek, and Latin but now it was in their own Elizabethan language and it was possible to own a copy and read it in one's own home. No longer was it necessary to seek out a library or cloister where the book was chained to a desk. The words of the Bible read by the minister formed a dramatic pageant of the heroes of faith, the immortal pioneers who were searching for the City of God.

Because preaching was Bible-centered, it opened up to the people a long-neglected and almost unknown library. This provided new power for the preacher and drew listeners who were hungry to hear a more vital message from the stereotyped pulpits of the kingdom. Biblical exposition was emphasized along with the necessity of Bible reading and study on the part of the people. Sermons became more appealing and religion took on a new relevance. The Pilgrims joined in this resurgence of interest in the Book. They read aloud from their Geneva Bibles at mealtime, by candlelight, and by the glow of fireplace embers, their children and servants gathered around them.

"It would be difficult to overemphasize the profound and varied consequences of continuous reading of Holy Writ by people of every rank and degree," wrote Carl Bridenbaugh.[14] The Geneva Bible and other translations brought the intellectual stimulus of exploring the sixty-six volumes of the Old and New Testaments, with consequent widening of intellectual horizons and deepening of moral and spiritual insights. It also presented to readers in their own tongue a new concept of what life meant, that they were part of a grand design established by the Creator. Their being took on new meaning as they learned to conform with the moral laws set forth in the Bible. To follow the laws of God promised a new life; to violate them meant death. It was one's duty to seek God, to obey God's rules, and to do God's will.

It was a new day of direct access to God through the scriptures which brought the thrill of adventure and discovery. Thomas Hobbes wrote in his *Behemoth*: "After the Bible was translated . . . every man, nay every boy and wench, that could read English thought they spoke with God Almighty (through the marginal notes as well as the text) and understood what he said, when by a certain number of chapters a day they had read the Scriptures once or twice over."[15]

The outpouring of English Bibles won the English the title of the greatest scripture-readers in Christendom. Following the Great Bible, authorized by Henry VIII, came the Geneva Bible of 1560. Copies were smuggled into England from the press of the Marian exiles who had fled England from the purges of Mary Tudor. Scholars like William Whittingham, Anthony Gilby, and Thomas Sampson translated the New Testament, using Greek, Latin, French, and English versions. Their Old Testament was a revision of the Great Bible compared with Hebrew texts. It was set in Roman type, divided into verses, and supplied with marginal notes and arguments of Calvinistic bent. There were engravings, maps, and descriptions of the Holy Land and other countries that offered a new global background to readers. No wonder the Geneva Bible became immensely popular and was called "the English Bible of the Elizabethan public, of the Scottish Reformation, of the English voyagers, and the first settlers in North America."[16]

For fifty years or more the Geneva Bible was popular in England and cherished by the Pilgrims. Their household inventories indicate that almost every family owned a copy. They searched its pages for inspiration and for guidance in daily living and agreed with William Ames that it was for "the instructing of all the faithful through all ages."[17]

The idiom of their Bible was intertwined in their daily living. For example, William Bradford wrote in much the same style as the eloquent, moving quality of this translation and of the King James Bible.

As the Pilgrims poured over their Geneva Bibles, the Anglicans and many of the unchurched were reading the Bishops' Bible and the King James Bible of 1611. This practice exerted profound influence upon English life, nurturing morality in the citizenry, shaping their speech as well as their conduct, and providing them with a treasured fund of common culture.

"The fact that the Bible was taken as a revelation of the divine will, and at the same time placed in the hands of every believer to read and interpret encouraged the individual to exercise his own wits. So long as he quoted Scripture he took high and unimpeachable grounds," wrote Ralph Barton Perry. "He could always appeal directly to God against any human authority, whether church or state. This biblical literalism did, no doubt, promote credulity and sanction the undisciplined vagaries of ignorance; but it taught the common man to conduct his own private search for truth, and to regulate his belief by the evidence presented to his own mind."[18]

CHAPTER 4

Outreach Toward Tolerance

I thought it better so to do than with the blind World
to Censure, Rail at, and Revile them when they neither
saw their Persons nor knew any of their [the Quakers]
Principles. But the Quakers and myself cannot close in
divers things, and so I testify to the Court that I am
no Quaker. . . . But withal I tell you that as I am no
Quaker, so I will be no Persecutor.

—James Cudworth[1]

The Pilgrims did not bring religious freedom with them
on the *Mayflower*. They were only seeking freedom for
themselves that they might worship according to the dic-
tates of their conscience. Having fled to the far corners of
the earth to find such a place, they knew they must protect
it from those of alien faiths who would again persecute
them, adventurers, fortune hunters, or mavericks who might
follow in their steps and try to set up utopias in their midst.
They did not come to the New World to establish a community open to all people of every type and persuasion.
It was to be a society where settlers were expected to be

sympathetic to their precepts. Those who were so minded were welcome.

Tolerance, like democracy, was an unpopular word, looked upon with suspicion in the seventeenth century. The Pilgrims were more tolerant than most of their peers; they deserve credit for their pioneering outreach. They did not permit people of all varieties of opinion to settle in their colony. Newcomers were not allowed to stay without permission, and troublemakers were asked to move on. In spite of strict rules, the Pilgrims were hospitable to all kinds of people, strangers, shipwreck victims, the needy and destitute, even enemies who had wronged them. In dealing with dissent and disorder they followed a flexible policy, showing leniency in many cases, endeavoring conscientiously to mete out justice.

The Pilgrim outlook had been tempered by encounters with dogmatism and bigotry in England. In Holland they learned something of liberality from the free air of Leyden and from their interchanges with the fundamentalists of Amsterdam. Their Leyden community withdrew from the bickering, agreeing with Robinson: "No family hath so many unskilled ones to meddle in it; as that of disputing in manner of religion." "We should affect strife with none," he admonished, "but study, as far as we can to accord with all; accounting it a benefit, when we can so do with any."[2]

Robinson's spirit of cooperation, sustained in Plymouth by the Pilgrims in their best moments, influenced the outlook of Congregationalism. Emphasis on charity, so rare on the battlefields of Christian history, and the inkling of a universal outlook led the Cambridge scholar and a small band of his associates to grasp the enlarging concept that variety and unity were possible in Christendom. He set a high aim before his people: "We must acknowledge but one brotherhood of all."[3]

Robinson's writings and leadership encouraged mediation. The leaven of a universal view was evident in his open mind and kindly personality. He wrote:

> Men are for the most part minded for, or against toleration of diversity of religion, according to the conformity which they themselves hold, or hold not with the country or kingdom where they live. Protestants living in the countries of Papists commonly plead for toleration of religion; so do Papists that live where Protestants bear sway: though few of either, specially of the clergy, as they are called, would have the other tolerated, where the world goes on their side. The very same is to be observed in the ancient Fathers, in their times: of whom, such as lived in the first three hundred years after Christ, and suffered with the churches, under heathen persecutions, pleaded against all violence for religion, true or false: affirming that it is of human right and natural liberty, for every man to worship what he thinketh God: and that it is no property of religion to compel to religion, which ought to be taken up freely; that no man is forced by the Christians against his will, seeing he that wants faith, and devotion is unserviceable to God: and that God not being contentious would not be worshipped of the unwilling.[4]

The Pilgrims separated from the Church of England because they believed this was the only way to have a true church, and they hoped that through their protest they might purify the mother church. But they were not rigid Separatists. They believed that in personal actions they could still attend services of the Established Church, listen to sermons, and join in worship. But they could not enter into official church actions such as sharing in the sacrament of the Lord's Supper. They could participate in the faith, but not in the order of the Church of England. They followed Pastor Robinson's policy:

> We who profess a separation from the English national, provincial, diocesan, and parochial church, and churches, in the whole formal state and order thereof, may notwithstanding lawfully communicate in private prayer, and other the like holy exercises (not performed in their church communion, nor by their church power and ministry) with the godly amongst them.[5]

The Pilgrims were more consistent than many Puritans, who wanted to reform the Church of England but did not dare break with it. Intellectual honesty forced them to separate, but they did not shun the mother church, as many Separatists did. They saw the wisdom of keeping lines of communication open. They visited other churches in Holland, and when in England worshiped with the Anglicans when there was opportunity. As private persons they believed they could partake with these other Christians in "private Christian duties."

This view helped develop an ecumenical outlook. Even Roger Williams could not accept this practice in Plymouth. Because he was for total separation, he was shocked to learn that the Separatist Pilgrims visited Anglican churches.

Edward Winslow emphasized the broad spirit of Robinson and the Leyden church:

> I was living three years under his ministry, before we began the work of Plantation in *New-England*. He [Robinson] was always against separation from any of the Churches of Christ, professing and holding communion both with the *French* and *Dutch* churches, yea, tendering it to the *Scots* also. . . . Ever holding forth how wary persons ought to be in separating

from a Church, and that till Christ the Lord departed wholly from it, man ought not to leave it, only to bear witness against the corruption that was in it. . . . He allowed hearing the godly Ministers preach and pray in the public Assemblies; yea, he allowed private communion not only with them, but all that were faithfull in Christ Jesus in the Kingdom and elsewhere upon all occasions . . . nay, I may truly say, his spirit cleaved unto them.[6]

The Leyden Green Gate church included quite a span of national Christians, who operated harmoniously together. There were members from English, Welsh, Scottish, Huguenot, French, Walloon, and Dutch churches. This afforded a base for international thinking. Church members were free to visit the Dutch churches and worship with them. A number learned to speak Dutch and became Dutch citizens. Moses Symonson, who came to Plymouth on the *Fortune* in 1621, was "a child of one that was in communion with the Dutch Church at Leyden." Godbert Godbertson, who arrived on the *Anne*, was a Walloon, a hat maker from Leyden. Philippe de la Noye, a *Fortune* passenger, was "born of French parents, and proving himself to be come from such parents as were in full communion with the French churches, was hereupon admitted to the Church of Plymouth." Francis Cooke's wife, Hester Mayhieu, was a Walloon from Leyden.

Speaking of the Reformed churches, Robinson wrote:

We account them the true churches of Jesus Christ, and both profess and practise communion with them in the holy things of God.[7]

To come nearer to our own times, how bitter was Luther against Zwingli and Calvin in the matter of the Sacraments! And how implacable is the hatred at this

day of them whom they call Lutherans against the followers of the other parties![8]
And so all Christians are one in Christ, and Christ one in, and unto them.[9]

The Leyden Pilgrim community drew some of the more moderate Separatists who were exiles in Holland. A number of the uncompromising ones stayed in Amsterdam, where the churches were more hidebound. The city of Leyden offered a liberal milieu. The fact that the Pilgrims chose Leyden as their home in Holland indicates that they favored an open community that was lenient toward dissent and permitted freedom of expression to Protestants, Roman Catholics, Jews, and atheists. Some of their critics derided them for moving to such a free city, which they called "a mingle mangle of religion" and "a cage of unclean birds." The broad outlook of Leyden rubbed off some of the provincial edges of the English refugees. The learning of the university exposed them to the best thinking of Europe. Bradford recorded:

> For these and some other reasons they removed to Leyden, a fair and beautiful city and of a sweet situation, but made more famous by the University wherewith it is adorned, in which of late had been so many learned men. . . . Being thus settled after many difficulties they continued many years in a comfortable condition, enjoying such sweet and delightful society and spiritual comfort together in the ways of God, under the able ministry and prudent government of Mr. John Robinson and Mr. William Brewster, who was an assistant unto him in the place of an Elder, unto which he was now called and chosen by the church. . . .[10]

So as they grew in knowledge and other gifts and graces of the Spirit of God and lived together in peace and love and holiness and many came unto them from divers parts of England, so as they grew a great congregation. And if at any time any differences arose or offenses broke out they were ever so met with and nipped in the head betimes, or otherwise so well composed as still love, peace, and communion was continued.[11]

Hornius stated that there were two types of Separatists: first, the Rigid Separatists or Brownists; second, the Semi-Separatists or Robinsonians, who after a while were called Independents and still retain the name. Thomas Prince explained:

> But had Hornius been duly acquainted with the generous principles both of the people, and their famous pastor [Robinson], he would have known that nothing was more disagreeable to them than to be called by the name of any man whatever; since they renounced all attachment to any mere human systems of expositions of the Scripture, and reserved an entire and perpetual liberty of searching the inspired records and of forming both their principles and practice from those discoveries they should make therein without imposing them on others.[12]

Pastor Robinson did not want his name applied to his followers. He disliked labels. As William Bradford put it:

> At first for the name, Independents, you are to know it is not a name of choice made by any of themselves, but a title imposed by others which are their opposite.
>
> Mr. Cotton saith [also] that it is no fit name for our churches, in that it holdeth us forth as independent from all others. Whereas, indeed, we do profess dependency upon magistrates for civil government and

protection, dependency upon Christ and his word for the sovereign government and rule of our administrations, dependency upon the council of other churches and synods when our own variance or ignorance may stand in need of such help from them.[13]

The Pilgrims did not like sectarian labels either and did not want to be called Brownists, Barrowists, Separatists, Robinsonians, or Independents. They did not hold that their church was the only true church, only that it was a true church of Christ, one of many in Christendom. Bradford stated in his *Dialogue* that the Pilgrims rejected the name Independents. It "was a nick-name of a badge of scorne." They did not consider themselves independent from civil authority in matters of civil government, neither did they set themselves apart from other Christians. They held "good correspondence with all sister churches by way of consociation, consultation, communion, communication, mutual consolation, supportation, and (in a word) in all things, duties & offices, as wherein Christ's kingdom is held up."[14]

Edward Winslow explained: "The primitive churches are the only pattern which the churches of Christ in New England have in their eye, not following Luther, Calvin, Knox, Ainsworth, Robinson, Ames, or any other, further than they follow Christ and his Apostles."[15]

William Bradford spoke of the unfair treatment heaped on the religious reformers of his time:

And to cast contempt upon the sincere servants of God they opprobriously and most injuriously gave unto and imposed upon them the name of Puritans, which it is said the Novatians (a third-century sect) out of pride did assume and take unto themselves. And lamentable it is to see the effects which have followed. Religion hath been disgraced, the godly grieved, afflicted, persecuted, and many exiled; sundry have lost their lives in prisons and other ways.[16]

Robinson was impatient with limitations and struggled for more open space to explore the larger implications of truth. He said: "The hearing of the Word of God is not so inclosed by any hedge, or ditch, divine or human, made about it, but lies in common for all, for the good of all."[17] The Pilgrims wished the Church of England no harm. They were not seeking its injury or destruction, only its reformation.

We do freely, and with all thankfulness, acknowledge every good thing she hath, and which ourselves have there received: the superabundant grace of God covering and passing by the manifest enormities in that church, wherewith these good things are inseparably commingled; and wherein we also, through ignorance and infirmity, were inwrapped.[18]

Edward Winslow denied that the Pilgrims ever boasted of their separation from the mother church. He pointed out that Robinson and Brewster did not ask inquirers to repudiate that church or any other body in order to enter their fellowship. He put up a stout defense against "all the injurious and scandalous taunting reports that are passed on us," and stated that "our practice is wholly grounded in the written Word, without any addition of human invention known to us, taking our pattern from the primitive churches."[19]

The Pilgrims loved England. Robinson said: "Yet for our country, we do not forsake it, but are by it forsaken and expelled by most extreme laws, and violent proscriptions, contrived and executed by the prelates."[20] They withdrew from the Church of England, which because of its corruptions was like Babylon, "but for the commonwealth and kingdom, as we honor it above all the states in the world, so would we thankfully embrace the meanest corner of it, at the extremest condition of any people in the kingdom."[21]

The Leyden Pilgrim congregation, which numbered between 350 and 500, was one of peace and unity. John Cotton wrote that the church at Leyden was in peace, and free from division.[22] Winslow spoke of the "wholesome counsel" that Robinson provided for the Leyden Pilgrims and "the sweet communion with the godly" of Holland. He denied that they were schismatics and said that

> the foundation of our New England plantations was not laid upon schism, division or separation, but upon love, peace, and holiness; yea, such love and mutual care of the church of Leyden for the spreading of the Gospel, the welfare of each other and their posterities to succeeding generations, as is seldom found on earth.[23]

Eighty-one of the Plymouth Pilgrims came from Leyden. Relatives, friends, and sympathizers who were drawn to their settlement made up the balance. Those who enjoyed some contact with Leyden developed into the key leaders of the colony. This nucleus carried over to New England concepts that they evolved during Holland days, along with a spirit of dedication of purpose and teamwork.[24]

The Pilgrims with the Leyden background included: William Brewster, John Carver, Samuel Fuller, Robert Cushman, Edward Winslow, William Bradford, Isaac Allerton, Jonathan Brewster, Love Brewster, Francis Cooke, George Morton, Nathaniel Morton, Thomas Blossom, Richard Masterson, Philippe de la Noye, Cuthbert Cuthbertson, Thomas Southworth, Constant Southworth, Thomas Rogers, John Goodman, Moses Fletcher, Degory Priest, William White, Thomas Tinker, John Tilley, John

Turner, John Jenney, Stephen Tracy, William Bassett, Moses Symonson, William Pontus, William Wright, Edward Bumpus, John Bradford, Isaac Robinson, and Thomas Willet. To this list of male settlers should be added the names of women, both single and married, and of the children who were born in Leyden and lived there for a time. These families were involved in shaping the course of Plymouth Plantation.

Pulpit and press were hot in this era with arguments and polemics. Clergy and professors issued tract after tract in this literary outpouring. The jungles of biblical quotations were studded with lurid outbursts against the Babylons of Rome and Canterbury, and the prostitutes of Puritanism, Separatism, Brownism, and a score of other banners. Amid this war of words, John Robinson kept a commendable stance. He wrote amid a battle over forms of baptism:

> But let all God's people be exhorted, and admonished to serve Him in modesty of mind, and meekness of wisdom, with reverence, and fear: avoiding, as the sands of humble hypocrisy, in pinning their faith and obedience upon the sleeves of others, so much more the rock of proud presumption: which is so much the worse than the other, as it is more dangerous for any to overvalue himself than another man.[25]

Robinson was impatient with litigation and feuding in religion and sought "peace and union above all else." As did Brewster, Bradford, Winslow, Fuller, Cushman, and Morton in Plymouth, he tried to replace divisiveness with cooperation:

> No family hath so many unskilled ones to meddle in it; as that of disputing religion. But we should affect strife with none, but study, as far as we can to accord with all, accounting it a benefit when we can so do with any.

We ought to be firmly persuaded in our hearts of
the truth and goodness of the religion, which we embrace in all things; yet as knowing ourselves to be
men, whose property is to err and to be deceived in
many things; and accordingly both to converse with
men in that modesty of mind, as always to desire to
learn something better, or further, by them, if it
may be.[26]

He stated that religious arguments were usually accompanied by bitterness and violence, and he wished to pacify
rather than alienate. One of Robinson's favorite sayings
was:

If in anything we err, advertise us brotherly, with desire of our information, and not, as our countrymen's
manner for the most part is, with a mind of reproach-
ing us, or gratifying others: and whom thou findest
in error, thou shalt not leave in obstinacy, nor as having a mind prone to schism. Err we may, alas! too
easily but heretics, by the grace of God, we will not
be.[27]

Robinson also observed:

Disputations in religion are sometimes necessary but
always dangerous; drawing the best spirits into the
head from the heart, and leaving it either empty of
all, or too full of fleshy zeal and passion if extraordi-
nary care be not taken still to supply, and fill it anew
with pious affections towards God, and loving towards men. We are therefore carefully to beware, and
earnestly to pray, that we may in controversies of
religion strive for God, and according unto God,
seeing in them we both may easily and do danger-
ously err.[28] . . .

And for men, how uncharitable are they towards

them in their persons, judging them as perishing without remedy, if they receive not their new gospel of
Anabaptistry and Free-will. As if the Word of God
came out of them, or to them alone.[29]

The Leyden Pilgrims accepted the articles of faith of
the Reformed Church of the Continent, and reached out
in fellowship to them—the Dutch, Walloon, Huguenot,
French, and Swiss—as well as to the Presbyterians of Scotland and refugee Presbyterians in Holland, which was quite
an outreach for this era.

The Leyden church practiced intercommunion with the
Church of Scotland. The Rev. David Calderwood, author
of the *Perth Assembly*, one of the liberal books published
by the Pilgrim Press in Leyden, attended the Green Gate
church while he was hiding in Holland from the soldiers
of King James I. Calderwood knew Robinson and came
to hear him preach. On one Sunday the Lord's Supper was
to be celebrated. Calderwood

stood up and desired he might, without offence, stay
and see the manner of his administration and our participation in that ordinance. To whom our pastor answered, "Reverend Sir, you may not only stay to
behold us, but partake with us, if you please; for we
acknowledge the churches of Scotland to be the
churches of Christ."[30]

Open communion is still a matter of debate among
twentieth-century Christians. Many sects close their ranks
when they hold communion. Some Christian denominations
have not yet been able to follow the ecumenical urge of
the Pilgrims.

Samuel Terry joined the Leyden church from the French
church. No fuss was made over the transfer of his membership. Other members were accepted freely from the Huguenot and Walloon fellowships.

Pilgrim faith was more than a criticism of the flaws in the Church of England. It consisted not in condemning others but rather in the edifying of themselves. Robinson explained:

> Our faith is not negative, nor consists in the condemning of others, and wiping their names out of the bead-roll of churches, but in the edifying of ourselves; neither require we of any of ours, in the confession of their faith, that they either renounce or in one word contest with the Church of England—whatsoever the world clamors of us in this way. Our faith is founded upon the writings of the Prophets and Apostles, in which no mention of the Church of England is made.[31]

He tried to think in terms of a universal church and said:

> If by the church be understood the catholic church, dispersed upon the face of the whole earth, we do willingly acknowledge that a singular part thereof, and the same visible and conspicuous, is to be found in the land, and with it do profess and practice, what in us lays, communion in all things, in themselves lawful and done in right order.[32]

In 1625 Plymouth Colony received a letter from the London Merchant Adventurers making three demands:

1. That since they were partners in trade they should also be partners in the government of Plymouth.
2. That the "French discipline," that is, the concepts of the French Calvinists or Huguenots, should be followed so "the scandalous name of the Brownists" should not be applied to Plymouth.
3. "That Mr. Robinson and his company may not go over to our Plantation unless he and they will recon-

cile themselves" to the Anglican church "by a recantation under their hands."

Bradford and his people stood firm, as did Robinson and the Leyden Pilgrims, refusing to recant. Bradford wrote an eloquent reply, pointing out that they had not dissembled to His Majesty or to the Adventurers about their affinity with the Reformed churches. They did agree in many ways with the Protestants of France and Holland, but they refused to be pinned down and limited to any one religious persuasion.

But whereas you would tie us to the French discipline in every circumstance, you derogate from the liberty we have in Christ Jesus. The Apostle Paul would have none to follow him in anything but wherein he follows Christ; much less ought any Christian or church in the world do it. The French may err, we may err, and other churches may err, and doubtless do in many circumstances. That honour, therefore, belongs only to the infallible Word of God, and pure Testament of Christ, to be propounded and followed as the only rule and pattern for direction herein to all churches and Christians.

And it is too great arrogancy for any man or church to think that he or they have so sounded the Word of God to the bottom, as precisely to set down the church's discipline without errour in substance or circumstance, as that no other without blame may digress or differ in anything from the same.[38] [Bradford in this last paragraph used a quotation from John Robinson.]

Winslow pointed out that the Pilgrims went out of their way to help the Presbyterians who came to Massachusetts in 1634. Thomas Parker and James Noyes were minister and teacher of a new church in Newbury. They "never had the least molestation or disturbance, and have and find as good respect from magistrates and people as other elders in the Congregational or primitive way." The Rev. Hubbard of Hingham also of Presbyterian leanings, was welcomed to a synod meeting "in all meekness and love" to discuss his theory of baptism.[34]

When inquiries reached Plymouth from Presbyterians in England and Scotland, who "groaned under the heavy pressures of those times," they were told that "they might be freely suffered to exercise their Presbyterian government amongst us." An agent was sent to survey the area near Ipswich and Newbury. The Pilgrims counseled with the agent of the Presbyterians, suggesting that they feel free to come, securing their own ministers, "that they might exercise their Presbyterian government at their liberty, walking peaceably towards us, as we trusted we should do to them."[35]

Those of the Congregational Way did not agree with the Anabaptists' insistence on baptism. This controversy was continued from England and Holland in the New World. Plymouth Colony, like the Bay, was afraid to grant free rein to new sects lest the unity of their ranks be weakened by contention. It soon became evident, however, that such restrictions were impossible. Deacon John Cooke, son of Francis of the *Mayflower* company, who married one of Richard Warren's daughters, turned Baptist. This caused a stir and a flurry of discussion. He moved to Dartmouth, where he was followed by some of the Howlands from Duxbury, and became a lay preacher. It was not long before Baptists were accepted as freemen.

Edward Winslow stated that the Bay (the Massachusetts Colony to the north) did have a law to banish Baptists, but not to whip them, and that Plymouth did have on its books such a law, but we never did or will execute the rigor of it upon any, and have men living amongst us, nay some in our churches, of that judgment; and as long as they carry themselves peaceably, as hitherto they do, we will leave them to God, ourselves having performed the duty of brethren to them.[36]

Winslow explained that one Baptist offender was whipped, " 'tis true we knew his judgment what it was; but had he not carried himself so contemptuously towards the authority God hath betrusted us with in a high exemplary measure, we had never so censured him."[37]

The Anabaptists were anathema to the Church of England, to the Presbyterians, to the Separatists, and to followers of the Congregational Way. These "double washers" were baptizing themselves and one another, administering a sacrament that should be performed only by ordained persons. They were losing sight of the weightier matters of the law in their overemphasis on a minor practice. In 1649 Obadiah Holmes, a Baptist from the Bay, moved to Rehoboth to start a Baptist church. A number of members withdrew from the Rehoboth church. The Bay Colony sent a petition to the court suggesting that they be more vigilant in checking the Baptists: "we feare maybe of other errors also, if timely care be not taken to suppress the same."[38]

The General Court of Plymouth issued an order to desist, and Holmes was told to file a bond for £10. The Massachusetts Bay caught Holmes performing baptisms according to his one and only way. He was ordered whipped on the charges of baptizing illegally and of offering the sacrament to Goodwife Bowdish in the nude.[39]

Feeling ran high against Anabaptists, who were considered disturbers of the peace. The intensity of resentment was expressed by Samuel Willard in 1681: "Experience

tells us that such a rough thing as a New England Ana-
baptist is not to be handled over tenderly. . . . If they
could get head among us, they would certainly undermine
the churches, ruine order, destroy piety, and introduce
prophaness."[40]

Sectarianism crept into the towns of Plymouth Colony,
causing dissension. In 1651 the court voted, in an effort
to restrain deterioration, to require church attendance.[41]
This legalistic approach did little to check the decline in
religious interest. Governor Bradford told the General
Court in 1655 that unless "some speedy course" were taken
to rekindle morality and faith he would resign as governor.
Due to respect for this eminent leader, the court tried to
stir townspeople to support their church and minister
through voluntary contributions. They ordered that clergy
who had problems with their people should not leave until
they counseled with the magistrates. If they could not persuade the people to do what was right, then they were "to
use such other means as may put them upon their duty."[42]

They were striving to build a community in harmony
with the will of God and believed that it was the obligation of the state to support religious order in accord with
God's will and to suppress what threatened it. John Robinson taught, and Bradford agreed, that it was the duty of the
magistrate to prevent dissension and preserve both tables
of the law.

There was less consultation in Plymouth between the
governor and the clergy than in the Bay Colony. Bradford
did confer with ministers on two occasions, but it was not
a common practice. This was done more in the Bay Colony,
where ministers like Cotton, Wilson, and the Mathers held
influential posts. This tradition of clerical importance was
not established in the early days of Plymouth. For five
years they were waiting for Robinson to arrive and for
someone to replace him after he died in 1625. The choices

of Ralph Smith and John Rayner did not bring men of commanding personality. Roger Williams and Charles Chauncy were noteworthy scholars and thinkers, but they stayed only a short time, so conditions were not conducive to a theocracy.

The Bay Colony enacted laws before 1650 making church attendance compulsory and setting up punishments for those who had "Contempt of the Word." Plymouth was less legalistic for the first thirty-five years. They had done well in Holland without support from the government and hoped to so continue in New England.

In 1645 a petition was presented to the court by William Vassall of Scituate "to allow and maintaine full and free tollerance of religion to all men that would preserve the Civill peace."[43] This effort to open the floodgates was opposed by Bradford, Winslow, Collier, and Prence. The other deputies favored the proposal: Standish, Browne, Hatherly, and Freeman. Governor Bradford held back voting on the petition and it was not acted upon. Although opposing freedom of religion, Bradford considered himself more tolerant than magistrates in England, where citizens were flung into dungeons for dissent and had ears and noses cut off, and offenders were paraded through the streets after being subjected to torture. He gave evidence of outreach toward tolerance, but he was not able, due to his obligation to the colony, to accept the concept of full toleration. It would, he believed with some of his associates, imperil what years of labor and sacrifice had created. The petition that expected too much for the time would lead to "sad consequences"—so Bradford, Winslow, and Prence felt. "It would eate out the power of godliness." It would open the colony to all types of nonconformers and "make us odious to all christian common weales."[44]

The petition was also rejected in the Bay Colony. Plymouth was not able to embrace such liberalism at this time, but gradually the people moved in that direction. The Baptists and the Quakers were soon accepted. Charges of sedition decreased. The right to follow the voice of conscience, cherished by the Pilgrims, was recognized as the right of other people as well.

Toleration was scarcely known in England and Europe. The precepts of uniformity were demanded almost everywhere. The regulation of dissent was considered to be imperative in a new colony, where the struggle to survive was vital and foremost in every consideration. Division was a threat to existing unity. New philosophies creeping into the colony brought the danger of disputation and divisiveness.

The Pilgrims spoke their minds freely and stood up for their rights, but they tended to follow common sense most of the time. They defended themselves, but did not proselytize. They depended on the spoken and the written word to present their cause.

In the midst of the spread of sectarianism the Quakers began their invasion. The Bay Colony took the lead in 1656, urging the New England Confederation, which included Plymouth, to prohibit their entrance. The Quakers startled the colonists with their contempt for religious and civil authority. They would have nothing to do with "pagan temples" and "steeple houses," or church bells "like market-bells, to gather the people that the priest may set forth his wares to sell." They rejected Christian ritual, ordained clergy, and educated ministers, who were called "priests" and "professors."[45] Edward Burrough, Quaker leader, dubbed ministers "the fountains of all wickedness abounding in the nation."[46] The Pilgrims bristled at this "crying down of ministry and ministers," since one of their basic precepts was the necessity for an educated religious leadership.

The Quakers upset the Pilgrims as they did other colonists. They were a puzzling lot, against much that the Pilgrims cherished—the Bible as the basis of all faith, learning, and the discipline of an organized society. Even Roger Williams, who had opened the doors of Rhode Island to them, could not endure their destructive ideas.

Moreover, the Quakers held the magistrates in low esteem and refused to take a public oath of allegiance, defying civil authority and creating a threat of anarchy in government. Unlike the respected Friends of later years, these followers of George Fox appeared as iconoclasts, protesting against order and provoking dissension. A Quaker matron strolled into the congregation at Newbury in the nude "to show the people the nakedness of their rulers." Another Quaker entered the meetinghouse in Cambridge with a bottle in each hand. He called out to the people, "Thus will the Lord break you to pieces," and he broke the bottles on the floor. The Pilgrims called these strange people "rantors, madmen, lunaticks and daemonackls." They and the other colonists were shocked and legislation against these subversive newcomers was passed.

The church in Sandwich had been without a minister for some time. In 1656 a nonresident and a Quaker, Nicholas Upsiall, appeared there as a missionary. He was brought before the court in Plymouth and found guilty of slander and disturbing public worship. Although he was not punished, he was told to leave the colony by spring.[47] Two women were charged with abusing the speaker during a Sunday service. One, who was up on a second offense, was sentenced to be whipped. The other was given a suspended sentence when she promised not to misbehave again.[48]

Because they were convinced that the Quakers would undermine civil and religious authority, the New England colonists feared them and tried through laws and threats to keep them out. The Bay Colony hanged four, including

Mary Dyer, whose statue stands today in front of the state house. George Bishop, a Quaker historian, wrote that Mary Dyer won the contest with her Puritan enemies: "Your bloody laws were snapt asunder by a woman, who, trampling upon you and your laws and your halter and your gallows and your priests, is set down at the right hand of God."[49]

Plymouth did not go to the extremes of execution, branding, beating with iron rods, burning books, or torture, but they did try fines and whipping. When the stern Thomas Prence became governor he tightened controls. Any settler bringing a Quaker into the colony was ordered by the court to pay twenty shillings each week as long as the intruder remained.[50] Anyone who refused to take the oath of fidelity to the government was to pay a fine of five pounds. In 1658 the court told two Quakers to leave Plymouth or face a whipping. Since the men returned a few days later the order was carried out.[51]

Humphrey Norton was "found guilty of divers horred errours, and was sentanced speedily to depart." After a stay in Rhode Island he returned and was again brought before the court. Governor Prence charged him with "many offenses against God." Norton retorted boldly: "Thou lyest, Thomas, thou art a malicious man. Thou art like a scolding woman, and thy clamorous tongue I regard no more than the dust under my feet."

Since Norton refused to take the oath before he testified, and since he was considered a threat to the peace of the colony he was sentenced to be whipped. He escaped the punishment by declining to pay the customary fee and was finally released. He wrote a sharp letter of rebuke to Prence and one to John Alden. To Alden he said:

I have weighed thy ways, and thou art like one fallen from thy first love; a tenderness once I did see in thee and moderation to act like a sober man, which through evil counsel and self-love thou art drawn aside from . . . like a self-conceited fool puffed up with the pride of his heart because he hath gotten the name of a magistrate. . . . In love this is written to dishearten thee in time before the evil day overtake thee; let it be so received from thy friend.[52]

The legal efforts to repress the Quakers, who called themselves "the people of God," did not work. They failed, as did the persecutions initiated by Elizabeth, James I, Charles I, the archbishop, the bishops, and the Star Chamber in their futile endeavors to stamp out Puritanism by whipping, torture, and burning. The Puritans had gone on meeting, preaching, and writing, defending their right to worship as they saw fit. A number of Pilgrims in Plymouth felt sympathy for the Quakers. They had known what it was to be branded as a heretical minority, to be considered outcasts, to be spied upon and manhandled.

The Pilgrims were more lenient in their treatment than the Bay. They were not shocked to see the laity carrying on worship services, since they had been trained in Leyden to participate in the church. For nine years lay members had run the Plymouth meetinghouse. However, they still held their deference for learned ministers and believed in the necessity of having a trained teacher to guide them in religion. Also, they were upset by the Quaker doctrine of the Inner Light, and strange "movings," the dependence upon guidance of the inner spirit as the ultimate authority. In contrast, they believed that the Bible was the center and guide for the church and for conduct. They could not accept the Quaker flippancy regarding government, the law, and the authority of the magistrates. The Quaker Way would, they felt, lead to anarchy.

William Penn spoke of the harsh reaction that his followers encountered:

> These things gave them [the Quakers] a rough and disagreeable appearance with the generality, who thought them turners of the world upside down, as indeed in some sense they were; but in no other than wherein St. Paul was so charged, viz. to bring things back to their primitive and right order again.[53]

The restrictions against the Quakers were not popular. The Pilgrim conscience could not accept them and severe treatment was tempered by time. John Cotton wrote that "the Pilgrims never made any sanguinary or capital laws against that sect as the colonies did."[54]

Needless to say, the Quakers began to moderate their extremisms and to follow saner practices. This led to less recrimination against them. Fortunately, the bark of the anti-Quaker laws was worse than their bite. The Pilgrims winced at cruel punishment and shared a sympathetic feeling for the persecuted. By 1690 Friends meetinghouses had been established at Sandwich, Rehoboth, Swansea, and Falmouth.[55]

Henry Fell, a Quaker, wrote a letter in 1657, when agitation was strong in Plymouth Colony, to Margaret Fell in Barbados: "In Plimoth patent there is a people not so rigid as the others in Boston, and there are great desires among them after the Truth."[56]

There was no one in Plymouth as violent against the Friends as the Rev. John Wilson of Boston who cried, "I would carry fire in one hand, and fagots in the other, to burn all the Quakers in the world."

A number of defenders of tolerance lifted their voices. One was James Cudworth of Scituate, who served as assistant governor in 1656-57 and as captain of the militia company. The captain spoke out against the trend toward "a State religion, a State ministry, and a State way of maintenance," arguing against Prence, John Alden, and others. He was asked by the court to explain why he had visited Quaker meetings and he answered:

> I thought it better so to do than with the blind World to Censure, Rail at, and Revile them when they neither saw their Persons nor knew any of their Principles. But the Quakers and myself cannot close in divers things, and so I signify to the Court that I am no Quaker. . . . But withal I tell you that as I am no Quaker, so I will be no Persecutor.

The court deprived Cudworth of his military command and disenfranchised him. But the people protested, so certain dependable persons from various towns were appointed "to repair to their [Quaker] meetings . . . and to use their best endeavors by argument and discourse to convince or hinder them."[57] In 1656 the General Court voted:

> Whereas some have deserved and others think it meet to permit some persons to frequent the Quaker meetings to endeavor to reduce them from the error of their Ways, the Court considering the premises do permit John Smith of Barnstable, Isaac Robinson, John Chapman and John Cooke of Plymouth or any two of them to attend the said meetings for the ends aforesaid at any time betwixt this Court and the next October Court.[58]

Isaac Robinson, son of Pastor Robinson, was placed on a committee to reason with the Sandwich Quakers, who were an active lot. Instead of converting them he defended them, and was consequently deprived of his town offices and his rights as a freeman.[59] His father would have been proud of Isaac, who took a stand for freedom of religion.

He had made his home in Barnstable, where he had been active in Henry Jacob's church, founded in London in 1616 on Scrooby-Leyden principles. He moved to Falmouth where he ran a tavern for many years.

In due time, the reaction swept away the controls attempted against the Quakers, and Governor Prence and his regime receded. Josiah Winslow, eldest son of Edward, who had been assistant governor from 1657 to 1672, was chosen governor in 1673 and so continued until 1680. He restored the civil rights of Isaac Robinson, which brought together the two sons of two eminent Pilgrim leaders, who had been close to each other. Winslow also restored the rights of Captain Cudworth, who was reelected assistant governor in 1674 and continued until 1680.

Timothy Hatherly of Scituate had been a resistor of Prence's efforts to suppress dissension. He was an esteemed member of the colony, having served as assistant governor from 1636 to 1637 and 1639 to 1657. It must have been a stormy session of the court when Hatherly was dismissed from his post after many years of service. Governor Winslow would have restored the civil rights of Timothy Hatherly, as he did for James Cudworth and Isaac Robinson, when he became governor, but Hatherly had died before the more liberal regime of Winslow came into being.

New Plymouth did not hang Quakers, but they did drive them out of the colony and threaten some with whipping. The hangings in the Bay and other severe moves to stamp out the Quakers, along with protests of saner leaders, led to revulsion against policies of suppression. The harassment ended in 1661, not only because of wiser judgments of the colonists but because of events in England.[60] Charles II became king in 1660 and the colonies were ordered to cease punishing Quakers and to send them back to England to be tried. There were no further efforts to control the

Friends. The fines that had been levied against former offenders were written off.[61]

William Bradford was disturbed by the waning interest in religion and the tendency toward contention, and wrote wistfully of the original unity and high purpose of the Pilgrim enterprise:

> O sacred bond, whilst inviolably preserved! How sweet and precious were the fruits that flowed from the same! But when this fidelity decayed, then their ruin approached. O that these ancient members had not died or been dissipated (if it had been the will of God) or else that his holy care and constant faithfulness had still lived, and remained with those that survived, and were in times afterwards added unto them. . . .
>
> I have been happy, in my first times, to see, and with much comfort to enjoy, the blessed fruits of this sweet communion, but it is now a part of my misery in old age, to find and feel the decay and want thereof (in a great measure) and with grief and sorrow of heart to lament and bewail the same. And for others' warning and admonition, and my own humiliation, do I here note the same.[62]

Bradford had upheld the Pilgrim enterprise since the days of his youth in Austerfield, when he was derided by friends for affiliating with the "fanatacticall schismatics" of Scrooby and the wrath of relatives who threatened to disinherit him. In Leyden he invested his estate in the corduroy manufacturing concern that he organized, working diligently at his business and studying at night with Robinson and Brewster. He had carried much of the load during the struggle to fund the crossing, to organize the company, and to get even a small number of the Leyden saints across to Plymouth. He had battled for survival of the colony through the starvation years, through the interminable disputes with the London Merchant Adventurers, the vicissitudes of fishing, fur-trading, and the corn and cattle trade, through the tribulations of the General Court and the meetinghouse. It had been a long and arduous pilgrimage.

In moments of reflection Bradford could detect flaws in the Plymouth annals that saddened him and shook his faith in human nature. Yet with the failures and transgressions, and the diminution of the dream of the City of God on earth, there were the faithful ones who cherished the vision in their hearts and kept it alive as they retold it by their hearths and in the pulpits of the steepled churches that graced the countryside and became the chief symbol of the faith of Scrooby, Leyden, and Plymouth. Something of that first fervor endured and made itself part of the ethos and mythos of America.

A life-sized statue of William Bradford was dedicated in Plymouth on Thanksgiving Day 1976 due to the leadership of Lawrence K. Geller and John G. Talcott, Jr. The bronze figure was executed by sculptor Adio Di Biccari after the 1920 design by Cyrus Dallin. It stands among the pine trees on the edge of the harbor, close to the landing place of the Pilgrims.

The Pilgrims made a long stride toward ecumenicity. Robinson had admonished that religious people should "not carry things as if the Word of God came from you or unto you alone."[63]

> For myself, this I believe in my heart before God, and profess with my tongue, and have before the world, that I have one and the same faith, hope, spirit, baptism, and Lord, which I had in the Church of England, and none other; that I esteem so many in that church, of what state, or order soever, as are truly partakers

of that faith, as I account many thousands to be, for my Christian brethren and myself a fellow-member of them of that one mystical body of Christ scattered far and wide throughout the world; that I have always, in spirit and affection, all Christian fellowship and communion with them.[64]

This was an inclusive concept of Christian kindredness for the early seventeenth century. One of Robinson's last efforts before his death, as he waited impatiently for the ship that was to carry him to Plymouth, was the uniting of his congregation with the English Reformed Church in Leyden. After his passing, his wife, Bridget, affiliated with this church.

Some of the Pilgrims remembered his words: "There is hardly any sect so anti-Christian or evil otherwise, in church profession, in which there are not divers truly, though weakly led, with the spirit of Christ in their persons, & so true members of his mystical body."[65] Existing in the midst of perils and hardships, the Pilgrim community managed to preserve its dream of a body politic built on the word of God.

"A basic toleration—even if at times veering off course—was something that could not be taken away from the Pilgrims," wrote Harry Ward.

They themselves had too long been despised and alienated in Europe not to appreciate the dignity and responsibility of each individual's conscience. Thus Myles Standish—military leader and assistant—was never required to join the church, and James Cudworth and Timothy Hatherly, though experiencing brief ostracism for their dissent, were thoroughly vindicated in having full freedom of conscience.[66]

William Hooke, a cousin of Oliver Cromwell, and the first minister of the church in Taunton in Plymouth Colony, made a statement on human liberty in "A Sermon preached upon a day of generall humiliation in the Churches of New England" in 1645, as he reacted to the injustices of Charles I:

> Brethren! Liberty is more precious than life, inasmuch as death is the common lot of all men, but servitude the portion only of men destined to misery. Seldom is it, that cruelty rests satisfied with bondage, but makes his progressions to further degrees of blood. . . . If any say, How are we concerned in the miseries of other men, so long as we are free. I say, it toucheth us.[67]

CHAPTER 5

The Pilgrim Family

Neither the distance of place, nor distinction of body, can at all either dissolve or weaken that bond of true Christian affection in which the Lord by his spirit hath tied us together.

—John Robinson[1]

The Pilgrim family was a school for children and servants for moral education and for vocational training, the hub of spiritual ties, pleasure, and amusement, a center for labor, health care, and community welfare. The Pilgrim colony was family-oriented. This is one basic reason for its success.

When the Pilgrim families were reeling under the blows of the Great Sickness the first winter, their loyalty to the orphans was demonstrated as they quickly took in the children who had been left homeless. Four entire families were wiped out by the epidemic. Only three married couples were left. Only five out of eighteen wives survived. Parents sacrificed for their children; that is why the youth came through as well as they did. Remaining men married widows, took in the little ones, and stood united against the rebuffs of the wilderness.

The fifty-one survivors were able to endure in large measure because they were part of firmly knit households. The tragedies of sickness, starvation, and Indian hostility almost broke the Jamestown colony under a succession of crises. The male settlers had a more tragic time of it because they were alone without their women and without the bond of offspring. William and Alice Bradford's example was characteristic of the settlers, who welcomed orphans into their homes when tragedy struck their parents. Bradford was taking care of Robert Cushman's son, Thomas, when the father died on a colony mission in London. He adopted the lad and wrote of the father: "And now we have lost the help of a wise and faithful friend." The Bradfords also raised Nathaniel Morton. These two youths developed into foremost leaders of the colony.[2]

The statue of the Pilgrim maid in Brewster Gardens beside the Town Brook in Plymouth represents what was unique in the Plymouth settlement. The colonists were sustained by a family comradeship.

Religion was an integrating force and a creative leaven in the Pilgrim family. There was a Bible in almost every home, the precepts of which established standards of conduct and faith, a panoply of belief under which men and women faced the testings of birth, sickness, death, housework, farm labor, hunger, sorrow, and joy. The Pilgrims endeavored to follow the admonition presented in their Geneva Bibles in the marginal note on Genesis 17:23: "Masters in their homes ought to be as preachers to their families, that from the highest to the lowest they may obey the will of God."

Church attendance was required in Plymouth, after the early beginnings, although Pastor Robinson opposed the use of compulsion in worship. The gathering of the people, sometimes fraught with resentment, accomplished much in integrating the life of the community and in providing a spiritual morale to confront hardship.

Special days were set apart in time of crisis, "solemn days of humiliation by fasting, etc., and also for thanksgiving as occasion shall be offered."[3] These people were children of the soil, and as they worked the earth with their hands and felt dependence on sun, wind, and rain, they lived in tune with the rhythm of nature. On the fringes of the unexplored forest and on the shores of an ocean with its ever-changing moods, they knew the wilderness life and were profoundly influenced by their dependence upon the natural order, the creation of their sovereign God.[4]

The serious-minded Pilgrims focused their vision on a super-mundane vista—their call to build the City of God on earth. Nevertheless, they were red-blooded, normal people and took pleasure in English amusements like bowls and pitch, stool ball, shuttlecock, pitching the bar, hoodman blind, foot-racing, and wrestling. Playing cards are mentioned in the court records. One man was fined for playing cards on Sunday, implying that he might have played on a weekday without breaking an ordinance. Dancing on the green and in the streets was popular at this time in England and countenanced by some of the Puritan divines. With their interest in good times, the Pilgrims may have done some dancing. They held frequent markets and fairs.

Men enjoyed the companionship of wives and children, planting and harvesting vegetables and grain, eating meat pie and corn pudding after laboring in the fields, sipping a mug of ale by the hearth while smoking fragrant tobacco they had cured, singing psalms and madrigals, listening to majestic words read from the Geneva Bible, sailing on the bay in pinnace or shallop, fishing for cod and haddock, and tramping the virgin forest. They knew the satisfaction that supports those who dwell in cottages built by their own hands, and the peace that comes through the independence of a self-sustaining homestead with one's own flour and meal, beans and peas, fish and wild game. They knew the sheer intoxication of breathing unpolluted air and the serene contemplation of the starry heavens on a summer night, free from the screaming brakes along a superhighway, the overhead roar of jet engines, and the pressure of noisy crowds.

Marriage was held in high esteem. Robinson wrote: "As marriage is a medicine against uncleanness, so adultery is the disease of marriage, and divorce the medicine of adultery."[5] Marriage was seen as the pattern for Christian life: "God hath ordained marriage, amongst other good means for the benefit of man's natural and spiritual life."[6] Robinson rejected the praise of virginity:

This is, indeed, the very dregs of Popery, to place special piety in things either evil, or indifferent, at the best; as is abstinence from marriage, and the marriage bed; which is no more a virtue than abstinence from wine, or other pleasing natural things. Both marriage and wine are of God, and good in themselves.[7]

"Differences will arise," wrote Robinson, "and be seen, and so the one must give way unto the other; this, God and nature layeth upon the woman, rather than upon the man."[8] "In the wife is specially required a reverend subjection in all lawful things to her husband. Eph. v. 22, &c. Lawful, I mean, for her to obey in, yea though not lawful for him to require of her."[9] Robinson said the love of a man toward his wife must be "like Christ's to his church, holy for quality, and great for quantity." This love must endure even when "her feelings and faults be great."[10]

The first Pilgrim marriage in the New World took place on May 12, 1621. Edward Winslow had been a widower only seven weeks, and his new wife, Susanna White, a sister of Deacon Fuller, had been a widow about twelve weeks after the Great Sickness had claimed their mates. In an established community it would have been considered good taste to wait awhile, but amid the perils of the wilderness it was imperative to hold the colony together. The marriage proved a fortunate one. A happy home was provided for Peregrine, the first white child born in New England, and his brother Resolved. Among their children was Josiah, who became the first native-born governor of an American colony.

Bradford described their wedding:

> May 12 was the first marriage in this place which, according to the laudable custom of the Low Countries, in which they had lived, was thought most requisite to be performed by the magistrate, as being a civil thing, upon which many questions about inheritances do depend, with other things most proper to their cognizance and most consonant to the Scriptures (Ruth iv) and nowhere found in the Gospel to be laid on the ministers as a part of their office. "This decree or law about marriage was published by the States of the Lowe Countries Anno 1590. That those of any religion (after lawful and open publication) coming before the magistrates in the Town, or state house, were to be orderly (by them) married one to another"—Petit's *History*, fol. 1629. And this practice hath continued amongst not only them, but hath been followed by all the famous churches of Christ in these parts to this time—Anno 1646.[11]

When Plymouth merged with Massachusetts, the clergy were authorized to solemnize marriages, but it was some time before the practice was widespread. In 1708 Josiah

Cotton and Hannah Sturtevant were married at Plymouth by Pastor Little.[12]

The betrothal or "precontract" was a brief ceremony before two witnesses. At this time the couple exchanged promises that they would marry. A period of time elapsed during which the banns were published. A betrothed couple were required to be loyal to their pledges. Sexual contact was forbidden, but the penalty for it was less than what was prescribed for single people. The couple were given a "portion" by their parents to help them establish a home of their own, in land, equipment, furnishings, or cash.[13]

Although weddings were removed from the church, they were an occasion for the assembling of family and friends. The ceremony was simple. The governor, or one of his assistants, joined the hands of the couple, asked if they took each other freely to be husband and wife, inquired if the parents approved, and then pronounced them man and wife.[14] Following the civil ceremony there was a social time, with food and drink.

In an effort to promote successful marriages, a law was passed in 1638 that no man should propose to a young woman until he had requested the consent of her parents, or her master, if she were a bond servant. Arthur Howland, Jr. was enraptured by the fair daughter of Governor Thomas Prence and Elizabeth did not discourage him. They kept company and he asked her to marry him. The stern governor was outraged and brought Arthur before the Court's Board of Assistants, accusing him of having "disorderly and unrighteously endeavored to obtain the affection" of his daughter. Arthur was fined five pounds, and to give surety for good behavior he was to deposit a bond of fifty pounds and agree that he would not again propose in the same fashion. The youth faced the rebuff in good spirits, and in time Elizabeth's father agreed to the marriage.[15]

John Saffin arrived at Plymouth Colony in 1644 at the

age of twelve. He grew up as the ward of Edward Winslow. When he was twenty-one he fell in love with Martha, daughter of Thomas Willet, an important figure in the colony. Willet told John that he would agree to their marriage if the young man would prove he could make a living. John set out for Virginia, and in four years he returned to Plymouth in a pinnace, with cash enough to please father and win Martha. He was a poet, as well as clever in business. On his homeward voyage he wrote:

> Sail, gentle pinnace; Zepheris doth not fail
> With prosperous gales; sail, gentle pinnace, sail!

The poet married Martha and they became part of the large Willet clan, which played an important role in the economy and culture of New England.

The man was accepted as head of the family. Women did not vote, but rights for women were more generous in Plymouth than in England, where they were unable to own property, make contracts, or bring a suit.[16] In Plymouth the law recognized that women deserved part of the family estate as in England, one third of the land and one third of the movable property. The Plymouth court occasionally altered the terms of a will to favor a widow. In 1663 widow Naomi Silvester was awarded a larger share of her husband's estate because she had been "a frugal and laborious woman in the providing of the said estate."[17]

In Plymouth the right of women to make contracts was upheld. They had legal interest in a limited type of ownership during marriage. Husbands did not include the clothing of wives in the property that was disposed of at their death.

An example of respect for the rights of a woman is found in the Colony Deeds, July 7, 1659. Robert Bartlett took a lease for ten years on the land of his late son-in-law, Richard Foster. He agreed to pay his grandson, Benjamin, then age "foure yeares," when he came of age. On this same day the widow, Mary Foster, and Jonathan Morey, whom she planned to marry, signed a prenuptial agreement about bringing up Mary's son, Benjamin. One of the conditions was that if Mary died before Jonathan, Benjamin should be at the disposal of Robert Bartlett (her father), Benjamin Bartlett, or William Harlow (uncles).[18]

Liquor licenses were granted to women. In 1663 Lydia Garrett of Scituate was licensed to "sell liquors to housekeepers." Mary Combe of Middlebury operated an ordinary. Goodwife Knowles ran a tavern. She was brought before the court "for selling strong waters for five or six shillings the bottle that cost but 35 shillings the case" and was fined ten shillings to be bestowed on "ye poor of Plymouth."[19]

An innkeeper in Taunton, James Leonard, was deprived of his license when his wife died, on the grounds that he was unfit to keep an inn. This indicates that his wife had played a major role in the tavern business.[20]

Bridget Fuller, wife of Dr. Fuller, who was married in Leyden in 1617, is believed to have served as a midwife. She also opened a small private school in 1634 and gave land for a church parsonage in 1667. An agreement was made on April 23, 1641 "between Bridget Fuller, widow and Nehemiah Smith concerning certain sheep which the said Nehemiah hath of the said Bridget to keep the half," indicating that Bridget operated a farm and that her rights were respected.[21]

Elizabeth Warren, the widow of Richard Warren who died in 1628 and who was assistant governor and one of the purchasers who held stock in Plymouth Plantation, was made a purchaser in her husband's place, succeeding to his rights:

It is agreed upon the consent of the whole Court that Elizabeth Warren Widow the relict of mr Richard Warren Deceased shalbe entred and stand and bee Purchaser instead of her said husband as well because that (hee dying before he had performed the said bargaine) the said Elizabeth performed the same after his decease as also for the establishing of the Lotts of land given formrly by her unto her sonns in law Richard Church, Robert Bartlett and Thomas Little in marriage with their wives her daughters.[22]

Elizabeth Warren was a businesswoman who owned extensive land and stock. In a list of the proprietors of the lands in what is now Little Compton, Rhode Island, dated March 1651, her name appears, and under the dates of March 22 and April 1, 1663, she and her son Joseph are entered as owners of the twelfth lot there. She was one of the purchasers of the tract of land which afterward became the town of Dartmouth, March 7, 1652. The marks of her horses were entered on the records on January 11, 1661, describing seven horses. She took one of her servants to court in 1635, which added a bit of spice to the routine of the plantation:

Thomas Williams, ye servant of widow Warren, was accused for spreading profane & blasphemous speeches against ye majestie of God, which wer these: ther being some discention betwen him and his dame, she after other things, exhorted him to fear God & doe his duty; he answered, he neither feared God, nor the divell; this was proved by witneses, and confessed by himselfe. This, because ye courte judged it to be spoken in passion & distemper, with reprove did let him pass.[23]

An active woman in the colony, Elizabeth Warren died October 12, 1673 at well over ninety years of age, having survived her husband by forty-five years and having lived to see at least seventy-five children, grandchildren, and great-grandchildren. "Mistris Elizabeth Warren an aged widow aged above 90 years Cam to her Grave as a shock of Corn fully Ripe she was honorably buried."[24]

Although a woman was not permitted to vote in the church or town government, and a man was considered head of the household and woman subject to him, Robinson did defend the female sex more than most contemporaries:

> Not only heathen poets, which were more tolerable, but also wanton Christians, have nick-named women, necessary evils; but with as much shame to men, as wrong to women, and to God's singular ordinance withal; when the Lord amongst all the good creatures which he had made, could find none fit and good enough for the man; he made the woman out of a rib of him, and for a help unto him, Gen. 11.20,21; neither is she, since the creation, more degenerated than he, from the primitive goodness. Besides, if the woman be a necessary evil, how evil is the man, for whom she is necessary.[25]

Pastor Robinson advocated more of a role for women in the church than they were given in the Church of England. He disagreed with the apostle Paul:

> Seeing that the apostle, ver. 34, 35 (I Cor xiv), enjoins women keep silence in this church exercise, not permitting them at all to speak; it seems most plain that he hath no eye, nor respect at all, to those extraordinary gifts and endowments of prophecy authorizing even women furnished with them, to speak publicly, and in men's presence, as appears in Miriam, Deborah, Huldah, Anna, as also even in Jezebel herself in regard order, and others![26]

Robinson also mentioned the Samaritan woman at the well, who talked freely with Jesus and so played a part in the New Testament. He felt that women should share in the life of the church:

> And for women, they are debarred by their sex, as from ordinary prophesying, so from any other dealing wherein they take authority over the man, 1 Cor. xiv. 34, 35; 1 Tim. ii. 11, 12, yet not simply from speaking; they may make profession of faith, or confession of sin, say amen to the church's prayers, sing psalms vocally, accuse a brother of sin, witness an accusation, or defend themselves being accused, yea, in a case extraordinary, namely where no man will, I see not but a woman may reprove the church, rather than suffer it to go on in apparent wickedness, and communicate with it therein.[27]

Family life-style followed an enviably simple pattern. There was plenty of healthy work for all to do. Every family member was expected to perform a variety of daily chores: cooking, curing meat, drying fruit, spinning, weaving, mending, sewing, tapping shoes, repairing tools, making soap, churning butter, preparing seed for planting, hoeing, weeding, reaping crops, storing the harvest, chopping wood, feeding fires, carrying water, building and maintaining shelters for man and beast, caring for cows, goats, sheep, pigs, and chickens. There was scant temptation to be idle or to indulge oneself since work was always to be performed in order to increase the security of the household.

The outdoor world was inviting at least eight months out of the year, offering an outlet that relieved family tensions. There was hunting in the forests for turkey, partridge, quail, and deer, and in the lowlands for ducks and geese. There was fishing in the ponds for perch, bass, and pickerel, and from a dory on the ocean for cod, haddock, and sole. Along the beach, clams, quahogs, scallops, and oysters were to be gleaned.

The family offered stability in the frontier world, a haven of companionship, although limited in facilities and luxuries. There were few divorces. The intrusions of technology and commercialism had not invaded this ancient sanctum. The home was self-sustaining. It was possible to survive for days on end without scurrying to a supermarket for supplies. Household members preserved and stored away grain and legumes, vegetables, smoked meat and fish, dried fruits, nuts, wool and flax for weaving, candles for light, and wood for fuel. These preparations nurtured pride in the household enterprise and a unity of spirit as members pooled their labor for the common good. Such efforts at planning and self-protection gave the family a feeling of confidence that together they could meet life's challenges.

Pilgrim households were large. Planned parenthood was a novelty and offspring were considered an asset as potential breadwinners. Family members were crowded into limited quarters in the early days of the colony, so privacy was at a premium. Young and old were together most of the time. The family was the center for teaching morality. Parents and masters were obligated by law to teach their children and their servants. The home was an adjunct to the meetinghouse in the building of Christian character, in inculcating spiritual values, and setting the example for righteous living. The Bible was read and prayers were offered daily, and churchgoing was supported. Youth were admonished and guided, and the unruly were disciplined. The morale of the colony was upheld by the unity of the family, and a sustaining faith was created, rooted in the spiritual values of the Bible.

Before there were formal schools, teaching of reading and writing took place in the home, along with vocational education. Here also the household arts were practiced. The home was the basis of the economy, the center for the work force. The family was the protector of society, opening its arms to the orphans, relatives in need, the aged, and the sick. This "little commonwealth" served as hospital, welfare department, and almshouse.

Plymouth was a poor colony, yet the first original cottages were graced by flower and herb gardens and by beds with sheets and pillowcases. Clothes were simple and carefully cherished, but some Pilgrims were from Leyden, a famous textile city, and knew good wool, corduroy, velvet, and cotton. Their inventories made clear that they loved colorful material, and their best costumes were attractive.

In spite of the original records that prove beyond doubt that Pilgrims dressed in bright colors and were against regulation of "gay apparel," that they wore red, blue, purple, green, and brown, liked silver buttons and buckles, pretty wools, velvets, and cottons, the concept of drab clothes and stern countenances prevails. Such a huddle of black figures was produced by the U.S. Postal Service at the time of Plymouth's 350th anniversary. Washington informed protesters that the artist who designed the colorless stamp was reflecting the painting "The Pilgrims Going to Church" by George Boughton. But, alas, the designer must have seen only a black and white reproduction of the original, which is in color. In happy contrast, the English created an anniversary stamp of the same scene using the proper hues of green, blue, red, and brown against a gaily colored ship, a more authentic picture than America's dark *Mayflower* and passengers.

The Pilgrims brought over furniture through the years in the ships that arrived steadily: oak chests, tables, beds, and chairs. Even in the early years they had carpenters like John Alden and Robert Bartlett, coopers, who knew how to build barrels and houses. These men made beds, stools, and chests, and utensils for the home and barn. Kenelm Winslow was a skilled cabinetmaker, and his furniture subsequently brought high prices in the antique market.

Cartoonists persistently portray these pioneers as grand-fathers and grandmothers, but the records show that the *Mayflower* company was a band of vigorous youth. When they landed in Plymouth, Howland was 21, Soule 21, Alden 22, Hopkins 22, Eaton 22, Winslow 25, Bradford 31, Allerton 34, Fuller 35, Standish 36, Warren 38; and there were youthful chaps like Doty, Leister, Cooke, Priest, Rogers, Brown, and others about whom we do not have a clear idea of age. Thirty-four of the "Pilgrim fathers" on the *Mayflower* were children.

Bradford told how he longed for "but a can of beer" when he was ill during the first winter, and how Captain Jones of the *Mayflower* passed word ashore that "he would send beer for them that had need of it, though he drunk water homeward bound." It was uncommon to drink water in this period since it was often unsafe. Bradford mentioned finding a spring during their exploration of Cape Cod, where they "refreshed themselves, being the first New England water they drunk of, and was now in great thirst as pleasant unto them as wine or beer had been in fore-times."[28]

The Pilgrims used beer and wine in moderation, being firmly against excess. They frowned on Thomas Morton and his men at Merrymount, who spent their profits from trading "vainly in quaffing and drinking" strong liquors with the natives, carousing with the Indian squaws, and selling firearms to the braves. Disturbed by the intemper-ance of their neighbors to the north, the Pilgrims took measures to disperse "some of the worst of the company."[29]

In 1646 Bradford wrote of the plentiful supply of wine that came to Plymouth from "Malaga, the Canaries, and other places, sundry ships landing in a year. So as there is now more cause to complain of the excess through abuse of wine, through men's corruption, even to drunkenness, than to any defect or want of the same."[30] In order to check drunkenness, laws were enacted and offenders brought to court.

These pioneers were guilty of "drinking" the "blessed weed." They had no knowledge of the adverse effects on health. One can scarcely begrudge them this small pleasure in the midst of their hardships. We know that Brewster owned a "tobacco case, tobacco box & tongs."

Even though the Pilgrims had to battle poverty and at times hunger, there is evidence that they lived with touches of beauty in their homes, dress, and social life. Isaac de Rasieres, secretary to Director General Peter Minuit of New Netherlands, visited Plymouth Plantation in 1627 to talk about trade with the Pilgrims. He noted the thrift of the settlers and the condition of the cottages and gardens, which gave him a sense of order and neatness.[31]

John Pory, secretary to the governor and council of Virginia, called at the plantation in 1622. He was a Cambridge University graduate, a member of Parliament, and the author of a book on Africa. Like de Rasieres, Pory was favorably impressed with the Plymouth people, feeling that they were above average in character.[32]

The tradition of the Christian family formed the core of survival in Plymouth Colony. It was men, women, and children together who were the home-builders, not just male settlers struggling alone to make a go of life in the wilderness. They crossed over with everything they possessed, staking all on the venture. They thought of themselves as permanent residents, not temporary sharers in a frontier community. They had come to stay, to put down roots, to stick it out through thick and thin. Women and children played a major role in the survival of Plymouth Plantation.

CHAPTER 6

Beginnings of Democracy

It is of human right and natural liberty for every man to worship what he thinketh God: and that it is no property of religion to compel to religion, which ought to be taken up freely; that no man is forced by the Christians against his will, seeing he that wants faith, and devotion is unservicable to God: and that God not being contentious, would not be worshipped of the unwilling.

—John Robinson[1]

The Pilgrim church was charged with radical experimentation since the people voted and elected their leaders. Both Bradford and Allerton wrote to England to defend the colony against enemies who claimed that they were a dangerous democracy, permitting even children to vote:

Touching our government, you are mistaken if you think we admit women and children to have to do in the same, for they are excluded, as both reason and nature teacheth they should be; neither do we admit any but such as are above the age of 21 years and they also but in some weighty matters, when we think good.[2]

There were democratic practices in the Pilgrim church. Robinson stated that "the highest church officers are but ambassadors of God, and interpreters . . . but neither an ambassador, nor interpreter . . . can command anything nor dispose of the least matter by his own authority." The practice of electing leaders and making them responsible to the people was a republican concept. Robinson insisted that the elders could not act separately, but only through the sanction of the congregation. The church "is never called the church of the elders, as they are called the elders of the church."[3]

The members of the church were all important since they were the priesthood of believers. "There is not the meanest member of the body but hath received a drop or dram of this anointing, so it is not the same to be despised, either by any member or by the whole."[4]

Edward Winslow pointed out that the Pilgrims were bound together by a special nexus developed by their persecutions in England and their discipline in Holland. Pastor Robinson said in his letter to the Plymouth portion of his parish: "Neither the distance of place, nor distinction of body, can at all either dissolve or weaken that bond of true Christian affection in which the Lord by his spirit hath tied us together."[5] What Robinson and Brewster wrote in 1617 to Sir Edwin Sandys was upheld by Bradford and his associates in Plymouth. They emphasized the fraternal bond that held them together in their enterprise.[6]

Their commitment was made in the form of a sacred covenant in the presence of God. In order to carry out their planting in the New World they were prepared to make further sacrifices. They were pledged to support one another in this mutual compact, undertaking the outfitting, the crossing, and the establishment in Plymouth of the friends left in Holland who wanted to cross over.

The Leyden Pilgrims who made it to Plymouth felt honor bound to bring over all those from Leyden who wished to come. This was a vast undertaking. They had no financial reserves and were dependent on further loans from the London Merchant Adventurers. Those in Plymouth had to meet principal and interest payments and contract further debts to keep their pledge to the Leyden people. Bradford wrote of the newcomers on the *Fortune* in 1621:

> These persons were in all thirty-five, which came at this time unto us from Leyden, whose charge out of Holland into England and in England till the ship was ready, and then their transportation hither, came to a great deal of money; for besides victuals and other expenses they were all newly appareled, for there was bought for them
>
> Of Kersey [cotton-wool], and
>   other cloth,   125 yards.
> Of Linnen Cloth,   127 ells.
> Of Shoes,   66 pair.
>
> Besides hats and other necessaries needful for them; and after their coming here, it was 16 months before they could reap any harvest, all which time they were kept at our charge which was not small: As the Lord sent these unto us, both to their and our comfort, so at the same time he sent many other godly persons into the land, as the beginning of a plentiful harvest, as will appear more fully hereafter.[7]

In 1633, when Edward Winslow was governor, it was voted that "whereas our ancient work of fortification . . . is decayed, and Christian wisdom teacheth us to depend

upon God in the use of all good means for our safety,"
every ablebodied male should perform or provide his share
in the building of a palisade around the original village.

The Pilgrim church had a tradition of discussion followed by decision of the majority. In the Green Gate
meetinghouse on the Kloksteeg in Leyden, the Pilgrims
had been trained to engage in open and free discussion.
They talked about whether they should leave Holland,
where they should try to settle (in Dutch territory on the
Hudson, in Virginia, or to the north beyond the bounds
of Jamestown), how they would finance this project, who
should go, and who should stay. In Plymouth they continued to talk over common problems and make decisions. As
church members they were part of Luther's priesthood of
believers, and followed Calvin's precept of the right of
individuals to judge for themselves. These beliefs formed
a seedbed of growth toward democracy.

The government checked on citizens in an effort to
control nonconformity when it threatened the public good.
Laws were not imposed by royal authority, but accepted
by the body of the people. In the contemporary sense,
Plymouth did not operate as a democracy, but it enjoyed
a representative government under law.

The democratic practices in the church were reflected
in the government of the colony. Before landing on Cape
Cod, forty-one men aboard the *Mayflower* signed the
Mayflower Compact, wherein was the promise to

> solemnly and mutually in the presence of God and
> one of another, Covenant and Combine ourselves to-
> gether into a Civil Body Politic, for our better order-
> ing and preservation and furtherance of the ends
> aforesaid; and by virtue hereof to enact, constitute
> and frame such just and equal Laws, Ordinances, Acts,
> Constitutions and Offices, from time to time, as shall

be thought most meet and convenient for the general good of the Colony, unto which we promise all due submission and obedience.[8]

Samuel Eliot Morison pointed out that the Mayflower Compact was an example of the compact theory of government and was "an experienced reality to North Americans who never heard of Jean Jacques Rousseau."[9]

When they had signed the compact, they elected Deacon John Carver as their first governor for that year. "After they had provided a place for their goods and begun some small cottages for their habitation, they met and consulted of laws and orders."[10] The settlers met once a year to elect the governor and, at first, one assistant. Voting was not restricted to church members, which indicated a liberal policy. The partisan spirit was not in evidence in the early elections. The community was small and integrated around a common cause. Public offices carried heavy responsibilities and there was no salary. The governor (Bradford, who was elected the second year, and for thirty terms thereafter) was granted his first salary in 1636, the munificent sum of £20 a year. Other officers received only living expenses while on duty.

The first law was recorded in 1623, establishing trial by jury. In 1636 a committee was appointed (four members from Plymouth, two from Scituate, and two from Duxbury) to draw up a code of laws. A declaration of rights was prepared, stating that they recognized only such laws as were enacted "by the consent of the body of freemen or associates, or their representatives legally assembled, which is according to the free liberties of the freeborn people of England."[11]

The "General Fundamentals" of 1636, adopted by the General Court of the freemen, formed the first bill of rights in America. The preamble stated that the Pilgrims came "hither as free-born subjects of the Kingdom of England." They laid claim to "all and singular privileges belonging to such." The Fundamentals read:

1. No laws may be made or taxes laid without the consent of the freemen "or their representatives legally assembled."
2. There will be "a free election annually" by the freemen to choose a governor and assistants.
3. Every person has a right to equal and impartial justice.
4. No one may be punished "in respect of limb, liberty, good name or estate" except by some express law of the colony or by virtue of the English common law.
5. All offenders are guaranteed a trial by jury "of twelve good and lawful men," and the defendant may challenge the jurors before the panel is formed.
6. No person may be condemned or sentenced without the evidence of at least two witnesses, or sufficient circumstantial evidence.
7. All sane persons of twenty-one years of age may dispose of their property by will.
8. The Congregational churches shall be protected and encouraged, and all towns must provide for their own ministers.[12]

During the early years of the colony the Pilgrims "administered justice with considerable informality but with a relatively rare degree of humanity."[13] There was not much crime during this period. Bradford stated that there were "some discontents & murmerings" and a few "mutinous speeches & carriages," but "they were quelled & overcome by the wisdome, patience, and just & equal carriage of things by the Governor and better part, which clave faithfully together in the maine."[14]

The Pilgrims, with their deference for the Bible, believed that "God gave right Judgment and true laws" to the Hebrews; yet they did not take over the Old Testament code with blind literalism. Five years before the Bay colonists drew up their law, Plymouth defined five capital crimes. The code in England listed 149. Capital offenses in Plymouth included: (1) "Treason or Rebellion," (2) "Willful Murder," (3) "Solemn Compaction or conversing with the divell by way of witchcraft, conjuration or the like," (4) "Willful & proposed burning of ships [or] howses," and (5) "Sodomy, rapes, buggery."[15] Plymouth refused to make adultery a capital crime. The only crimes that brought the death penalty were murder and buggery.

The General Court in 1623 made an effort to control trade by ordering that no one should sell or transport lumber without the permission of the governor and the assistants. Artisans and skilled workers were told not to do any work for strangers until the basic needs of Plymouth had been met. In 1626 it was decreed that no corn, beans, or peas should be transported or sold out of the colony without permission. When the first livestock came over, it was ordered that no animals were to be sold beyond the boundaries of Plymouth. Wages were fixed by the governor and the assistants. Private enterprise was practiced under certain governmental restrictions.[16]

The Pilgrims shared the Puritan concept that government should regulate the corrupt nature of human beings and that civil magistrates, once elected, were servants of God. Citizens should defer to the magistrates, who were expected to maintain the purposes of God. Civil officials were to uphold the covenant with God; hence, they were respected by the people. Even Roger Williams felt that anarchy would prevail if all were politically equal. He denied that the magistrates had any power in the affairs of religion and that the king had any right to grant land to the settlers. These challenges, plus his insistence on complete separation from the Church of England, caused the Bay authorities to order him banished from the colony in 1635. It is doubtful that Plymouth Colony would have expelled him. They considered it the ultimate punishment to deprive a citizen of land and home. Certainly they would not have censored him for being an extreme Separatist.[17]

Robinson taught that "the Christian magistrate hath his power of magistracy from God, which his Christianity serves to sanctify, and direct: so, undoubtedly, he is to use it for God and his honour."[18] Bradford asked: "Was it lawful for a magistrate to meddle in religion?" He quoted from the reformer Peter Martyr, who stated that "the prince should have the book of law and that both tables were committed to the magistrate's power." It was the duty of the magistrate to require people to "live well and virtuously." Bradford quoted Robinson, who said that the magistrate was the preserver of both tables of the ten commandments and could punish breaches of both of them.[19] The magistrates were respected and expected to assume authority. The freemen were protected against their domination, because they could vote them out of office if they overstepped. The authority of the magistrates was checked in 1636; in 1639 the governor and the board of assistants were deprived of the right to control the granting of land.

An intellectual self-reliance, encouraged by direct access to the Bible and to God, gave confidence to the individual, which tended to counteract the tendency of the select few to dominate the church or state. Leaders were all elected by the voters, and when they tended to violate their authority and exert oligarchic dominance, they could be voted out of power.

While the Pilgrims objected to ecclesiastical control

over the churches, they respected the authority of the state. Robinson said that when civil authorities acted in harmony with the precepts of religion they did so with God's sanction. He wrote that the magistrate "may alter, devise, or establish nothing in religion otherwise than Christ hath appointed, but [he may] use his lawful power lawfully to the furtherance of Christ's kingdom and laws." The magistrate was bound by the sacred nature of authority to carry out the will of God.[20]

The first freemen were the forty-one men who signed the Mayflower Compact. Some of these were hired workers like John Alden, others were indentured workers like John Howland, Edward Doty, Edward Leister, and George Soule. Each following year others were made freemen. They had to be twenty-one years or over and of a good reputation.

The settlers were divided into sojourners, inhabitants, and freemen. It was voted in 1656 that freemen of the various towns should be permitted to "propound" new candidates for admittance. Two years later there was an amendment to the effect that the candidate should be accepted by the court "upon satisfactory testimony from freemen of his town." After standing "propounded" for a year, he would be considered a freeman "if the Court shall not see cause to the contrary."[21]

Although the freemen were a minority, they formed the base for a representative government under law. They met at least once a year as a court or general assembly, and they elected their governor, deputy governor, secretary, treasurer, coroner, constables, and Board of Assistants. By 1633 four out of five male taxpayers were or would be freemen. Plymouth held no property qualifications for freemen. As the colony grew, deputies were elected to represent the people. In 1638 the right to choose the deputies was extended to every man who had taken the oath of fidelity, was head of a household, and was a settled resident.[22]

As early as 1638 six neighboring settlements had been formed outside the original plantation. There was feeling that too much power lay in the General Court dominated by Plymouth village. It was agreed that an assembly of towns should be set up, giving Plymouth four votes and the new communities two votes each. This assembly met four times a year. Its representatives or "deputies" formed a kind of lower house. The governor and the assistants came to be called the "Bench," which was something like an upper house.[23] During the seventy-two years of the colony, Plymouth had only six governors, all of whom were fortunate choices. These men lived close to the people, who knew their leaders personally.

The covenant principle of church organization tended to promote democratic ways as members committed themselves in a pact of mutual support and interdependence. The granting of land in fee simple also tended to create an independent yeomanry. The holding of individual land differed from the plantation system of Virginia and the patroon system of New York, and struck a blow at oligarchy in state and church.[24]

The Bay Colony drifted closer to dominance by the magistrates than did Plymouth, where civil officials were tied up with the citizens. The fundamental law of England was cherished by the colonists, and that law proved a safeguard against tyranny and protected the people from arbitrary acts by government. The clergy in Plymouth did not lean toward theocratic control. John Robinson had been very much one of the people. Roger Williams resisted dogmatism. Charles Chauncy was concerned with an intellectual and meditative religion, not with power politics. John Cotton was attentive during his long ministry to the nurture and care of his flock. The other ministers were not dominant personalities.

Church and state were separate entities that grew up together "like two twinnes." They both had the same basic purpose, to establish the commonwealth of God. Ministers were not permitted to hold public office. They were sometimes consulted by the magistrates, but the civil authorities made the final decision.[25] In 1642 Bradford records an outbreak of wickedness, "of sundry notorious sins especially drunkenness and uncleanness." Richard Bellingham, governor of the Bay, wrote to Bradford, asking him to counsel with his elders "and give us your advice in them" regarding how to deal with "heinous offenses in point of uncleanness." Governor Bradford replied that he had discussed the matter with his Board of Assistants "and we have referred the answer of them to such Reverend Elders as are amongst us, some of whose answers thereto we have here sent you enclosed under their own hands; from the rest we have not yet received any."[26]

Written considerations on how to deal with sodomy were sent in by Ralph Rayner of Plymouth, Ralph Partridge of Duxbury, and Charles Chauncy of Scituate. Their replies, in which they referred to noted scholars, quoted in Greek and Latin, stated that sodomy was a grave crime, but they all insisted that torture should not be applied to extort a confession. They upheld the precept of English law: "No man can be compelled to accuse himself." This civil right was later incorporated in the Fifth Amendment of the U.S. Constitution.

The clergy served as a board of advisers on such matters as capital punishment. The magistrates in turn were expected to support the ministers in their efforts to control moral offenses. In Plymouth, civil authorities took over certain functions of the ecclesiastical realm, such as the recording of births, marriages, and deaths, the rite of marriage, and the granting of divorces. This tended to keep the church from encroaching upon the state. Separation of church and state was made clear in 1633 when John Doane was elected and ordained as a deacon. He resigned his post as assistant governor, since he could not serve in both spheres.[27]

Bradford, elected for one-year terms as governor, with his personality and leadership qualities might have become a lord protector of the plantation like Penn and Baltimore in their colonies. But he remembered with aversion the dominance of lords and bishops and held to the democratic ways of the Leyden heritage. As a result, he avoided the evils of theocracy. He wrote in one of his verses:

Oh, how great comfort was it to see,
The churches to enjoy free liberty!
A prudent Magistracy here was placed,
By which the Churches defended were and graced;
Whilst things thus did flourish and were in their prime,
Men thought it happy and a blessed time,
To see how sweetly all things did agree,
Both in Church and State, there was an amity,
Each to the other mutual help did lend.[28]

The Pilgrims practiced freedom of expression as they spoke out against the regimentation and the abuses of the Church of England, and as they defended their Separatist position in oral debate and in the books they published. John Robinson engaged in public disputation at the University of Leyden. The meetinghouses in Leyden and in Plymouth encouraged members to stand up and speak their minds. They were a frank and independent people who dared to use strong rhetoric. Robinson confronted his critics, meeting their invectives with vigor. Bradford firmly accosted John Lyford, the conspirator against the colony. He rebuked the timid settlers, who wanted luxury and an idyllic existence in Plymouth, as he did the hypocritical London Merchant Adventurers.

The thought of the Separatists "was saturated with democratic feeling."[29] The Pilgrims brought these egalitarian tendencies with them to the New World. They did not openly champion this avant-garde precept, but John Wise, a minister in the Bay Colony, wrote later of the Congregational Way: "It seems most agreeable in the light of nature, that if there be any of the regular government settled in the church of God it needs be a democracy. This is a form of government, which the light of nature does highly value, and often directs to, as most agreeable to the just and natural prerogatives of human beings."[30]

Plymouth had its influx of "Strangers" like Lyford and Oldham, who were out of harmony with the purpose of the colony. A split was threatened between the planters and the particulars, who paid their own way and in some cases did not fit the ideology. It was natural for discontents to pull up stakes in England, leave their problems there, and move to a faraway colony. Morton and Gorton were men of this type, who battled against the Pilgrims because they disliked their philosophy and tried to undermine the future of Plymouth by spreading charges in England.

Drinking was permitted in the colony, but drunkenness was forbidden. There was a five-shilling fine for the first offense, the second was doubled, and the third tripled. Drunkenness was spelled out: "By drunkenness it is to be understood one that lisps or falters in his speech by reason of overmuch drink, or that staggers in his going, or that vomits."[31]

Regulations restricted the use of tobacco to house, taverns, and the fields. Smoking was prohibited in the meetinghouse. Men were fined for "drinking tobacco" in the highway.[32]

Fines were sometimes assessed for absence from public

worship. In 1659 there were a number of cases where parishioners stayed away in order to express their sympathy for the Quakers, whom they felt were getting unfair treatment. This was the period when Thomas Prence was governor, and he departed for a time from the tolerant policies of Bradford and Winslow.

The sabbath was strictly observed from sundown on Saturday to sundown on Sunday. Everyone was expected to attend church. Work, games, and amusements were forbidden. Sabbatarianism was not peculiar to Plymouth. The Puritans in England protested in 1618 until the Declaration of Sports was withdrawn, many clergy refusing to read the document from the pulpit as ordered by the king. When reissued by Charles in 1633, it was publicly burned. In 1643 people were forbidden under penalty to be present on the Lord's Day at any wrestling, shooting, bowling, ringing of bells for pleasure, masques, wakes, church ale games, dancing, and such other pastimes.[33]

William Bradford was disturbed that punishment should be necessary in the community the Pilgrims had established and that misconduct should occur among good people. He concluded that possibly there was no higher degree of bad conduct in Plymouth than elsewhere, but that their system of checking on wrongdoing was more meticulous so that defections were promptly noted and offenders censored and consequently brought to light.[34]

Their rules governing social conduct appear rigorous in the twentieth century, but they were not too disagreeable to the majority of the public then. Enforcement of the law and punishment were limited to an insignificant minority. There were court disputes about boundaries, livestock, debts, and slander, but major crimes were few. Some strayed from the straight and narrow path, but their deviation from the law appears mild to twentieth-century Americans.

The practice of justice was more humane in Plymouth than in many areas of the world at that period. Plymouth never employed torture, never burned a criminal alive, never punished a witch, never applied the cruel practices that were common in other countries. A very small number found guilty of murder were hanged. Troublemakers like Lyford, Oldham, and Morton were shown considerable mercy in view of their offenses. They were told to move out of the colony and settle elsewhere. Some were placed in the stocks and some were whipped, but in a good many instances the breaches of peace that were brought before the court were dealt with in common sense and a degree of forbearance. A case in point is that of Mercy, the teen-age daughter of Robert Bartlett, and her friend Sarah Barlow, who were sued by James Clarke for slander and brought before the court on October 22, 1668:

James Clarke complaineth against Sarah Barlow and Marcye Bartlett, in an action of slander and defamation, to the damage of two hundred pounds for reporting that they saw the said James Clarke kisse his mayde, and vse other uncuiell carriages that he acted towards her in the field vppon the Lords day.

This was refered to be ended by the majestrates by mutuall consent of each of the pties, whose determination and judgment is as followeth:

In reference to the complaint of James Clarke against Sarah Barlow and Marcye Bartlett, for defaneing him in makeing report of vnseemly familiarities between him and his mayde, the Court, haueing fully considered the matter, and compared the testimony relateing thereunto, and takeing notice how the pties that haue charged him haue, one or both of them, said and unsaid or greatly varyed in their relations about it, doe declare, that we judge they have defamed and slaundered him therein, because the things charged by them doth in noe measure appear by testimonie; and also their way of devoulging it was manifestly scanderlous, although there had bine some appaerances of truth in their report, and therefore for this theire misdemeanor doe amerce them ten shillings appece to the Kinge. (On the margin) This was non suited because the said Marcye Bartlett was found under couert barud.[35]

The shillings were not collected for the crown since the girls were underage. James Clarke was not excommunicated from the church. The potential for quite a rumpus existed, but it was handled in a calm fashion. The gossipy girls were put in their place. James Clarke was left with only a problem to square with his wife. The hysteria that might have been created by a teenage blowup, as in Salem, was avoided, through the horse sense of the magistrates.

A study of court records indicates that the magistrates did not follow the letter of the law too strictly and that they were not heartless in most instances in meting out punishment. A spirit of mercy was often in evidence.

Arthur Peach, the runaway indentured worker who murdered an Indian and was hanged for it with his two co-conspirators, left Stephen Hopkins' maidservant, Dorothy, pregnant. Hopkins refused to carry out his bargain to clothe and feed her and keep her in his home. He was brought before the court, where he himself had sat in judgment on others, charged with contempt, and ordered confined to his house. He was released after he paid £3 to John Holmes, who assumed charge of Dorothy and her child for the two years yet to be covered by her contract. The young mother was arraigned later for unlawful maternity and sentenced to be whipped twice. The first attempt was halted when the victim fainted, and the penalty was remitted.[36]

Proof of regeneracy was not required for status of a freeman as it was in the Bay Colony. The Massachusetts General Court voted soon after settlement that only church members could vote in elections and hold office. In Plymouth Colony, no statement of qualification for freemanship existed until 1656 when candidates were required to secure approval of the freemen in their town before sending their names to the General Court.[37]

Plymouth did not require church membership for one to become a freeman. Peregrine White, born aboard the *Mayflower* in 1620, became a freeman in 1652, but did not join the church until 1698.[38] By 1670 Baptists were among the freemen. Even Quakers were eventually included, but they were disbarred during the period of intense hostility that swept the colonies. When Thomas Prence became governor, an applicant for freeman was required to wait a year to be admitted. The court directed that no Quaker could be admitted and converts to this faith and even sympathizers would be disenfranchised.[39]

Plymouth did not set up a rigid list of requirements for membership in the church. Candidates were not expected to face cross-examination in the Christian faith. They were supposed to be "converted," that is, separated from the world and dedicated to Christian precepts, and ready to "own the covenant," but forced to accept no formal creed or to testify extensively. John Robinson wrote about salvation: "A man can say this only of himself certainly because he only knows his own heart but of others morally and in the judgment of charity which is according to outward appearance and which may deceive."[40]

In Leyden and during the early days in Plymouth, candidates for membership were not put through an examination but only required to agree to the confession of faith and accept the covenant.[41] There were later efforts to tighten requirements. After John Cotton arrived in Plymouth in 1667, after the Leyden Pilgrims had passed away, individuals were asked to make a public statement on their religious experience. But Cotton stated that while he was pastor no one who sought membership was ever refused.[42] In light of this testimony it appears that Plymouth was more liberal than some of the early New England churches in drawing the lines between "Saints" and "Strangers."

Class structure in Plymouth was more flexible than in England. Robinson pointed out in his farewell letter, which was influential in developing the Mayflower Compact:

> Whereas you are become a body politic, using amongst yourselves civil government, and are not furnished with any persons of special eminency above the rest, to be chosen by you into office of government; let your wisdom and godliness appear, not only in choosing such persons as do entirely love and will promote the common good, but also in yielding unto them all due honour and obedience in their lawful administrations, not beholding in them the ordinariness of their persons, but God's ordinance for your good; not being like the foolish multitude who more honour the gay coat than the virtuous mind of the man, or glorious ordinance of the Lord.[43]

There was no royalty in Plymouth and there were no hereditary posts or firm class barriers, as in England. Plymouth did possess its own gentry, made up of men of education, means, and social standing. This included the six governors: John Carver, William Bradford, Edward Winslow, Thomas Prence, Josiah Winslow, and Thomas Hinckley; the deputy governors created in 1680: James Cudworth and William Bradford, Jr.; and the assistant governors: Isaac Allerton, Richard Warren, Myles Standish, Stephen Hopkins, John Howland, John Alden, John

Doane, William Gilson, William Collier, Timothy Hatherly, John Browne, John Jenney, John Atwood, Edmund Freeman, William Thomas, Thomas Willet, Thomas Southworth, and others. The secretaries were Nathaniel Souther, Nathaniel Morton, Nathaniel Clarke, and Samuel Sprague. The treasurers were William Paddy, Myles Standish, John Alden, Constant Southworth, and William Bradford, Jr.

The freemen were fortunate most of the time in their choice of officers. They seemed to pick candidates with natural leadership qualities. A small group of "select men," to use John Robinson's phrase, provided direction for the colony.

In the church the ruling elders were William Brewster, Thomas Cushman, and Thomas Faunce, three stalwart figures who guided the church of Leyden and Plymouth from 1609 to 1746. The deacons were Robert Cushman, Samuel Fuller, John Carver, Richard Masterson, Thomas Blossom, John Doane, William Paddy, John Cooke, Robert Finney, Ephraim Morton, and Thomas Faunce.

These citizens, and others who were prominent in church and community and in farming, trading, and shipping, formed the gentry of Plymouth. A good number of them lived relatively prosperous lives. Several from the ranks of artisans, and even indentured servants, managed to climb the ladder of recognition, indicating that the hurdles of rank were not as insuperable in the New World.

In 1627 there were fewer than 209 settlers in the Plymouth Plantation Colony. In 1630 there were possibly 250. Farming was still grouped about the village, but the settlers were beginning to think of moving to larger land holdings.[44] Plymouth soon sprawled out from the original stockade village into nearby settlements, forming twenty towns in all, each eventually with its own church: Plymouth (1620), Scituate (1636), Duxbury (1637),

Barnstable (1639), Sandwich (1639), Taunton (1639), Yarmouth (1639), Marshfield (1641), Rehoboth (1645), Eastham (1646), Bridgewater (1656), Dartmouth (1664), Swansea (1667), Middleborough (1669), Edgartown (1671), Tisbury (1671), Little Compton (1682), Freetown (1683), Rochester (1686), Falmouth (1686), Nantucket (1687).

William Bradford was naturally dismayed as his people spread forth like growing chicks from a mother hen. He wrote, "This I fear will be the ruin of New England, at least of the churches of God there." But during this diaspora there was sufficient leaven of the Scrooby-Leyden-Plymouth origins left to build new meetinghouses and preserve the heritage.

In 1646 Bradford gave vent to his democratic feeling when he learned of the tottering regime of Charles I, and, with Charles' defeat in the civil war, of the impending collapse of the dominance of the Church of England:

> Do you not see the fruits of your labours, O ye servants of the Lord? That have suffered for His truth, and have been faithful witnesses of the same, and ye little handful amongst the rest, the least amongst the thousands of Israel? . . . The tyrannous Bishops are ejected, their courts dissolved, their canons forceless, their service cashiered, their ceremonies useless and despised, their plots for popery prevented and all their superstitions discarded and returned to Rome from whence they came, and the monuments of idolatry rooted out of the land. . . . Are not these great things? Who can deny it? . . . Hallelujah![45]

Charles' execution in 1649 was followed by the Commonwealth and Protectorate. Soon after the death of Lord Protector Oliver Cromwell, the Restoration took place in 1660, and Charles II came to the throne. At his death,

James II was crowned in 1685. His efforts, as a Catholic, to suppress the Church of England caused widespread hostility. The opposition called William, ruler of the Netherlands, and his wife, Mary, a daughter of King James, to take over the country. James fled to France and the "Glorious Revolution" came to England in 1689.

Plymouthians resented paying taxes to a distant government and worried over the state of their land. Their patent of 1629 was not a royal charter that gave them the rights of self-government. They feared that moves would be made against their churches of the Congregational Way. In October 1691 the crown issued a new charter for the Massachusetts Colony, ordering the annexation of Plymouth. Thus, at length, after seventy-one eventful years, the Pilgrim Story entered a new epoch.

CHAPTER 7

Church of the People

As the Lord's free people joined themselves (by a
covenant of the Lord) into a church estate, in the
fellowship of the gospel, to walk in all His ways made
known, or to be known unto them, according to their
best endeavors, whatever it should cost them, the Lord
assisting them.

—William Bradford[1]
The Scrooby Church Covenant, 1606

William Bradford stated that the Pilgrim church was
modeled on the New Testament and early Christianity:
"They came as near the primitive pattern of the first
churches as any other church of these latter times hath
done, according to their rank and quality."[2]

The people could form their own church. They were
the church. Hence the name Congregational. The congregation was the church. The people chose their minister,
their officers, and their organization, and ran the enterprise
free from outside state or ecclesiastical control. "The
people are a free people, and the church a free estate

spiritual, under Christ the king; the ministers the church's, as Christ's servants; and so by the church's provision to live, and of her, as labourers to receive wages."[3]

The Pilgrims believed that:

To make a reformed church, there must first be a reformed people: and so there should have been with you [the Established Church] by the preaching of repentance from dead works, and faith in Christ: that the people, as the Lord should have vouchsafed grace, being first fitted for, and made capable of the sacraments, and other ordinances, might afterwards have communicated in the pure use of them: for want of which, instead of pure use, there hath been, and is at this day a most profane use of them.[4]

The Church of England was composed of all residents of the parish, irrespective of their spiritual condition or training. They were "gathered generally," encompassing many false and dead members, and consequently they could not be "the true visible body of Christ."[5] This motley crew was composed of all sorts, "clapped and clouted together." How could a true church be made up in this arbitrary manner, including all within the parish perambulation?[6]

It seemed ridiculous to hold that

every subject of the kingdom dwelling in this or that parish, whether in city, or country, whether in his own or other man's house, is thereby, *ipso facto*, made legally a member of the same parish in which that house is situated: and bound, will he, nill he, fit, or unfit, as with iron bonds, and all his with him, to participate in all holy things, and some unholy also, in that same parish church.[7]

Ungodly, profane persons could not create a true church. The true church was composed of "persons called out of the state of corrupt nature into that of supernatural grace." To form a church, people had to separate themselves from idolatry, corruption, and the secular and join together in "the fellowship of the gospel."[8] The gathering of the visible church came about when people "separated themselves from the unsanctified world into the covenant and fellowship of the gospel, by free and personal profession of faith and confession of sins."[9]

The gathering of a church could be brought about by the preaching of the gospel. This was the only outward means. Where "two or three faithful people do arise, separating themselves from the world into the fellowship of the gospel and covenant of Abraham, they are a church truly gathered." Even a small unit was significant. Size did not determine the importance of a church.[10]

Members had to be prepared intellectually and spiritually by "the preaching of the Word and fitted as spiritual stones for the Lord's building, and so join in covenant, by voluntary and personal confession of faith, and confession of sins."[11]

How was a true church founded? "By coming out of Babylon, through the mercies of God, and building ourselves into a new and holy temple unto the Lord." Members were not gathered by the service book or by popish priests, but through the preaching of the word they were quickened to separate from the secular world.[12]

Robinson spoke of the true church as "a company of faithful and holy people, with their seed, called by the Word of God into public covenant with Christ and amongst themselves, for mutual fellowship in the use of all the means of God's glory and their salvation."[13]

The Pilgrims of the Scrooby fellowship followed the words of Paul: "Come out from among them, and be ye separate [2 Cor. 6:17, KJV]." The Church of England as they knew it was a jumble of the pious and the impious, "a confused heap." There was no choice but to march out of that false church and create a true one. "By this we hold and affirm, that a company, constituting though but of two or three, separated from the world, and gathered in the name of Christ, by a covenant made to walk in all the ways of God known unto them, is a church, and so hath the whole power of Christ."[14]

The "Saints" were a people set apart for the purpose of building a community patterned after the heavenly city.

> The main ends for which the Lord gathereth and preserveth his church upon earth are that he might have a peculiar people, separated unto himself, from all other peoples, to call upon his name in faith and to glorify him, their heavenly Father in their holy conversation, whom he also might glorify in the end of their faith, the salvation of their souls.[15]

Robinson explained that the word church came from the Hebrew word *kahal*, and the Greek *ecclesia*, signifying "a company of people called out of the state of nature, into the state of grace, out of the world, into the kingdom of Christ."[16]

Those belonging to the Church of England called Separatists like the Pilgrims "the hasty Puritans" because they were in the vanguard, having made an overt break with the establishment.

The Pilgrims did not advocate complete democracy in the church. There was a mingling of the "aristocratic" and the "democratic." The church was administered by "certain choice men," chosen by the people. Elders were selected to serve as teachers and helpers of the minister. They should "be apt to teach in public assembly." They must take decisions to the people for action. They did not rule the church.

Deacons were chosen, following the New Testament

custom. The power of church leaders was limited to the right to persuade, and that right belonged to the people also. Church officials were not like public magistrates who could demand obedience. They were "not Lords over God's heritage to rule like princes," but "ministers and servants of Christ."[17]

"The meanest member thereof" was not expected to submit if the minister did not live up to accepted responsibilities. The clergy were not to be obeyed as the magistrates were, "but for the reason of the commandment, which the ministers are also bound in duty to manifest, and approve unto the consciences of them over whom they are set."[18]

The Pilgrims spoke out against the unscrupulous practices of parish priests:

> Their sale of orders and institutions and . . . of dispensations for pluralities, and non-residence, of licences to preach up and down the country, and to marry at times by their canons prohibited; of pardons and absolutions, when men are excommunicated, and sometimes when they are dead, before they can have Christian burial; with the extorted fees, and purse-penalties, the very sinews of their kingdom, do clearly pronounce against them, and they and their subordinates are merchants of that great city Babylon, trafficking for all manner of wares, and for the souls of men.[19]

They believed that excommunication, when necessary, should be handled by the individual church, not by the bishops and the hierarchy, where it was so often abused. Robinson pointed out that the "bishops' courts played with excommunication like a child with a rattle." Arch offenders went free while honest people were often expelled from the church for mere trifles. Exorbitant fines were levied and bribes exacted.[20]

The power of censure and excommunication had been grossly abused in the Established Church. The Pilgrims placed this authority in the hands of the people, who were to follow the advice of Jesus: "If he refuses to listen to them, tell it to the church [Matt. 18:17, rsv]." "The People have power to censure offenders: for they that have power to elect, appoint, and set up officers, they also have power, upon just occasion, to reject, depose, and put them down."[21]

In cases of discipline, the officers consulted with the offender and then brought their suggestions to the people. The offender might be sent to talk with Elder Brewster, where he or she would be counseled and admonished. If efforts at repentance and reconciliation failed, dismissal from the church was considered as the last resort.

People could be restrained by the magistrates in outward behavior, but in religious actions the proper guide was not the civil authority, since moral motivations lay in the "faith and devotion in the heart of the doers."[22]

The authority of the civil magistrate required obedience, but not the officer of the church. The elected leaders of the congregation had no such authority. They had only the right to persuade, and this right also belonged to the people. If they were wronged, they had the right to defend themselves and to speak before the church body.

The Pilgrims operated on the thesis that church and state should employ different officers and follow different methods because they fulfilled separate functions. The church stood for the kingdom of God on earth. The authority of its leaders was spiritual because that kingdom was not of the world. The church should not endeavor to carry out the will of God through force, but only through spiritual means: persuasion, exhortation, and admonition.

The most radical form of censorship was expulsion from the church.[23]

They contended that they

cannot find in the Scriptures the least colour for the offices of archbishops, bishops, suffragans, deans, archdeacons, half-priests, or English deacons; nor that the duties of celebrating marriage, purifying women, burying the dead, reading the service-book in manner and form, are laid upon the ministers of the gospel, as duties to be done in their offices, nor that the provincial and diocesan officers may intrude into their office, which are set over particular congregations, and deprive them of the power of government; nor the deacons to administer the sacraments, nor that any of them may intrude into the office of the civil magistrate, as they all do less or more, in meddling with matters of marriage, divorce, testaments, or with injuries, as they respect the body, or outward man.[24]

This confusion of duties blocked the main obligation of the minister, which was to be a teacher of the word of God to the people. The outward works of the church were outlined in the *Catechism* of William Perkins, which was used by the Pilgrims in teaching: "1 Prayer, 2 The reading and opening of the Word, 3 The sacraments, 4 Singing of Psalms, 5 Censures, 6 Contributions to the necessities of the saints."[25]

The Pilgrim church organization appeared to contemporaries to be a swing to the far left in democratic procedure. John Robinson explained that they did not practice pure democracy, so that a chaos of controversy prevailed, and even women and children voted. He said, "the external church government was under Christ, the only mediator and monarch thereof." The elders were elected by the male members. "The elders publicly propound and order all things in the church." The elders lawfully met separately from the congregation when necessary "to deliberate on such things as concern her welfare." Women and children did not vote, as critics charged "but only men, and them grown, and of discretion."[26]

False accusations were hurled at the Pilgrims. Robinson and his associates repudiated the charge that their church was a democratic bedlam. He pointed out that three forms of political theory were followed: First, the monarchical, where supreme authority rested in the founder, Christ. Second, the artistocratic, where the authority was in the hands of a few select people elected by the congregation. Third, the democratic, where the decisions were shared by the members. This step toward democracy was more advanced than anything in the Church of England at that time.

The Plymouth church held frequent business meetings. Policies were openly discussed and then voted upon. All sorts of problems were propounded: the use of contributions, procedures in worship, discipline, and the state of the church in general.[27]

The purity of the church was all-important. It is not clear what tests were applied to those who sought membership, besides the search to determine saving grace at work in their lives. The pure church was marked by the faith and grace evidenced by its members.[28]

The Pilgrims not only sought the purification of the church from oppressive controls of a hierarchy, excessive dogma, the constraint of deadly formalities, and the blight of banalities; they also stood for positive action, the championing of humanity's obligation to know and to serve God.

Members were asked to share in a covenant which they made with one another that they would obey the will of God. Robinson taught that the "Saints," or members, were a holy people who had parted with evildoers. As God's people, they were set apart in a special fellowship; they were "knit together" in a solemn duty to "exhort, comfort, admonish and reprove one another." They had left the Church of England because it was polluted, accepting the unprepared and unrepentant, and infected with impurity.[29]

The concept of purity pervaded the life of the church. Members were obligated to seek pure company and a pure leadership. As members of a "holy fellowship every one is made a king, priest, and prophet, not only to himself but to every other, yea to the whole." The priesthood of believers made every person important. Members had the right to choose their leaders and their ministers and to dismiss them. The minister was subject to the gathered church and its people. Christ gave his power "first to the body of the church" and then by delegation to the ministry. Authority came first to the "body," the church members, and then to the "eye," the minister. "In the church, the officers are the ministers of the people, whose service the people is to use for the administering and executing of their judgments."[30]

The Pilgrims carried to the New World no written confession, declaration of faith, or creed. They made use of the Scrooby covenant. It was not until 1676 that a more formal covenant was set up. This was during King Philip's War and was recommended by the General Court. A Day of Humiliation "was set apart" and the proposal was made that all should renew a covenant engagement with God in the face of the evils that confronted the colony.

They believed that everyone was called to engage in the discipline of work and in the discipline of faith. Everyone had a "particular calling" to contribute through work. There was also a "general calling," in which all Christians must serve, that is, "the building of the church." As

William Perkins put it: "Though men . . . fondly imagine that this duty is proper to the ministers, yet the truth is, it belongs not only to them, but to everyone."[31]

Plymouth was more liberal in its standards of admission into church membership than some in the Bay, and was not too strict in asking "proof of election." Bradford in his *Dialogue* has the young men ask the ancient men (who had come from Leyden), "Wherein doe they [the Separatist churches] differ from the Judgement or practice of our churches here in New England?" The ancient men answer: "Truly for matter of practice Nothing att all that is in any thinge materiall these [the Bay], being Rather more strict and Ridged in some proceedings about admission of Members and things of such Nature than the other."[32]

Bradford upheld the position of Robinson, who pointed out the difficulty of judging the inner state of a person's piety: "A man can say this only of himself certainly because he only knows his own heart but of others morally and in the judgment of charity which is according to outward appearance and which may deceive."[33]

Edward Winslow stated that the church in Plymouth sought "to see the grace of God shining forth (at least seemingly, leaving secret things to God) in all we admit into church fellowship with us, and do keep off such as wallow in the mire of their sins, that neither the holy things of God, nor the communion of the Saints may be leavened or polluted thereby."[34]

The Pilgrims opposed the dominance of the mother church by the prestigious class of prelates and bishops, and the monarchical controls of the court. They were a people's movement, struggling to evolve more democratic practices. The elected officers were "not lords over God's heritage." They were not to rule like princes over their subjects. In contrast, they were "ministers and servants of Christ" and were subject to the will of the people who elected them. It was proper for members who were "doubtful of anything in the officers' administration, to propound their doubt for satisfaction." Members had the right to admonish them concerning their duties and to demand that problems be solved and evils corrected.

The duties of the minister to the congregation were to keep order and sustain the faithful. Robinson wrote that his role "stands in feeding, and not in begetting." He was not obligated to preach to those outside, but to care for the flock who made him their minister.

The elders, chosen by the people because they were "apt to teach in public assembly," served as teachers and assistants to the minister. They were to oversee the administration of the sacraments and were supposedly qualified to teach in the pastor's absence or illness. Elected for life, they were still subject to the people and had to take all decisions to them for final action. The elders were not the ultimate authority; their function was purely moral. In the Plymouth church

> the Ruling elders with the Pastor made it their first spetiall worke together to passe through the whole towne from family to family to enquire into the state of soules and according as they found the frame either of the children of the church or others, soe they applyed counsells, admonitions, exhorting, for in divers with whom God had begun his work, it prevailed to stirre them up to lay hold of the covenant.[35]

In keeping with the practice of the early church, deacons were elected by the congregation. They took care of the church funds and distributed them for the support of the pastor, the care of the needy, the propagation of religion, and the administration of the Lord's Supper.

The covenant of membership obliged each person to be

responsible for the work of the church and for its reputation. Each member had the right to participate and was commissioned by Christ which "so makes every one of them severally kings and priests and all jointly a kingly priesthood." Belief in the priesthood of all believers emphasized the dignity of membership.[36]

Ordination was regarded as important, since it was sanctioned by the Bible. They ordained their pastors, teachers, and elders by the laying on of hands. Henry Jacob, who lived with the Pilgrims in Leyden, spoke of ordination as "a holy sign [although] of less dignity and inferior nature" to the sacraments. John Robinson was ordained by his own congregation when it was established in Leyden.

When the church was being organized in Salem in the summer of 1629, Governor Bradford and a group from Plymouth were invited to attend the ordination of the minister and teacher. They were caught in a high wind as they sailed north, but they arrived in time to extend the hand of fellowship on behalf of their church. Governor John Endecott had set apart "a solemn day of humiliation for the choice of pastor and teacher." After a time of "prayer and teaching," the two candidates spoke of their "calling." Persuaded that the two men were qualified, they were elected by the members. Mr. Skelton was chosen pastor and Mr. Higginson teacher. The next day was "appointed for another day of humiliation for the choice of elders and deacons and ordaining of them."[37] This must have been similar to the practice of the Leyden-Pilgrim church.

John Cotton wrote of the ordinations in the Boston area in much the same pattern. The nominee "then with the Presbytery of that Church if they have any, if not two or three of the gravest Christians among the Brethren of that Church being deputed by the body, do in the name of the Lord Jesus ordain him into the Office, with imposition of hands, calling upon the Lord, to accept and own him."[38] The minister was then given a charge to serve the people and extended the hand of fellowship into the church.

During their unfair treatment in England, caused by the spying, malicious accusation, arrest, fines, and imprisonment, the Pilgrims never advocated reprisals against their persecutors or resorted to violence in any way. They did not hate the mother church, their country, or their king, although they were harassed by them. They did not plot to bomb the royal palace or violate altars, stained-glass windows, or images.

It was clear that they were a peace-loving fellowship: "Neither good intent, nor events, which are casual, can justify unreasonable violence."[39]

In the early years church attendance was not compulsory at Plymouth. During this period in Virginia, Governor De La Warr ordered two sermons each Sunday, accompanied by an elaborate ritual, with a service on Thursday and prayers twice each day. General Thomas Dale established a rigid discipline in an effort to check laziness, idleness, and refusal to work. Shootings, burning at the stake, hanging, and breaking on the wheel so terrorized the settlers that they changed some of their habits. Under Dale's regime the first offense at swearing brought a whipping, the second a bodkin thrust through the tongue, the third the death sentence.[40]

Robinson believed that the state should not enforce church attendance:

Considering that neither God is pleased with unwilling worshippers, nor Christian societies bettered nor the persons themselves neither, but the plain contrary in all three . . . by this cause of compulsion many became atheists, hypocrites, and familists, and being at first constrained to practice against conscience, lose all conscience afterwards. Bags and vessels overstrained break, and will never after hold anything.[41]

However, in the 1660s regulations and restrictions were imposed. The records of Plymouth Colony state:

It is ordered that if any in any lazey, slothful or prophane way doth neglect to com to the publick worship of God shall forfeit for euery such default ten shillings or bee publicly whipte.

Whosoever shall prophane the Lords day by doeing any servill worke or any such like abusses shall forfeit for every such default ten shillings or be whipt.[42]

It was stipulated that a fine be levied on those who traveled on the Lord's Day "except they can give a sufficient reason for theire soe doing." Another ordinance stated that "noe ordinary keeper in this Govrment shall draw any wine or liquor on the Lords day for any except in case of necessitie for the reliefe of those that are sicke or faint or the like for theire refreshing, on the penaltie of paying a fine of ten shillings for every default."[43]

With the coming of more new settlers and the weakening of the original idealism, efforts were made under Governor Thomas Prence to increase orthodoxy. The court passed rules to ban travel on the sabbath, punish dozing during church services, and prohibit smoking near the meetinghouse: "That any psons goeing to or coming from the meetinges within two miles of the meeting house shall pay twelve pence for every such default to the Collonies use."[44]

If Elder Brewster had been alive at this time, he might have taken a stand against such limitations. His inventory shows that he owned a smoker's kit. His home was close by the first meetinghouse and he might have welcomed Governor Bradford and others there after church for a chat. The men enjoyed their long-stem clay pipes filled with their home-grown weed. Bradford might have served a mug of ale from his "great beer bowle worth three pounds" or his "other beer bowle" worth two pounds, filled from his "brewing tub." With the passing of Bradford, snoopy laws crept in, after the pattern of the Bay.

The Pilgrims insisted that the church should be independent of the state. Taxes were not to be used to pay the clergy, but ministers should be employed by the members of the church, who should contribute to their support. Robinson said, and the Pilgrims followed his policy:

> All free persons and estates should choose their own servants, and them unto whom they give wages, and maintenance for their labours and service. So it is betwixt the people, and ministers: the people a free people, and the church a free estate spiritual, under Christ the king, the ministers the church's, as Christ's servants; and so by the church's provision to live, and of her, as labourers to receive wages.[45]

He taught:

> The Lord hath ordained that they which preach the gospel, should live of the gospel. We do willingly leave unto you [the Established Church] both your priestly order, and maintenance, content in ourselves with the people's voluntary contribution, whether it be less or more, as the blessing of God upon our labour, the fruit of our ministry, and a declaration of their love and duty.[46]

In the 1640s legislation in the Bay Colony indicated that the relation of ministers to their flocks was changing, as was the authority of the dominies. Formal systems to provide support for the church were tried. Institutional protection replaced the former voluntary personal bonds between clergy and people.

With the declining interest in religion, attempts were made to guarantee collection of ministerial salaries. Although Plymouth had opposed tax support of the clergy, in 1655 Rehoboth asked the General Court to force citizens to contribute. James Cudworth of Scituate complained: "Now we must have a State-Religion . . . a State-Minister and a stateway of Maintenance; And we must worship and serve the Lord Jesus as the World shall appoint."[47]

Plymouth Colony was small and poor and faced problems in providing for its ministers. The General Court in 1657 moved for the first time a law ordering compulsory support of the church and clergy. Ups and downs had been commonplace in collecting maize and wampum to take care of the pastors. Ministers received minimum stipends, yet some of them in early New England managed to exist in relative refinement and to even accumulate modest estates.

Deacon Samuel Fuller's son, Lieutenant Fuller, protested when such a law was passed: "The devil sat at the stern when it was enacted." Such efforts failed to provide for the church, and the people clung to private support.[48]

CHAPTER 8

Pilgrim Ethics

Thus out of small beginnings greater things have been produced by God's hand that made all things of nothing, and gives being to all things that are; and, as one small candle may light a thousand, so the light here kindled hath shone unto many, yea in some sort to our whole nation.

—William Bradford[1]

Ethics were of major importance in Pilgrim religion. Pastor Robinson stated that God did not look with partiality on "chamber religion towards him, which is not accompanied in the house, and streets, with loving-kindness, and mercy and all goodness towards men."[2]

With the same vivid sense of God's nearness, the Pilgrims believed that they were called by God to play an active role in life. There was a calling for every lawful work—a general calling to the Christian life and a particular calling to this or that state of life. "God is a God of order" and expects everyone to assume some post and carry on the work of the world. This gave one the sense of counting for something.

When a man knows himself to be orderly called to a condition in life, he both sets himself more cheerfully and roundly to the works thereof, wherein he is assured he serves God's providence by his order, and appointment; and with faith expects a blessing from God upon his endeavors in that organized life in which his hand hath set him.

The gifts of a man enable him to his office; his grace sanctifies both the gifts and office to the person; his inward calling persuades his heart to undertake the outward in desire to glorify God, and in love to men.[3]

William Perkins, whose catechism was studied by the Pilgrims, taught: "Set thy heart to seek God's kingdom, follow the Word and labor therein for regeneration and doubt not, but if thou be upright and diligent in thy lawful calling, thou shalt find sufficient for this life."[4]

Lowly jobs were regarded as important and not beneath the dignity of anyone. The sense of working with God in one's daily tasks gave an ethical meaning to labor. Due to original sin, human beings were destined to eat their bread by the sweat of their brow (see Genesis 3:19). Because of Adam's sinful progeny, people should not pass their days in idleness "without exercising themselves diligently in some lawful calling."[5]

This Calvinism was harsh theology, but in spite of the penalty placed on the legendary Adam and the inconsistency of a vengeful sovereign deity, the Pilgrims found satisfaction in their work. They believed that idleness bred mischief and labor brought strength of body and vigor to the mind, and they felt it was "a shame for a man not to work and exercise himself in some one or other lawful calling." The Pilgrims accepted the work ethic and respected the words of Robinson: "He that without his own labour either of body or mind, eats the labour of other men's hands only, and lives by their sweat, is but like unto lice, and such other vermin."[6]

The work ethic, questioned in an era of high technology, mass production, unemployment, and concern for leisure, was an imperative in the wilderness. All members of the community were compelled to exert themselves by scarcity of shelter and food, by isolation from commodities and neighbors, by the rigorous climate, and by the constant threat of disease. The bolstering provided by John Calvin added moral motivation to the wilderness warning: work or die.

The Pilgrims enjoyed the curt and pithy marginal notes in their Geneva Bibles, such as this one which condemned tramps and freeloaders: "Vagabonds, which do nothing but walk the streets, wicked men, to be hired for every man's money to do any mischief, such as we commonly call the rascals and very sink and dunghill knaves of all towns and cities. . . . Into what country and place soever they come, they cause sedition and tumults."[7]

To twentieth-century readers Pilgrim ethics may appear rigorous. They were strict. Religion was a discipline. But the people were not as somber and stern as usually portrayed. They avoided the ascetic restrictions that John Calvin passed on to them and enjoyed the normal appetites of life.

The Pilgrims' thanksgiving celebration, held the first autumn in gratitude for their slender harvest, was a happy occasion of feasting, games, and fellowship with some ninety of their new neighbors, the Wampanoags. There is no evidence that the celebration was accompanied by a religious service. No meetinghouse had been built at that time. No doubt prayers were said in the cottages, and possibly Elder Brewster added a note of spiritual commemoration. It was not a pagan harvest festival, however, where ale and wine flowed freely. The Pilgrims had a meager store of such drinks, and would not have served them to their native neighbors. They were averse to public holidays that reflected the carousing they had witnessed in England. The first Thanksgiving was a spontaneous, happy gathering which made it clear at the start that the Pilgrims knew how to have a good time.

Captain Emmanuel Altham of the *Little James*, who was one of the London Merchant Adventurers, paid a visit to Plymouth in 1623. He wrote a description of the village and reported on William Bradford's wedding. Soon after the *Mayflower* had landed in Provincetown, Bradford's young wife, Dorothy, lost her life. He married Alice, the widow of Edward Southworth. The Pilgrims invited the Wampanoags to come to this party. Massasoit arrived with his queen, who was one of his five wives, together with four other chiefs and one hundred twenty braves with their bows and arrows, four bucks, and a turkey. The guard of honor greeted them with a salute from their matchlock muskets and then stored all weapons in the governor's house.[8]

Captain Altham spoke of the "very good pastime" entertainment staged by the Indians and of the feast of "twelve pasty venisons, besides others, pieces of roasted venison and other such good cheer." Following the marriage ceremony, conducted by the governor's assistant, the crowd enjoyed the venison, turkey, home-made wine, nuts, plums, and grapes. The natives danced for their hosts. It was the second big social function the Pilgrims had staged and no doubt it proved to be good public relations with their native neighbors, who became loyal friends for many years.[9]

John Cotton, minister of the Stump Church in Boston, Lincolnshire and later of the First Church in Boston, New England, came out in 1625 for dancing: "Dancing (yea, though mixt) I would not condemn, only lascivious dancing to wanton ditties and in amorous gestures and wanton dalliances, especially after great feasts, I would bear witness against."[10] Cotton spoke here for the enlightened Puritans, which would include the Pilgrims. These men were not crusaders against pleasure. They opposed excess (drunkenness, gluttony, libertinism) but not happiness, a cup of wine, a mug of ale, madrigals, and tripping the light fantastic. Dancing was enjoyed in every hall and on every village green. It would have been extremism to rule out dancing in the New World. It does not seem incongruous with Plymouth's ideology that settlers might have joined in song and dance.

The Pilgrims did not celebrate the holy days of Christmas, Easter, and Whitsunday in the tradition of pagan revelry, for they objected to the extraneous usages taken over from folklore and non-Christian conventions that were contrary to the spirit of Christianity. They could not countenance the levity that they encouraged. They also pointed out that these were not dates that could be verified by the Bible or history.

Champions of the joy-killer Pilgrim image have cited the incident of Bradford's encounter with Christmas 1621 in the Plymouth village, twisting this report into anti-pleasure propaganda. The young governor's account reads:

> And herewith I shall end this year only I shall remember one passage more, rather in mirth than of weight [indicating in advance that he was not crusading]. On the day called Christmas Day, the Governor called them out to work as was used. But the most of the new company excused themselves and said it went against their consciences to work on that day. So the Governor told them that if they made it a matter of conscience, he would spare them till they were better informed; so he led away the rest and left them. But when they came home at noon from their work, he

found them in the street at play, openly; some pitching the bar, and some at stool-ball and such sports. So he went to them and took away their implements and told them that it was against his conscience that they should play and others work. If they made the keeping of it matter of devotion, let them keep their houses; but there should be no gaming or reveling in the streets. Since which time nothing hath been attempted that way, at least openly.[11]

Laws were not enacted against play in Plymouth. It was the responsibility of the governor to keep people working together for the common good. On Christmas 1620 they came ashore from the *Mayflower* to start the first cottage on their plantation in the wilderness, "some to fell timber, some to rive, and some to carry, so no man rested all day." That was a time of emergency which had to be employed in constructive labor. On Christmas 1621 the situation was equally critical. The village was still unfinished. Winter was closing in. Daylight hours were short and cold. Every minute was precious in the struggle to provide shelter from the rigors around them. This was not a time to loiter but a time for all to take ax and hammer in hand, chop down oaks and pines, rive timber and planks, and frame another cottage. Settlers were crowded together like sheep. If the great cold came before more houses were erected, another epidemic might sweep them all away.

By contract with the Adventurers, the land was to be held in common and worked in common. All were obligated to share. Every able male must work unless he held moral scruples against labor on Christmas. If he did, he should stay in his own house and not undermine morale by flaunting his irresponsibility. There would be time to play later.

Some legislation was set up in 1623, but the first codification of law came in 1636. This legislation was based on

English law, but scholars recognize certain advances such as marriage by civil authority, equal descent for children, provision for widows, and the recording of land deeds.[12]

At this time there were no rules spelled out against profaning the sabbath, regulation of dress, card-playing, or "night walking." In later years, when the original idealism of the plantation had ebbed and the unity of tradition had been blurred, there were greater efforts to control behavior. The original Pilgrims had passed on and the second and the third generations plus newcomers filled their places. The *Books of Laws* of 1685 took over regulations that had been adopted in the Bay, such as the prohibition of card-playing and regulation of clothing. Sabbath observance was spelled out: "no unnecessary servile work," no "unnecessary traveling," no "buying or selling," no "Sunday sports."[13]

Along with this tightening up it should be pointed out that there were also laws to protect the accused and to limit the authority of the magistrates.

Strict observance of the sabbath was not peculiar to Plymouth. The medieval church upheld the tradition that forbade labor on Sunday. Nicholas Bownd, rector of Norton in Suffolk, wrote a book, *True Doctrine of the Sabbath*, and the word Sabbatarian was coined before the Pilgrims set sail for Holland. The Puritans also insisted that the Lord's Day should be dedicated to worship. Stephen Hopkins' breach of the sabbath was reported on October 2, 1637

> for suffering men to drink in his house upon the Lord's day, before the meeting be ended, and also upon the Lord's day, both before and after the meeting, servants & others to drink more than for ordinary refreshing is respited until the next Court, that the testimony of John Barnes be had therein.

Mr. Stephen Hopkins, psented for suffering servants and others to sitt drinkeing in his house, (contrary to the orders of this Court), and to play at shovell board & such like misdemeanors, is therefore fined fourty shillings.[14]

On July 5, 1638 "Web Adey, being presented for breach of the Saboth, as above, by workeing two seuall Saboth dayes, one after another, and for disorderly liveinge in idlenesse & nastyness, is censured by the bench to sitt in the stocks during the pleasure of the bench."[15]

Stocks were used for public exposure and punishment throughout New England, as they were in England. Capital punishment was sanctioned for a limited number of crimes, but seldom used. In Plymouth Colony "serious crimes were less common than in the Bay Colony and the constable's whip less in evidence."[16]

Thomas J. Wertenbaker stressed the oppressive regulations of dress among the Massachusetts Bay Puritans. In 1634 the General Court prohibited the use of apparel "with any lace on it, silver, gold or thread, slashed clothes, other than one slash in each sleeve and another in the back; also, all cutworks, embroidered or needlework caps, bands and rails, all gold and silver girdles, hat-bands, belts, ruffs, beaver hats."[17]

In contrast, Plymouth Colony enacted no rules against "gay apparel" in the 1636 codification of laws. While in Holland the Pilgrims had been disgusted with the dissension in the Ancient Church in Amsterdam. The Separatists there engaged in a disputation called the Millinery War over the hats, ribbons, high-heeled boots, and luxurious gowns of Pastor Francis Johnson's wife. This disturbance was one reason the Pilgrims moved to Leyden. They had seen enough of Calvinist efforts to regulate dress. It was not until the *Book of Laws* was published in 1685 that some legislation was set up regulating clothing and prohibiting card-playing. With the passing of the original leadership there was a tendency to follow the tighter rules of the Puritan neighbors.[18]

Contemporary readers rebel at the restrictions regarding conduct and dress set up by the Puritan community. But it is well to recall that English society in this era was tightly operated by monarchs, bishops, clergy, and royalty, and that legal and social restraints limited individual freedom. It is interesting to compare contemporary society with its ever-multiplying governmental bureaucratic regulations that straitjacket citizens.

The Pilgrim community may have enjoyed more freedom than moderns who find paperwork so complex and tax laws so intricate that they must consult accountants and lawyers and pay sizable fees to manage a simple household. Plymouth settlers were free from the presence of investigators, wire-tappers, computer experts, tax agents, and the necessity for licenses for fishing, hunting, clamdigging, oystering, driving, and the requirements for Social Security numbers, ID cards, passports, and countless forms. Legal red tape surpasses the simple framework of seventeenth-century Plymouth. During the first sixty years one volume would have contained its laws. Today an entire library would be required to hold the rules that govern citizens in Massachusetts.

Plymouth's efforts to restrain the frailties of the flesh preserved a state of law and order that is envied by twentieth-century Americans. Vandalism, robbery, mugging, rape, kidnapping, terrorism, and murder are seldom listed in the records. Contemporaries may well view with admiration the ability of the Pilgrims to preserve peace with their simple system of justice and wonder if the country would be better off today if it had more moral controls and fewer in the realms of economics and politics.

Cushman reminded the Pilgrims, as they assembled for one of their services in December 1621, of their ethical obligations "that you are not in a retired, monastical course, but have given your names and promises one to another, and covenanted here to cleave together in the service of God and the King."[19]

From the days of harassment in their English villages, to the landing on the wharves of Amsterdam, where they were compelled to find shelter and jobs, to the task of financing their voyage and settlement in the New World, to their December disembarkation on Plymouth Rock, the Pilgrims were tried and tested in the development of their own realistic Christian philosophy.

The sense of honor bred by their ethical concepts was given a rigorous challenge in their new conflict over money with the London Merchant Adventurers. Tedious negotiations continued over a number of months. The exiles in Leyden were eager to push on to the New World, while the Adventurers demanded every possible security on their investment. Two deacons, John Carver and Robert Cushman, struggled to revise the terms of the loan agreement, particularly the requirement that for seven years the Plymouth settlers must work on a communal basis with all profits going to the lenders. Unable to alter the terms or to secure any other loan, the contract was reluctantly signed.

On arrival in Plymouth the settlers faced the superhuman task of building homes, planting crops, and starting debt payments. The first ship that came, the *Fortune*, was loaded with beaver pelts, clapboard, and other timber worth £500, but she was seized by French pirates and stripped of her cargo. Robert Cushman went ashore in London empty-handed to face the hostile Adventurers. The next ship, the *Little James*, was likewise loaded with merchandise and furs. She, too, was taken by Barbary Coast pirates, and the crew members were sold into slavery. Myles Standish, who was aboard, reached London, where he spent several months trying in vain to raise money. He managed to negotiate a loan of a mere £150 at 50 percent interest.

For the first three years Plymouth settlers were forced by their agreement with the London Merchant Adventurers to practice a communal economy. Resentment ran high, as Bradford recorded:

> For this community was found to breed much confusion and discontent and retard much employment that would have been to their benefit and comfort. For the young men that were most able and fit for labour and service, did repine that they should spend their time and strength to work for other men's wives and children without any recompense. The strong, or man of parts, had no more in division of victuals and clothes than he that was weak and not able to do a quarter the other could; this was thought injustice. The aged and graver men to be ranked and equalized in labours and victuals, clothes, etc., with the meaner and younger sort, thought it some indignity and disrespect unto them. And for men's wives to be commanded to do service for other men, as dressing their meat, washing their clothes, etc., they deemed it a kind of slavery, neither could many husbands well brook it. Upon the point all being to have alike, and all to do alike, they thought themselves in the like condition, and one as good as another; and so, if they did not cut off these relations that God hath set amongst men, yet it did at least much diminish and take off the mutual respects that should be preserved amongst them.[20]

The economy of "all being to have alike, and all to do alike" proved a failure. It took them only three years to return to private enterprise. Every family was assigned a parcel of land according to the number of members. There was an immediate change, for

> it made all hands industrious, so much more corn was planted than otherwise would have been by any means the Governor or any other could use. . . . The women now went willingly into the field, and took their little ones with them to set corn; which before would allege weakness and inability, whom to have compelled would have been thought great tyranny and oppression.[21]

In spite of sincere efforts by the settlers, the London debt kept growing in a terrifying manner. Isaac Allerton was dispatched to London in 1626 to explain the determination of the colony to pay the obligation in spite of piracy, sickness, and bad fortune, and to see what could be done in refinancing the millstone that hung around their necks. Allerton took over a cargo of furs on the *Marmaduke* and returned with a document signed by forty-two Adventurers who agreed on a settlement of £1,800 plus an old debt of £600. Calculating a pound at $50 value, the obligation came to about $120,000. This was an enormous amount for some 180 people to assume. Eight of the Pilgrims signed as guarantors. These "undertakers" included William Brewster, William Bradford, Myles Standish, Edward Winslow, John Howland, Isaac Allerton, John Alden, and Thomas Prence.

The colonists owned the plantation subject to this huge mortgage. In support of the "undertakers" all freemen were to pay three bushels of corn or six pounds of tobacco each year to help carry the load. They also granted the "undertakers" a monopoly of the fur trade to meet the payments. One trading post was set up in 1627 at Aptuxcet on Cape Cod. In 1630 a second was established at the mouth of the Penobscot River in Maine, and soon after another at Augusta on the Kennebec. In 1632 a post was created at Windsor on the Connecticut River. The fur trade paid most of the London debt.

Over twenty-five years of struggle with these "debts hopeful and desperate" ensued. The Adventurers heaped rebuke upon the settlers. Ship after ship brought letters of condemnation and exhortation, urging them to send more furs, to pay faster, to dwell in love "without secret whisperings and complaining one of another," and to "pluck up your spirits and quit yourselves like men."[22]

Even the diplomatic Bradford fired back hot replies. The Pilgrims had undertaken a colossal task through their borrowing. They financed not only the expedition of the *Mayflower* and the *Speedwell* but also other subsequent expeditions. This required more and more capital from London since Plymouth was not yet self-supporting. Eventually a good number of the Leyden friends reached Plymouth. This mutual sharing was, in Bradford's words, "a rare example of brotherly love, for they never demanded, much less had any payment of all these great sums thus disbursed." There were numerous mishaps and additional demands for funds. Accounting was soon in a muddle and the interest rate was high. The account piled up like a dark cloud that threatened a hurricane. Bradford wrote:

> Being thus deeply engaged, and a few only of us being bound to make payment of all, yea in a double bond: for besides our formal bonds, it was our credits and honesty, that made our friends rest and rely upon us, assuring themselves, that if we lived and it was possible, we would see them have their monies: Therefore we thought it our safest and best course to come to some agreement with the people, to have the whole trade consigned to us for some years; and so in the time to take upon us, to pay all the debts and

set them free: Another reason which moved us to take this heavy burthen upon our shoulders was, our great desire to transport as many of our brethren of Leyden over to us, as we could, but without this course we could never have done it, all here being (for peace and unity's sake) made joint purchasers with us, and every one thereby had as much interest as ourselves, and many were very opposite here against us in respect of the great charge.[23]

Again we knew, that, except we followed our trading roundly, we should never be able to do the one or the other; therefore we sought means to have our patent enlarged, and to have some good trading places therein; that if we could not keep them thereby wholly to ourselves, yet that none should exclude or thrust us wholly out of them, as we well knew that some would have done, if we now had not laid hold of the opportunity: Therefore Mr. Allerton was sent over to prosecute these things, and to acquaint those few of our friends in England, whom the year before were joined purchasers with us, what agreements we had made and concluded with our people, and for what ends, and so to offer them to be our partners in trade and the whole business; writing our letters unto them for that end.[24]

Not all the London Merchant Adventurers were like Thomas Weston. Some of them, such as William Collier and Timothy Hatherly, liked the Pilgrims and came over to cast their lot with them. After some four bad years of "losses and crosses at sea," due to the pirates and storms and all the ill luck Plymouth faced in shipping furs and shingles back to London, the partnership was broken up. James Sherley and forty-one others bought the shares of those who wanted out. They wrote Plymouth that they still owed £1,400. The poor settlers did not know how they had arrived at this figure. Bradford calculated that they did it by charging 40 percent profit on all the cattle and goods sent over, taking 30 percent commission on all the fur, fish, clapboard, and sassafras sold—"a thing thought unreasonable by some."

Finally after these years of harassment, hard labor, and strict economy, the "undertakers" managed to rid themselves of this thorn in their flesh. They might have reneged on the note and it would have been impossible for the Adventurers to collect. But they stood behind their promise and their signatures. The Pilgrim ethics confronted a rigorous test and stood firm. The bulk of the debt was paid in 1645; the final claim of one Adventurer was met in 1648. To conclude this settlement Winslow and Prence sold their own houses and other "undertakers" sold some of their land.[25]

Captain John Smith was in London in 1626 when the Pilgrim debt was being renegotiated by Isaac Allerton. When he was consulted, he said that the Virginia Company had invested £200,000 (approximately $10,000,000) in that colony and had not received one pound in return from the planters there. He also reported that some £2,000 ($100,000) had been invested in Plymouth by the Adventurers as a loan.[26]

This record is testimony to the fact that the Pilgrim work ethic proved to be good economics as well as a noble precept. Their stubborn will, broad backs, and willing hands created the first self-sustaining colony in America. Samuel Eliot Morison estimated that the Pilgrims paid back some £20,000 worth of beaver and other goods to discharge a debt of £1,800, due to the high interest demanded by the London Merchant Adventurers.[27]

The concept of the "Saint" in Pilgrim ethics was not that of Christian history or of the Church of Rome, but simply a church member who followed the Christian Way, a person of moral stamina. Many in the early years of the colony achieved this status. The "Strangers" who came over to join them usually entered into the fellowship of the church. There were black sheep, of course, as found in every body of human beings. Weaknesses were revealed in the records of the church and court. Legal proceedings were largely concerned with minor conflicts over property, business, slander, quarrels, violations of wage and price controls, drunkenness, and the frailties of the flesh. The colony was law-abiding and there were few capital crimes.

Community life, organized about the meetinghouse, promoted togetherness. The town was small and the people shared in the government and religious life. They knew one another and worked and prayed together. "Holy watching" was practiced since everyone was his or her neighbor's keeper and harmony and teamwork were necessary for the safety and preservation of the colony.[28]

The Christian Way was not defined by the Pilgrims in an elucidation of creed and ritual. The true disciple was called to demonstrate virtue while busy with the tasks of life. As a social being he was in the midst of the battle for truth and right.[29]

When William Brewster died in 1843, at the age of seventy-seven, William Bradford, who had been his pupil and co-worker for forty years, wrote:

> He was wise and discreet and well spoken, having a grave and deliberate utterance, of a very cheerful spirit, very sociable and pleasant amongst his friends, of an humble and modest mind, of a peaceable disposition, undervaluing himself and his own abilities and sometimes overvaluing others. Inoffensive and innocent in his life and conversation, which gained him the love of those without as well as those within, yet

he would tell them plainly of their faults and evils, both publicly and privately, but in such a manner as usually was well taken from him. He was tender-hearted and compassionate of such as were in misery, but especially of such as had fallen unto want and poverty either for goodness and religion's sake or by the injury and oppression of others, he would say of all men these deserve to be pitied most, and none did more offend and displease him than such as would haughtily and proudly carry and lift up themselves, being risen from nothing and having little else in them to command them but a few fine clothes or a little riches more than others.[30]

Brewster assumed Robinson's role, as a lay preacher, in Plymouth, "where he taught twice each Sunday" for nine years until a minister arrived. He stood by through change and transition. "Many were brought to God by his ministry. He did more in this behalf than many that have their hundreds a year do in all their lives."[31] As one of the English gentry, Brewster met hardship unflinchingly like Governor John Carver, who helped plant the crops.

He was willing to bear his burthen with the rest, living many times without bread or corn many months together, having many times nothing but fish and often wanting that also; and drunk nothing but water for many years together; yea till within five or six years of his death. And yet he lived by God's blessing in health till very old age. And besides that, he would labour with his hands in the field as long as he was able.[32]

Brewster was a product of the Pilgrim ethics. His life and spirit speak more convincingly than a library full of sermons, the most elaborate ecclesiastical accoutrements, and the most profound theological dialectic.

William Bradford, the Austerfield orphan and teenage pupil of Robinson and Brewster, never flaunted his ego in his classic journal, America's first great book. "His steadfastness of character and humane outlook should qualify him for the status of a real saint," a title he would promptly reject. His contemporary, Cotton Mather, explained why the governor, who knew Dutch, French, Latin, and Greek, was zealous in his study of Hebrew "because he could see with his own eyes the ancient oracles of God in their native beauty."[33] He knew that Bradford was well versed in history, philosophy, and theology, and added, "But the crown of all was his holy, prayerful, watchful and fruitful walk with God, wherein he was examplary." It was recorded that "he was a common blessing and father to them all."[34]

Deacon Samuel Fuller, active in the Leyden church and in Plymouth, was the physician of the colony and helper of newcomers in the Bay. He gave his life fighting the pestilence of 1633. "After he had helped others, Samuel Fuller, who was their surgeon and physician and had been a great help and comfort unto them [died]. As in his faculty, so otherwise being a deacon of the church, a man godly and forward to do good, being much missed after his death."[35]

Edward Winslow—printer, author, ambassador of the colony, statesman under Oliver Cromwell after his return to England for a second career, chief of commissioners to capture the Spanish West Indies—dying off of Jamaica, was buried at sea in 1655. He wrote *Good News from New England* in 1624, *Hypocrisie Unmasked* in 1647 (to defend the colony against false criticism), *New England Salamander* in 1647, and *The Glorious Gospel Among the Indians in New England* in 1649. He helped launch the Society for the Propagation of the Gospel in New England.

Winslow was known for his "abilities of presence, speech, courage and understanding."[36] His portrait, painted in London in 1651, hangs in Plymouth in Pilgrim Hall, together with paintings of his son, Josiah, and his wife, Penelope, made at the same time. This collection provides insight into the personalities of three Pilgrims, who appear as cultured, intelligent people in attractive attire.

John Carver, a merchant of Doncaster, York, married a sister of John Robinson's wife and moved early to Leyden. He was no doubt instrumental in prevailing on the Pilgrim exiles in Amsterdam to shift to Leyden. He was a deacon in Leyden and chief negotiator in making plans and financing the *Mayflower* voyage. Regard for Carver was expressed by the *Mayflower* passengers when they elected him governor before they landed on Cape Cod. He helped initiate the good-neighbor policy with the Wampanoag Indians, which led to their famous peace treaty. He died in the spring of 1621, from sunstroke, working in the fields with the other settlers, setting the pattern of democratic leadership, which was followed by Bradford. He was remembered as a leader "of singular piety, and rare for humility."

Robert Cushman, a wool-comber from Canterbury, emerged as a lay leader in Leyden, serving as a deacon. He labored with Deacon Carver in England against grave odds, trying to arrange for the voyage to the New World. Having crossed on the *Fortune* in 1621, Cushman gave a sermon to the settlers on the "Danger of Self Love," which was published in December 1621 in London, the first book on the Pilgrim colony. He was called "their right hand with their friends, ye Adventurers." Back in London in 1625, battling with the London Merchant Adventurers over the terms of the debt and the colony payments, Cushman died, probably of plague.

Thomas Cushman was adopted by William Bradford when his father, Robert, died on this mission. He married

Mary Allerton, daughter of the enterprising and prosperous Isaac, and they were the parents of seven children. Succeeding William Brewster as elder and holding this important office from 1649 to 1691, Thomas Cushman was described as "very studious and solicitous for the peace and prosperity of the church, and to prevent and heal any breaches."

Jonathan Brewster, son of William Brewster of Scrooby, arrived from Leyden on the *Fortune* in 1621 as a widower, and in 1624 he married Lucretia Oldham. He was chosen as agent for the Pilgrim trading post at Windsor, Connecticut but later removed to New London, where he founded a trading post at Groton. He was a deputy to the Connecticut General Court and the father of eight children.

Love Brewster, born in Leyden in 1611, came over on the *Mayflower*. He married Sarah Collier, daughter of William Collier, a leader in the colony, and they lived in Duxbury. His interest in religion is indicated by his library which included the Bible, catechisms, works by Calvin, Perkins, Ainsworth, biblical studies, and sermons.

Thomas Prence, a carriage-maker from London, crossed on the *Fortune*, married Patience Brewster, and had five children. He later married Mary Collier, from another leading family, and produced four children. Prence served as a purchaser and an "undertaker" and held many key posts. He had four wives in all. As governor, he followed the more tolerant Bradford, who called him "a terrour to evil doers." Although Prence was firmly against the Baptists and Quakers, he was a studious man with a large library of religious books, and died with a sizable estate.

John Faunce, who came on the *Anne*, married Patience Morton. They had nine children, including Ruling Elder Thomas Faunce, who took up the mantle of Elder Thomas Cushman, "an aged and goodlie leader."

Thomas Blossom, a deacon in Leyden and Plymouth, died in the epidemic of 1633, "a holy man and experienced saint."

Richard Masterson, a Leyden and Plymouth deacon, came over on the second *Mayflower* with Thomas Blossom and died with him in the same pestilence. He was "a man of rare abilities, a second Stephen to defend the truth against gainsayers, and one who had expended most of his estate for the public good."

Francis Cooke, who married Hester Mayhieu, a member of the Walloon church in Leyden in 1613, arrived on the *Mayflower*. Their son was prominent in the church. During the brief furor against the Baptists around 1657, he moved to Dartmouth where a good many Pilgrims had acquired land. He embraced the Baptist persuasion and preached in the area.

George Soule, another good *Mayflower* citizen, lived in Duxbury to the age of eighty, and was the father of seven children.

Thomas Southworth, born in Leyden, became a stepson of William Bradford. He married the daughter of Plymouth's Pastor Rayner and was a leader in the fur trade, holding numerous offices. He died in 1655, "rarely endowed both in sacred and civil respects."

Constant Southworth, another stepson of Bradford, married Elizabeth Collier, daughter of William Collier, and served as treasurer of the colony and as assistant governor. He was the father of eight children, and died in Duxbury in 1679.

William Paddy, chosen as the first treasurer of Plymouth, in 1653,

> was a precious servant of Christ, of a courteous behavior to all men, and . . . instrumental in his place for common good, both in the church (being some-

times by office a deacon of the church in Plymouth) and in other respects very officious. . . . He, having a great temporal estate, was occasioned thereby to have abundance of business upon him . . . a precious servant of Christ.[37]

William Collier, former London brewer who served as assistant governor, was reported to be the richest man in the colony. He died in 1670, having "lived a godly and holy life until old age." Collier was an advocate of religious toleration.

Nathaniel Morton came on the *Anne* with his father, George, a prosperous merchant from the Scrooby area. At the death of his father, he was brought up by Bradford and Samuel Fuller. He was secretary of the colony from 1647 to 1685 and wrote *New-Englands Memoriall*. Morton was one of the wealthy men of the colony and died owning vast lands. He was "very religiously tender and careful in his observations of the Sabbath day and of speaking truth."

William Bassett, a master mason, was married in Leyden in 1611 and arrived on the *Fortune* in 1621. His inventory of 1667 reveals interest in religion. Among his books were the writings of John Robinson and Ainsworth, concordances, biblical commentaries, Reformation writings, and sermons.

Isaac Robinson, son of Pastor Robinson, born in Leyden, came over in 1632 with the London church founded in 1616 by his father's friend, Henry Jacob. He married Margaret Hanford, a niece of Timothy Hatherly, founded Falmouth on Cape Cod, and moved to Martha's Vineyard, where he operated a tavern. He returned to Barnstable to the old London church modeled after the one in Leyden, where he died at the age of ninety-four. Judge Samuel Sewall of Boston made a journey to see him and presented him with a gold piece in honor of his famous father.

James Cudworth, son of the Rev. Ralph Cudworth, fellow of Emmanuel College, Cambridge, was a liberal in the colony and opposed persecution of the Quakers and Baptists. Serving as assistant governor, he died of smallpox in London in 1681 while on charter business for the colony.

Thomas Williams, a Merchant Adventurer from Yarmouth, Norfolk, served as assistant governor and died in 1651, "a well-approved and well rounded Christian," implying that he was a pillar of the church.

John Atwood died in 1644 with an inventory that listed extensive property, a good library, and a substantial fortune, including much valuable pewter. He was described as a "godly man, singularly endowed with the grace of patience, and leaving a large estate, became a useful benefactor of the Colony of New Plymouth. He departed this life expressing his great faith in Christ and a cheerful expectation of the restoration of his body at the general resurrection in glory."[38]

John Browne, Sr. and his son, John Browne, Jr., came in 1635. They died in 1662, leaving large inventories. The son had an estate valued at £300.00.11, including 9 oxen, 20 cows, 2 heifers, 8 calves, 2 bulls, 9 yearlings, 1 mare and colt, 1 yearling mare, and 18 sheep. This indicates quite an establishment. John Browne, Sr. had accumulated an estate worth £655. Listed among his possessions were a bed "in the parlour worth £24, 8 India Table Cloths, 4 great wooden chairs, halfe a dozen of cushens, 2 carpetts, pcell of books valued at £4.10.0, 3 pewter bowles, 11 pewter dishes & a pewter plate, 9 peeces of pewter, 13 peeces of pewter, 3 pewter candlesticks, 9 spoones, and a silver bowle valued at £4.10.0."[39] His farm stock at Rehoboth included:

6 oxen valued at	£40.00.0	11 swine	10.6.0
3 bulls	16.10.0	1 mare & a yearling	
4 steeres & 1 bull	24.00.0	mare coult	21.00.0

2 yeare old heiffers	14.00.0	1 mare & a horse	
4 cowes	19.00.0	coult	17.00.0
14 cowes	70.00.0	1 black stan horse	11.00.0
10 calves	10.00.0	2 horses	24.00.0
10 yearlings	25.00.0	1 mare	17.00.0
18 ewes & lambes		1 younge mare 2 year	
weathers & 1 ram	8.12.0	old	10.00.0

In the boom days when Plymouth was selling cattle to the Bay, an ox was valued at £8.10. During this period the Pilgrims made money, improved their economic status, and gleaned funds to pay off their London debts.[40]

Timothy Hatherly served as assistant governor and governor. He stood with Cudworth against persecution of the Quakers. Hatherly favored "free and full toleration of religions to all men that will preserve the civil peace and submit unto the government."

Josiah Winslow, son of Edward, was educated at Harvard. He married Penelope, daughter of Herbert Pelham, treasurer of Harvard College. Josiah and his wife traveled with his father in England and later he served as assistant governor and then governor. He took the place of Myles Standish as commander of the Pilgrim army. He died in 1680, "a true picture of wisdom, courage and generosity. A worthy and well accomplished gentleman, deservedly beloved of the people, being a true friend of their just liberties, generous, facetious, affable, and sincere, qualities incident to the family."[41]

Thomas Willet, born in 1605, the son of the Rev. Andrew Willet, arrived in Plymouth on the second *May-flower*, "an honest young man." He married Mary Browne, daughter of John Browne, gentleman and Plymouth magistrate. Browne was a friend of Sir Henry Vane, and after his death he served as steward of Vane's estate in Lincolnshire. Willet held various offices at Plymouth, was a member of the New England Expeditionary Force against the Dutch along the Hudson, and was chosen as the first English mayor of New York. He was the father of twelve children, who lived on his estate in Swansea that included some one thousand acres and a large manor house, which contained forty paintings, twenty-six chairs, thirteen featherbeds, a sizable library, and much silver.[42]

Isaac Allerton, a London tailor, was active in the Leyden church. He arrived on the *Mayflower*. In 1620 he married, most strategically, Fear Brewster, daughter of the esteemed elder. He was chosen assistant governor in Plymouth in the early years. Serving as a purchaser and "undertaker," he journeyed to London to renegotiate the debt. While acting as accountant for the colony, he yielded to the temptation to pad his books, making double entries. He even got the finances of his father-in-law, Elder Brewster, in disorder and managed to hoodwink the Pilgrims for many months as they were "abused in their simplicity." Allerton deserted them and launched into shipping and trading ventures on his own, "having brought them into the briars, he leaves them to get out as they can."[43]

When Allerton returned to Plymouth "the church called him to account for these and other gross miscarriages. He confessed his fault and promised better walking, and that he would wind himself out of these courses as soon as he could." A new accountant was found and he departed from the colony to start again as a merchant in New Amsterdam and in New Haven, building up a fortune in trade with Virginia and the West Indies. He is reported to have died insolvent.

It is obvious from these brief biographical insights that the Plymouth Colony had a gentry comparable to that of English life, people of some culture and means. The idea that settlers were poor and simple people needs correction. A number of these men became prosperous for their time and enjoyed a comfortable living. They were not peasants in England; most of them were landowners, yeomen, farmers, merchants, and artisans when they came over. They were granted land, and this tended to promote democratic practices and encourage initiative and private enterprise.

Plymouth lacked a harbor, and shipping never flourished. Most of the Pilgrims were farmers. In spite of their light and rocky soil they did well with corn and cattle but they were not very successful at fishing, making little profit from the sea.

Josiah Winslow wrote in 1680 that a few estates were worth £1,000, "if any are worth £2,000, such are very rarely found." Although the economy did not expand as it did in the Bay, Plymouth settlers were better off than they would have been if they had stayed in England. Most of them owned their own land, house, and livestock. Governor Josiah Winslow stated that "we are fed and Cloathed and our people are Generally Growing in their estates."[44] Wills and inventories indicate that Plymouth achieved a successful economy and that the growth of wealth increased after the first rigorous years.

Most of the Pilgrims were workers, forced to hard labor by the exigencies of the harsh environment of the terrain and climate. Certain colonists proved to be good businessmen, like William Bradford, Myles Standish, Thomas Prence, John Browne, William Collier, William Paddy, and Thomas Willet. They faced rugged competition in the fur trade and had to be ingenious and persistent. This trade fell off, and in 1660 the colony sold its tract of land on the Kennebec for £400. The Pilgrims had been considered the best fur traders between the Saint Lawrence and Hudson Bay. Due to their business acumen they found a way to pay off their enormous debt with the help of the beaver and the Indians.

Although religious motivation was powerful in the founding and survival of the colony, economic factors also entered into the achievement of a self-sustaining settlement, a community that was eventually to be debt free. The practicalities of human nature had to be coped with. There were suits over pigs that invaded neighbors' corn patches, debtors who defaulted on debts, regulation of wages and prices, bargaining over cattle, grain, and furs. Plymouthians were subject to the same moral conflicts and compromises that Robert Keayne explained in his *Apology*.

Keayne was a London tradesman who arrived in Boston in 1635 and set up business as an importer. In this period of demand he sold at the highest prices he could get. In 1639 he was charged in the General Court with "taking above the six-pence in the shilling profit; in some cases above eight-pence; and in some small things, above two for one." Due to the public protest at his profit-taking he was fined £200. He was even brought before the church and admonished "for selling his wares at excessive rate, to the dishonor of God's name."[45]

In his will Keayne reflected on the enigma that faced a pillar of the church who went every Sunday and even kept notes on the sermons of his minister—the distinguished John Wilson. Should his Christian ethics restrain him from seeking to make profit and accumulate as much wealth as ambition and effort could bring him?[46] The code of the meetinghouse answered yes. In Plymouth Colony also the aggressive businessman discovered that there were conflicts between Christian profession and daily practice, private gain and public good.

If the "Saints" in general upheld the Pilgrim ethics, what of the "Strangers"? It should be pointed out that the cleavage was not wide between these two classifications. "Strangers" were non-members on leaving England or Holland, but most of them joined the church in Plymouth.

They knew in advance that this was a community deeply concerned with religion. Even the indentured workers who came on a contract, which obligated them to pay back their travel expenses before they could be free to work and live on their own, must have felt some affinity with the Pilgrim cause or they would not have signed up.

This is one reason the Plymouth settlement faced fewer violent dissensions than the Virginia Colony. The community was a religious one, with some fifteen years of intellectual and spiritual discipline in England and Holland before they set foot on Plymouth Rock.

Most of the "Strangers" developed into stalwart supporters and some into leaders like John Alden, "a hopeful young man," a cooper, a barrel-maker, and carpenter from Harwich, Essex, who was hired by the *Mayflower* expedition. He married Priscilla Mullins around 1622 and moved to Duxbury in 1632. Serving as assistant governor and treasurer, Alden lived until 1686, when he died at the age of eighty-seven, leaving many heirs.[47]

John Howland was one of John Carver's servants, an indentured worker who came on the *Mayflower*. He apparently inherited the estate of Governor Carver, and he married Elizabeth Tilley from Leyden. He was a purchaser, "undertaker," and assistant governor, and he established the Kennebec trading post.

Richard Warren, a London merchant, arrived on the *Mayflower*; his wife, Elizabeth, came with her five daughters on the *Anne* in 1623. The Warrens had two sons in Plymouth, the largest family in the early days of the plantation. "Grave Richard Warren" died in 1628, but his wife carried on and became the resourceful matriarchal head of a large and successful family. Warren was involved in the early exploration and development of the settlement and served as assistant governor. His wife, sons, and daughters were active in the church and community. Bradford called

Warren "a useful instrument." Nathaniel Morton wrote that Warren "during his life bore a deep share of the Difficulties and Troubles of the first Settlement of the Plantation of New Plymouth."[48]

Robert Bartlett, a wine cooper from Stopham, Sussex who came on the *Anne*, married Mary, the oldest daughter of Richard Warren, in 1628. They and their eight children lived in the Hobshole section of Plymouth, where Elizabeth Warren, widow of Richard, built up a clan with extensive holdings. Robert was a substantial citizen, farmer, surveyor, and landowner. His family and descendants were active in the church.

Stephen Hopkins, from Gloucestershire, had made one trip to the New World, having been shipwrecked on Bermuda from 1609 to 1610. He was accused of leading a mutiny on this unfortunate voyage. Making his way back to England, he joined the *Mayflower* people. One of few who had any knowledge of America, Hopkins helped Standish in the explorations of Cape Cod. He also journeyed with Edward Winslow when the Pilgrims sent a medical contingent to doctor Massasoit. The father of seven, he served as assistant governor for a number of years. Two servants, Edward Doty and Edward Leister, came with him on the *Mayflower* as indentured workers. In later years he had several bouts with the authorities regarding sabbath observance and drinking.

It was inevitable that some misfits should make their way to Plymouth. John Billington was the chief transgressor. He

> was arraigned, and both by grand and petty jury found guilty of wilful murder, by plain and notorious evidence. And was for the same accordingly executed. This, as it was their first execution (1630) amongst them, so was it a matter of great sadness unto them.

. . . He and some of his had been punished for miscarriages before, being one of the profanest among
them, they came from London, and I know not by
what friends shuffled into their company. His fact was
that he waylaid a young man, John Newcomen, about
a former quarrel and shot him with a gun whereof
he died.[49]

The large number of stalwart characters in the group
is as noteworthy as the small number of failures.

Myles Standish was from an Old English family who
were Roman Catholics. Although he never became a member of the church in Plymouth, he was a disciple of John
Robinson, attended church, and was active in deliberations
affecting church and community. As head of the colony's
small military force, he was a leader in exploration and
trade and a dependable figure. He also served as assistant
governor and treasurer, and favored religious toleration.
Small of stature and reputedly hotheaded, Bradford wrote
of him, "A little chimney is quickly fired." Captain Standish
left a comfortable estate: a dwelling and land valued at
£140, and an extensive library for a military man and a
non-church member.

Although little is recorded of the Plymouth Colony
women, we know that they did their "women's work" with
strength and courage. They gave birth to the children,
nursed the sick, cooked and scrubbed, labored in the fields,
created beauty in flower gardens and needlework, sustained
disheartened husbands, marshaled their families to the meetinghouse every Sunday, taught from the Good Book, and
upheld faith in the Almighty.

They form an assemblage equal in full measure to the
Pilgrim fathers: Mary Brewster, Catherine White Carver,
Alice Carpenter Bradford, Bridget Lee Fuller, Susanne
Fuller Winslow, Barbara Standish, Mary Clarke Cushman,

Elizabeth Warren, Elizabeth Tilley Howland, Elizabeth Hopkins, Priscilla Mullins Alden, Patience Brewster Prence, Fear Brewster Allerton, Esther Dewbury De La Noye, Hester Mayhieu Cooke, Elizabeth Kendall Godbertson, Ann Elson Blossom, Mary Goodall Masterson, Mary Browne Willet, Jane Collier, Margaret Hanford Robinson, Lydia Hatherly, Elizabeth Collier Southworth, Elizabeth Rayner Southworth, Dorothy Browne, Ellen Newton Winslow, Elizabeth Ring Deane, Juliana Morton Kempton, Martha Bourne Bradford, Mary Warren Bartlett, Sarah Carey Jenney, Patience Morton Faunce, Constance Hopkins Snow, Lucretia Oldham Brewster, Mary Allerton Cushman, Faith Clarke Dotey, Mary Chilton Winslow, Mary Becket Soule, Margaret Oldham Bassett, Priscilla Carpenter Wright, Juliana Carpenter Morton, Lydia Cooper Morton, Mary Carpenter, Wybra Hanson Pontus, Elizabeth Savory Eddy, Elizabeth Warren Church, Lydia Hicks Bangs, Tryphosa Lee Tracy, and others.[50]

These mothers of New England will be remembered as long as the story of America's beginnings is retold. Pilgrim ethics produced a company of high-principled women and men. Their resourcefulness and stamina formed cornerstones in the foundation of the nation and were an inspiration to later Pilgrims who sought escape from old-world tyranny.

CHAPTER 9

No One Turned Away

If in anything we err, advertise us brotherly. . . . We
must acknowledge but one brotherhood of all.

—John Robinson[1]

During the first three decades of Plymouth Colony, no
stranger was turned away and the plantation endeavored
to extend hospitality to those who came seeking a haven.[2]

The Pilgrims assumed the role of the coast guard on
Cape Cod during the shipwreck of the *Sparrowhawk* in
1627. This small vessel, about forty feet in length, was
loaded "with many passengers and sundry goods bound
for Virginia." They became lost at sea because the captain
was sick with scurvy, and they were out of food, beer, and
water and had burned the last bit of wood. The passengers
panicked with the fear that they would starve or die from
disease. When they ran ashore in Pleasant Bay, they tried
to salvage their goods and hoped to repair the ship. Some
Indians led their delegation to Plymouth.

The settlers gave them pitch, oakum, and spikes to mend
the boat, and corn and other food and articles to trade

with the Indians. After they had repaired the *Sparrow-hawk*, it was rendered unseaworthy by further storms. So they once more entreated Plymouth so "that they might have leave to repair to them and sojourn with them till they could have means to transport their goods. . . . Considering their distress, their requests were granted and all helpfulness done unto them; their goods transported, and themselves and goods sheltered in their houses as well as they could."[3]

This was quite an undertaking in the midst of winter hazards, and the village was crowded with its usual inhabitants. It is a wonder that they could take in twenty-seven or more. These people were not of the persuasion of Plymouth. Most were Irish. Messrs. Fells and Sibsey appeared to be of the gentry and had brought servants with them. The colony gave them land and set them to work planting corn and vegetables. Their entertainment was fraught with hardship for the hosts. There were

> many untoward people amongst them; though there were also some that carried themselves very orderly all the time they stayed. So they both did good, and received good one from another. And a couple of barks carried them away at the latter end of summer. And sundry of them have acknowledged their thankfulness since from Virginia.[4]

The adventure with the Irish immigrants from the *Sparrow-hawk* was evidence that the plantation was open to all in need who came in the early years.

John Winthrop wrote in his *Journal* that "Plymouth extended a helping hand to a shipwrecked shallop of Richard Garret in December 1630 and its passengers from Boston who were in a wintry storm."[5]

Thomas Weston was one of the most obstreperous troublemakers faced by the Pilgrims. He was an ironmonger from London who showed up in Leyden and offered to raise money as a loan from London businessmen to help finance the journey of the *Mayflower* and the *Speedwell*. He ended up as president of the London Merchant Adventurers, who made the loan and caused so many years of debt-grubbing for Plymouth. Weston proved to be one of the super-critical Adventurers, and was fond of lecturing the Pilgrims. Eager to make more profit out of the expedition, he sent a fishing vessel, the *Sparrow*, to the New World. A crew of seven came on the shallop from this ship to Plymouth in 1622 with an appeal from Weston to house and feed these men and to give them seed corn and supplies. The Pilgrims took them in and "gave them as good as their own."

The *Charity* brought sixteen more men whom Weston had sent over with letters of rebuke, and the announcement that he was establishing his own colony on the southern part of Boston Bay. He asked Plymouth to take care of his men while the *Charity* sailed to Virginia and returned,

> which was the most part of that summer, many of them being sick, and all of them destitute of habitation, and unacquainted with this new beginning. At the ship's return from Virginia, by the direction of the said Mr. Weston their master, they removed into the Massachusetts Bay, he having got a patent for some part there, yet they left all their sick folks at Plymouth, until they were settled and fitted for housing to receive them. They were an unruly company, and no good government over them, and by disorder fell into many wants.[6]

Deacon Cushman had warned the colony that Weston's crew "are no men for us." In spite of the counsel and Weston's double-talk, Plymouth took in the motley clan.

There were soon many complaints about "the unjust and dishonest walking of these strangers," who stole the crops and devoured them. The Pilgrims suffered "secret back-bitings, revilings, etc.," as they took care of their unappreciative guests.[7]

Plymouth breathed a sigh of relief when the *Charity* returned from Virginia and sailed away with the *Swan*, taking the Weston gang, except for a few who were sick. They were bound for the north to Boston Bay where they were to build their colony of Wessagusset.

Weston's men "made havoc with their provisions" so that they were soon trading their blankets and clothes to the Indians for food, and cutting wood and fetching water "for a cup full of corn." Some became servants to the Indians. Others stole from them. Alarmed by the turmoil among their neighbors, Plymouth sent an expedition to investigate. Armed violence resulted in the first encounter of the Pilgrims with the Indians. This tragic story is told in Chapter 10.

Sometime after the collapse of his settlement, Weston came back on a fishing vessel "under another name, and the disguise of a blacksmith." He was shipwrecked in a storm between the Merrimac River and Piscataqua "and barely escaped with his life." He fell into the hands of Indians "who pillaged him of all he saved from the sea, and stripped him out of all his clothes to his shirt. At last he got to Piscataqua [Strawberry Bank, Portsmouth] and borrowed a suit of clothes, and got means to come to Plymouth."[8]

The people he had criticized and cheated saw "a strange alteration there was in him, to such as had seen and known him in his former flourishing condition, so uncertain are the mutable things of this unstable world. And yet men set their hearts upon them," Bradford philosophized, "though they daily see the vanity thereof."

After much discourse he desired to borrow some beaver. . . . They [the Pilgrims] pitied his case, so they let him have 100 beaver skins which weighed 170-odd pounds. . . . Thus they helped him when all the world failed him. . . . But he requitted them ill, for he proved after a bitter enemy unto them upon all occasions, and never repaid them anything for it to this day, but reproaches and evil words.[9]

A Captain Robert Gorges pitched a colony on the place that had been deserted by Weston. He arrested Weston on various charges. When Gorges threatened to ship him back to England, Weston asked Bradford to intercede and was allowed to keep his ship. He paid a final visit to Plymouth, but as he departed he "gave them a quib behind their backs for their pains." He sailed for Virginia and died in Bristol "of the sickness of that place."[10] Thus ended the stormy encounters with this schemer, who was requited good for evil in generous measure.

In 1625 Captain Wollaston brought a load of colonists on the *Unity* to found Mount Wollaston, north of Plymouth. The captain sailed to Virginia with most of his indentured servants and sold their contracts to the planters there. Thomas Morton took over the colony and invited the remaining indentured workers to a feast. "After strong drink & other junkets," according to the Pilgrim account, he suggested they get rid of the agent who had been left in charge and form their own settlement.[11]

Morton was a gentleman adventurer who had practiced law in London, knew prominent figures in England, was well versed in literature, and penned his own poems. The spot was renamed Mare Mount, but was soon called Merrymount. The men started to live "in riotous prodigality, quaffing & drinking both wine & strong waters in great excess, and, as some reported, 10 pounds in a morning."

To celebrate the renaming of the settlement, a maypole was installed and the Indians were invited to share in the festivities with a barrel of beer and "all good cheer," and plenty of dancing.

Plymouth felt that Morton had "more craft than honesty" and "had been a kind of pettifogger of Furnival's Inn." It was reported that the Merrymounters "fell to great licentiousness and led a dissolute life, pouring out themselves into all profaneness." In order to support their gay existence, the settlers sold "fowling pieces, muskets, pistols," and shot to the Indians. Plymouth colonists were alarmed as Merrymount armed the natives, "inviting the Indian woman for their consorts, dancing and frisking together like so many fairies." They were concerned that "discontents would flock to him [Morton] from all places, if this nest was not broken."[12]

"So they mutually resolved to proceed, and obtained of the Governor of Plymouth to send Captain Standish and some other aid with him, to take Morton by force." Morton gave one version of his capture and Standish another. The captain claimed that Morton and his men had locked themselves in their house, too drunk to lift their muskets. Morton ran out with a loaded carbine and Standish "stepped to him, & put by his piece, & took him." There was one casualty—a drunken chap ran his nose onto the point of a sword and lost a little blood.[13] Morton was brought to Plymouth and was sent by ship to the Isle of Shoals and then on to England. Charges were not lodged against him there, and he returned to Massachusetts the next year. He was a vocal defender of himself and later in England wrote his *New England Canaan*, in which he attacked the Pilgrims with wit and satire.

Merrymount Morton proved an active propagandist against Plymouth. Edward Winslow was assigned the defense of the colony. He replied to the charge that the

Pilgrims crossed over to Plymouth for reasons of self-gain by countering that they came for spiritual reasons, to escape "the hierarchy, the cross in baptism, the Holy Days, the Book of Common Prayer, etc."[14]

In dealing with Morton's charge that Plymouth held a faulty patent, Winslow was in a vulnerable position. He journeyed to England in 1635 with the hope that he might improve the lot of the colony and answer some of Morton's accusations. He carried a petition to the Lords Commissioners for the Plantations in America, urging support in restraining France and Holland in their efforts to expel the English colonists.

Morton had written that the Pilgrims permitted lay people to have too much authority in the church: "The Church of the Separatists is governed by Pastors, Elders and Deacons, and there is not any of these, though he be but a cow keeper, but is allowed to exercise his gifts in the public assembly on the Lord's day, so as he do not make use of any notes for the help of his memory."[15]

Morton presented a caricature of the Plymouth settlers. Winslow wrote in a similar vein, accusing Morton of penning "lascivious rhymes" and sponsoring a "school of atheism" at Merrymount. The author of *New England Canaan* had sufficient contacts at court and at Canterbury to win the attention of the archbishop. He lodged charges against Winslow, who was brought before Archbishop Laud. Morton supported the plan to send Sir Fernando Gorges to New England as governor general "to disturb the peace of the churches and to overthrow the proceedings and further growth, which was the thing they aimed at."[16]

So it came about that Winslow was ordered to appear before Archbishop Laud and answer the charges that he had preached as a layman in the Plymouth church and had married people as a magistrate. The ambassador from the New World admitted that he had done both and defended his position. His testimony offended His Highness, who ordered Winslow locked up in Fleet Prison "where he lay seventeen weeks or thereabouts, before he could get released." He chafed at this confinement since time was precious, as he had many important assignments to carry out for the plantation.[17]

Later, for some strange reason, the dissembling Isaac Allerton brought Morton back to Plymouth with him from a trip to London. He lodged him in his house and employed him as a secretary until pressure mounted and "he was caused to pack him away. So he went to his old nest in Massachusetts." He was soon charged by Governor Winthrop and sent back to England as a prisoner to Exeter jail. His house was demolished by the Bay. Morton was free again and spread his charges against the Pilgrims around England. He returned once more to Plymouth and was permitted to live with one of the settlers for four shillings per week, with the understanding that he would "begone as soon as winter breaks up." He was not a popular resident and "had little respect amongst them and was slighted by the meanest servants," yet he was tolerated as another creature who needed shelter and food. He journeyed to Maine, where he returned to his former practices. He was sent to jail in Boston and died in 1647.[18]

The Pilgrims demonstrated the golden rule in sharing their meager substance with their enemies.

On March 9, 1627, Isaac de Rasieres, secretary of the New Amsterdam Dutch Colony, wrote Governor Bradford a letter:

> We have often before this wished for an opportunity
> or an occasion to congratulate you and your prosper-
> ous and praiseworthy undertakings and government
> of your colony there. And the more, in that we also

have made a good beginning to pitch the foundation of a colony here, and seeing our native country lies not far from yours, and our forefathers divers hundred years ago have made and held friendship and alliance with your ancestors . . . as may be seen and read by all the world in the old chronicles.[19]

The Dutch magistrate asked if they could trade together, selling merchandise from Holland and buying furs from Plymouth.

Governor Bradford replied on March 19, 1627 in a cordial vein, expressing

no small joy to hear that His Majesty hath not only been pleased to confirm that ancient amity, alliance and friendship, and other contracts formerly made and ratified by his predecessors of famous memory, but hath himself (as you say) strengthened the same with a new union, the better to resist the pride of that common enemy the Spaniard, from whose cruelty the Lord keep us both, and our native countries. . . . Yet are many of us further obligated by the good and courteous entreaty we have found in your country, having lived there many years with freedom and good content, as also many of our friends do to this day. For which we, and our children after us, are bound to be thankful to your nation and shall never forget the same, but shall heartily desire your good and prosperity as our own forever.[20]

Bradford expressed interest in trade with the Dutch colony and asked if they were interested in buying "tobacco, fish, corn or other things, and what prices you will give, etc."

Shortly afterward, de Rasieres arrived by sloop at the Pilgrim trading post located at Aptuxcet on Cape Cod. He crossed the portage on foot but grew weary and sent a messenger to Plymouth stating that he had not walked that "far this three or four years, wherefore I fear my feet will fail me." Governor Bradford promptly dispatched the shallop to bring the honored guest from Scusset River to Plymouth harbor.

The village turned out in full force to welcome this distinguished visitor from Holland. He was greeted in his own language and toasted royally. Judging by the dislike of his legs for walking, he may have been a portly figure like one of Rembrandt's rotund burghers. The Pilgrims were happy to make his mission a time for feasting on venison, turkey, and seafood, accompanied by their best red and white wines.

De Rasieres brought precious gifts, such as woolen goods, linen, sugar, and wampum.[21] He proved to be an adept salesman in introducing the shell money made by the Indians to the south. The visitor convinced the settlers that this novelty would work magic in trade with their neighboring Indians. The wampum was manufactured out of the hard-shell clam or quahog and the shells of sea snails and formed into beads that were hung in strings of purple and white. This *wampumpeag* formed the currency that became the popular means of exchange in the area. Plymouth started producing the product and held a monopoly for a time. The Dutchman's mission brought unexpected dividends.

Later the Dutch spoke to the Pilgrims about their trading post on the Connecticut River as "a fine place both for plantation and trade, and wished them to make use of it." The Indians in that area had also mentioned trade with Plymouth. When some of the Dutch heard that Plymouth planned to make such a move, they changed their minds and "endeavored to prevent them, and got in a little before them and made a slight fort and planted two pieces of ordnance, threatening to stop their passage."[22]

When the Pilgrim boat arrived with the materials aboard to build their trading post, the Dutch stopped them and threatened to fire on them if they sailed up the river. The Plymouthians answered that "they must obey their order and proceed; they would not molest them, but would go on." They went upstream, "clapped up their house quickly and landed their provisions and left the company appointed, and sent the bark home, and afterwards palisadoed their house about and fortified themselves better."

In time the Dutch sent an armed force

> in warlike manner, with colours displayed, to assault them, but seeing them strengthened and that it would cost blood, they came to parley and returned in peace. . . . They did the Dutch no wrong, for they took not a foot of any land they bought, but went to the place above them and bought that tract of land which belonged to these Indians which they carried with them, and their friends, with whom the Dutch had nothing to do.

Shortly thereafter, in 1634, the Dutch moved some of their men to an Indian settlement to the north to winter with the hostile natives, hoping to engage them in trade. The enterprise failed. A devastating epidemic visited the Indians and nearly a thousand died. The Dutch almost starved in the ice and snow before they could get away. They reached the Pilgrim trading post in February, where they were "kindly relieved, being almost spent with hunger and cold. Being thus refreshed by them [their English hosts] divers days, they got to their own place and the Dutch were very thankful for this kindness."[23]

The trading post on the Connecticut was in the charge of Jonathan Brewster when further complications evolved. Neighbors in the Bay hankered after land along the Connecticut. They had learned of the smallpox epidemic that had wiped out many Indians and considered it a good time to establish a colony. The Dorchester people set their minds on the spot that the Pilgrims had purchased from the natives, where they had built their trading center and established their business.[24]

Jonathan Brewster wrote to Governor Bradford that "the Massachusetts men are coming almost daily, some by water and some by land. . . . Some have a great mind to the place we are upon." Brewster could scarcely believe that they wanted to take the Pilgrims' land since there were thousands of acres still unclaimed, but the Puritans were determined. He tried to "withstand them," since they "held here a chargeable possession," striving to "keep that [which] we are settled upon."[25]

The Dorchester settlers began to pitch themselves upon the Pilgrims' land and near their houses. Bradford protested to the Bay; challenging their claim that God had providentially led them to this spot picked by Plymouth and caused them to "cast a covetous eye upon that which is your neighbors' and not yours." The Pilgrims managed to practice restraint, although they were tempted at times to fire a volley from their flintlocks. Bradford wisely reasoned:

> To make any forcible resistance was far from their thoughts—and to live in continual contention with their friends and brethren would be uncomfortable and too heavy a burthen to bear. Therefore, for peace sake, though they conceived they suffered much in this thing, they thought it better to let them have it upon as good terms as they could get. And so they fell to treaty.[26]

The Pilgrims got the short end of the bargain. They were allowed to retain their house and have the sixteenth part of all they had bought of the Indians, and the others should have all the rest of the land.

Soon after this unneighborly treatment by the Puritans from Dorchester,

> two shallops under Captain William Cooper were making their way to the Connecticut settlement, loaded with goods from Massachusetts of such as removed thither to plant, were in an easterly storm cast away in coming into this harbor, in the night. The boats' men were lost and the goods were driven all along the shore, and strewed up and down at high water mark.[27]

When what had happened to the Dorchester settlers' belongings was reported, Governor Bradford and his associates dispatched aid to the stricken Puritans on Brown's Island Shoal. The Pilgrims "caused them (and their things) to be gathered up and drawn together, and appointed some to take an inventory of them, and others to wash and dry such things as had need thereof, by which means most of the goods were saved and restored to the owners."

A few weeks later thereafter they were challenged again in a test of their faith. "Afterwards another boat of theirs [the Dorchester immigrants] going thither likewise, was cast away near into Scusset, and such goods as came ashore were preserved for them." This was further evidence that the Pilgrims were long-suffering and forbearing and knew how to "go the second mile." Bradford wrote of the Dorchester people: "Such crosses they met with in their beginnings, which some imputed as a correction from God for their intrusion, to the wrong of others, into that place. But I dare not be bold with God's judgments in this kind."[28]

Father Gabriel Druillettes, a priest of the Jesuit order from Quebec, paid a visit to Plymouth in 1651. He came on a mission from Canada to see if the federation and Indian groups would join in support of the French in an alliance against the Mohawk Indians. He stopped to see John Winslow, who was in charge of the Pilgrim trading post on the Kennebec River, was cordially received there, and journeyed on to Boston and to Plymouth. Governor William Bradford entertained the priest in his own home. Since it was Friday, he thoughtfully prepared a fish dinner. He gave the Jesuit traveler a warm reception and cordial conversation on the subjects of history and theology.[29]

New Plymouth demonstrated the motto of John Robinson: "Advertise us brotherly."

CHAPTER 10

Native Neighbors

And we, for our part, through God's grace, have with equity, patience, justice, and compassion carried ourselves towards them [their Indian neighbors], as that they have received much favor, help, and aid from us, but never the least injury or wrong by us. . . . And when any of them are in want, as often they are in the winter, when their corn is done, we supply them to our power, and have them in our houses eating and drinking, and warming themselves.

—Robert Cushman
December 12, 1621[1]

Pilgrim leaders were naturally apprehensive about the Indians in New England. Brewster, Carver, and Standish had no doubt read the writings of Richard Hakluyt and Captain John Smith. A few native Americans had been brought to England. In 1605 Captain George Weymouth returned from a voyage to the New World with five Indians who proved a novelty in Plymouth, Devon. In 1608 Captain Edward Harlow carried some Indian captives to London. The Pilgrims had heard of the bitter conflicts of the Virginia settlers with the local tribes. They were cautious as they explored Cape Cod after their landing at Provincetown.[2]

The first encounter was a mild attack of arrows amid screams of hostility, but the hidden foe fled after brief fire from flintlock muskets. On this expedition the white explorers took a kettle of corn that the natives had buried, with the pledge that they would return the seed and the pot, which they did.

The Pilgrims sympathized with the Cape Indians who had suffered a raid by Captain Thomas Hunt in 1614. Hunt had come over with Captain John Smith and had taken a number of the Nausets and sold them into slavery in Spain. The Pilgrims condemned Hunt as "a wretched man that cares not what mischief he doth for his profit."[3]

On a visit to the Nauset Indians on Cape Cod, the Pilgrim company met a mother who had lost three sons to the English pirates. She

> could not behold us without breaking forth into great passion, weeping and crying excessively. We demanding the reason of it, they told us she had three sons who, when Master Hunt was in these parts, went aboard his ship to trade with him, and he carried them captives into Spain [Squanto at that time was carried away also] by which means she was deprived of the comfort of her children in her old age. We told them we were sorry that any Englishman should give them that offense, that Hunt was a bad man, and that all the English that heard of it condemned him for the same; but for us, we would not offer them any injury though it would gain us all the skins in the country.[4]

During a journey to the Massachusetts Indians to the north, Squanto, their faithful guide and interpreter, would have had us rifle the savage women, and taken their skins and all such things as might be serviceable for us; for (said he) they are a bad people, and have oft threatened you. But our answer was: Were they ever so bad, we would not wrong them, or give them any just occasion against us.

Having well spent the day, we returned to the shallop, almost all the women accompanying us to truck, who sold their coats from their backs, and tied boughs about them, but with great shamefacedness (for indeed they are more modest than some of our English women are). We promised them to come again to them, and they to us, to keep their skins.[5]

Robert Cushman recorded the peaceful efforts to bring Massasoit and other Indian sachems in the area into the empire of King James and their success in winning their allegiance to His Majesty.

Neither hath this been accomplished by threats and blows, of shaking of sword and sound of trumpet, for as our faculty that way is small, and our strength less, so our warring with them is after another manner, namely by friendly usage, love, peace, honest and just carriages, good counsel, etc., that so we and they may not only live in peace in that land, and they yield subjection to an earthly prince, but that as voluntaries they may be persuaded at length to embrace the Prince of Peace, Christ Jesus, and rest in peace with him forever.[6]

The Pilgrims revealed statesmanship when, within one week after they had met their first Indian neighbor, they signed an enduring treaty with Massasoit, sachem of the Wampanoags.

One sunny March day in 1621, Chief Massasoit and

some sixty of his braves visited Plymouth Plantation. He was greeted by Elder Brewster and Captain Standish, who conducted him to a place of honor in one of the small cottages, where they had "placed a green rug and three or four cushions." Governor Carver entered at the beat of drum and sound of trumpet. They drank "strong water" together and ate "a little fresh meat."[7] Then the peace treaty, that was to last for fifty-five years, was signed. It provided:

1. That neither he nor any of his should injure or do hurt to any of our people.
2. And if any of his did hurt to any of ours, he should send the offender, that we might punish him.
3. That if any of our tools were taken away when our people were at work, he should cause them to be returned, and if ours did any harm to any of his, we would do the like to him.
4. If any did unjustly war against him, we would aid him; and if any did war against us, he should aid us.
5. He should send to his neighbor confederates, to certify them of this, that they might not wrong us, but might be likewise comprised in the conditions of peace.
6. That when their men came to us, they should leave their bows and arrows behind them, as we would do our pieces when we came to them.

Lastly that doing this, King James would esteem of him as his friend and ally.[8]

The Pilgrims deserve credit for this honorable beginning of human relations in the New World. This agreement was followed by similar trading and military alliances with other Indian tribes. It was not easy for the new settlers to adjust to the formidable natives, these "tall and proper men" in their strange attire and weird customs.

On December 13, 1621 Deacon Robert Cushman delivered a sermon in Plymouth that was printed in London the next year, in which he recorded the goodwill that existed between the settlers and their neighbors:

> They were wont to be the most cruel and treacherous people in all these parts, even like lions; but to us they have been like lambs, so kind, so submissive, and trusty, as a man may truly say, many Christians are not so kind nor sincere. . . .
>
> And we, for our parts, through God's grace have with that equity, justice and compassion carried ourselves towards them, as that they have received much favor, help, and aid from us, but never the least injury or wrong by us. . . . When any of them are in want as often they are in the winter, when their corn is gone, we supply them to our power, and have them in our houses eating and drinking, and warming themselves.[9]

During recent years Thanksgiving Day in Plymouth has been made a pretext for demonstrations by small groups of Indians and their supporters who lay the blame for their discontent upon the Pilgrims. *The New York Times* reported on November 27, 1970 that

> on Thanksgiving Day a group of about 200 Indians [a figure larger than local witnesses estimate], determined to make Thanksgiving a day of national mourning for the American Indians, buried Plymouth Rock under several inches of sand. "That damed rock," said one demonstrator, motioning to the stone shelter that protects Plymouth Rock, "I'd like to blow it up. It was the start of everything bad that has happened to the American Indians."[10]

Once again the Pilgrims bore the brunt of false accusation. Like the rock that has withstood many a storm, they have grown accustomed through the years to being made the scapegoats by distorters of facts and proponents of emotional crusades.

In contrast to the peaceful landing of the Pilgrims, the Jamestown settlers came ashore in the spring of 1607 to be greeted by a violent attack from the Indians, a hostility that continued for months. By autumn half their company was dead from plague and from Indian arrows.

The Virginia Indians were aggressive in their effort to exterminate the English. They abused their captives. John Smith's associate, George Caseen, on a journey of exploration, was captured. He was scalped, the skin was ripped from his body in strips, and he was burned as the Indians danced around him. Smith was about to be beaten to death when Pocahontas, daughter of Powhatan, saved him. The queen of the Apponattock Indians invited the English to a feast and slew the guests. Indian women inflicted cruel torture on the victims they caught.[11]

It is unfortunate that the American Thanksgiving Day has been seized upon by a few contemporary Indians as a day of protest misdirected against the Pilgrims, who, along with the Quakers in Pennsylvania, proved to be among the best representatives of the white race in early America.

During the 350th anniversary of Plymouth in 1971, a reenactment of the signing of the Pilgrim-Wampanoag peace treaty of 1621 was presented with descendants of both groups cooperating in complete goodwill. The colorful dramatization marked one of the bright moments in history. It was followed by a brotherhood luncheon and a service of worship in the Indian church at Mashpee on Cape Cod.

Alden T. Vaughan states:

The rapid success of the Pilgrims in establishing cordial relations with the neighboring tribes is remarkable. Not only did the men of New Plymouth win the sincere friendship of most of the Indian leaders, but they managed within a few hectic years to set a model for interracial diplomacy that was followed, with varying success, by the later Puritan colonies. Justice, tolerance, decisiveness, and amity became the keynotes of Plymouth's Indian policy.[12]

On landing at Plymouth no Indian welcoming committee appeared, as some historic paintings erroneously indicate. The Great Plague of 1616-1617 killed thousands of the New England Indians. This was one reason that the Pilgrims met no resistance on landing. The Patuxet band of Wampanoags, who lived in the area, had been wiped out. Squanto was their sole survivor. It was several weeks before the first native, Samoset, appeared. He brought the English-speaking Squanto, who had been sold as a slave in Spain, escaped to England, where he was befriended, and finally was sent back with some English fishermen to New England. The Pilgrims were well rewarded for the warm reception they gave him. He became their indispensable interpreter, guide, and tutor in fishing, planting, and exploring. Bradford called him "a special instrument sent of God for their good." This loyal friend died suddenly in September 1622 while on an expedition to Cape Cod. He

fell ill of an Indian fever, bleeding much at the nose (which the Indians take for a symptom of death) and within a few days died there; desiring the Governor [Bradford] to pray for him that he might go to the Englishman's God in Heaven; and bequeathed sundry of his things to sundry of the English friends as remembrances of his love; of whom they had a great loss.[13]

Hobomok, a Wampanoag, proved a devoted friend of the Pilgrims. He "came to live among them, a proper lusty man, and a man of account for his valour and parts amongst the Indians, and continued very faithful and constant to the English till he died." Hobomok brought word that Corbitant, sachem of the Pocasset, one of Massasoit's subjects, had imprisoned Squanto and planned to kill him. Bradford sent Captain Standish and a group of men with Hobomok as their guide, since they could not "suffer their friends and messengers thus to be wronged." On arrival they announced that they had come to avenge the alleged death of Squanto, "but would not hurt any but those that had a hand in it." They discovered that Corbitant was away and that Squanto had only been threatened with stabbing and had not been killed. "So they withheld and did no more hurt, returning to Plymouth with Squanto and many other known friends," including a few who had been wounded, who had their wounds dressed and cured. "After this they had many gratulations from divers sachems and much firmer peace."[14]

The sturdy Hobomok, who was also threatened by the knife of Corbitant, formed an attachment to Captain Standish and moved to his farm in Duxbury, where he lived until he died in 1642, braving the "enticements, scoffs and scorns" of certain of his people, loyal to the Pilgrims, still "seeking after their God . . . leaving some good hopes in their hearts that his soul went to rest."

The foremost Indian leader of the area, Massasoit, a wise ruler, took a liking to the Pilgrims. From the time he signed the mutual treaty of peace with them he was a frequent visitor at the plantation, helping with the first thanksgiving and sharing in Bradford's wedding. There

Pilgrim Rock, Clark's Island in Plymouth Bay where the Pilgrims held their first religious service in the New World. Courtesy of the Pilgrim Society.

The Mayflower Compact of 1620 in the handwriting of William Bradford from Nathaniel Morton, *New-Englands Memoriall*, 1669. Courtesy of the Pilgrim Society.

MAYFLOWER COMPACT

In the Name of God, Amen. We whose Names are underwritten, the Loyal Subjects of our dread Sovereign Lord King James, by the Grace of God, of Great Britain, France and Ireland, King, Defender of the Faith, &c. Having undertaken for the glory of God, and advancement of the Christian Faith, and the Honour of our King and Country, a Voyage to plant the first Colony in the Northern parts of Virginia; Do by these Presents solemnly and mutually, in the presence of God and one another, Covenant and Combine our selves together into a Civil Body Politick, for our better ordering and preservation, and furtherance of the ends aforesaid; and by virtue hereof to enact, constitute and frame such just and equal Laws, Ordinances, Acts, Constitutions and Officers, from time to time, as shall be thought most meet and convenient for the general good of the Colony; unto which we promise all due submission and obedience. In witness whereof we have hereunto subscribed our Names at Cape Cod, the eleventh of November, in the Reign of our Sovereign Lord King James, of England, France and Ireland the eighteenth, and of Scotland the fifty fourth, Anno Dom. 1620.

John Carver	Samuel Fuller	Edward Tilly
William Bradford	Christopher Martin	John Tilly
Edward Winslow	William Mullins	Francis Cook
William Brewster	William White	Thomas Rogers
Isaac Allerton	Richard Warren	Thomas Tinker
Myles Standish	John Howland	John Ridgdale
John Alden	Susan Hopkins	Edward Fuller
John Turner	Digery Priest	Richard Clark
Francis Eaton	Thomas Williams	Richard Gardiner
James Chilton	Gilbert Winslow	John Allerton
John Crackston	Edmund Margeson	Thomas English
John Billington	Peter Brown	Edward Doten
Joses Fletcher	Richard Bitteridge	Edward Lester
John Goodman	George Soule	

GOVERNOR BRADFORD'S COPY OF THE MAYFLOWER COMPACT

Preserved in his handwriting in his History of Plymouth Plantation.

OVER 300 YEARS AGO!

The "Compact," with the signers, as first printed in Morton's Memorials at Cambridge, Mass., in 1669, an official publication of Plymouth Colony. The order of signing the original manuscript is not known.

"The Embarkation of the Pilgrims" by Charles Lucy. Courtesy of the Pilgrim Society.

"The *Mayflower* and the *Speedwell* in Dartmouth Harbor, Devon, England" by Leslie Wilcox, 1927. Courtesy of the Pilgrim Society.

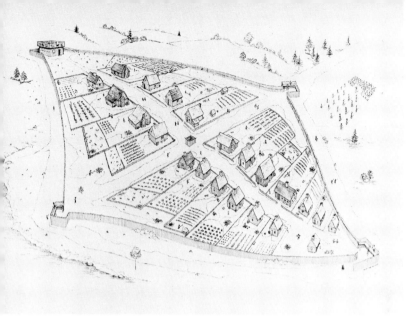

Plymouth Plantation as it is believed to have looked about 1630.
Courtesy of Charles Mathewson, the artist.

Portrait traditionally called "President Charles Chauncy," Plymouth
minister and second president of Harvard College; attributed to
Nathaniel Smibert. Courtesy of the Harvard University Portrait
Collection.

"A Seventeenth Century Dutch Printing Press" by Abraham Von Wert. Courtesy of Leiden Archives, Leiden, Holland.

Roger Williams, a minister among the Pilgrims and founder of Rhode Island. Courtesy of the Rhode Island Historical Society.

Leiden University Library in 1610. Courtesy of Leiden University Press.

"Abbey Square, Middleburg, Holland" by Jacob Cats. Courtesy of Leiden Archives, Leiden, Holland.

astellum	5. Coll Iesu	9. Bibliot Trinitatis	13. Eccl Sᵗ Andreæ	17. Aula Claræ
ogor Castelli	8. Bibliot divi Iohannis	10. Eccl Sᵗ Michaëlis	14. Eccl Bᵗ Mariæ	18. Aula Katharinæ
ll Sᵗ Petri	7. Coll divi Iohannis	11. Eccl S S Trinitatis	15. Eccl Sᵗ Edvardi	19. Coll Reginense
oll Magdalen	8. Coll Trinitatis	12. Coll Caij	16. Sacel Coll Regalis	20. Montes Hogm̃.g̃og

The Prosp

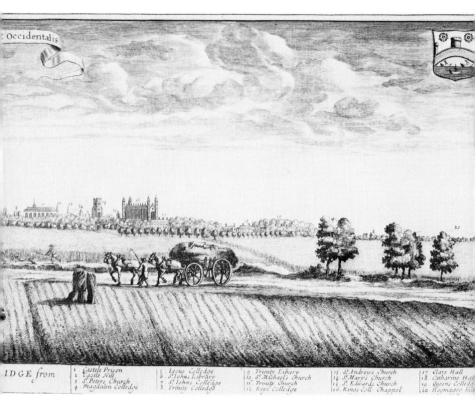

The following image labels appear:

IDGE from

1 Castels Prison
2 Castle Hill
3 St Peters Church
4 Magdalen Colledge

5 Jesus Colledge
6 St Johns Library
7 St Johns Colledge
8 Trinity Colledge

9 Trinity Libary
10 St Michaels Church
11 Trinity Church
12 Kings Colledge

13 St Andrews Church
14 St Marys Church
15 St Edwards Church
16 Kings Coll. Chappel

17 Clare Hall
18 Catharine Hall
19 Queens Colledge
20 Hogmagog hill

The Prospect of Cambridge from the West, a seventeenth-century
view of the university that furnished leadership for the Pilgrims.
Courtesy of Cambridge University Library.

The Pilgrim Pathway, Scrooby to Babworth, where the Pilgrims
walked to and from church. Courtesy of the Rev. Edmund F.
Jessup and the Hon. R. H. Williamson.

The statue of William Bradford, near Plymouth Rock; dedicated Thanksgiving 1976. Courtesy of the Pilgrim Society.

Frontispiece of William Bradford's *Dialogue*. Courtesy of the Pilgrim Society.

was open communication between Plymouth and the Grand Sachem's domain to the west.

When word came that he was "sick and near unto death," a delegation was sent to visit him, with Hobomok as guide and interpreter. Edward Winslow discovered that Massasoit was critically ill and set to work to doctor him. He found that the chief had not slept for two days and had been constipated for five days. He placed a conserve liquid on his swollen tongue in his furry mouth until the chief was able to swallow. At Massasoit's request he shot geese and ducks and made him some English pottage "such as he had eaten at Plymouth." He dispatched messengers to Plymouth to bring chickens for the preparation of broth, asking Dr. Samuel Fuller for suggestions and some liquor to strengthen Massasoit. He searched the countryside for herbs and made sassafras broth.

Pleased with his progress under the youthful physician, Massasoit sent Winslow to doctor his people who were ill.

> He caused me to spend [my strength] in going from one to the other, amongst those that were sick in the town: requesting me to wash their mouths also, and give to each of them some of the same [that] I gave him, saying, they were good folk. This pains I took with willingness; though it were much offensive to me, not being accustomed with [to] such poisonous savours.

Upon his recovery Massasoit "brake forth into these speeches, 'Now I see the English are my friends, and love me; and whilst I live I will never forget this kindness they have shewed me.' "[15]

The Pilgrims thought of the Indians as descendants of the ten lost tribes of Israel, although they may have spoken of them as savages and heathens. They considered them victims of their primitive environment and backward because they were under the control of Satan. They were not damned forever but were capable of salvation. They did not seek to destroy them or to enslave them but rather to enlighten and liberate them from the power of the devil. They harbored no imperialistic design against the red people, who were not viewed as a foreign race but as part of God's family.[16]

During their discussions in Holland, as the Pilgrims planned their move to the New World, they made it clear that they intended to befriend the Indians. They stated that they desired to help in "the propagating and advancing the gospel of the kingdom of Christ in those remote parts of the world."[17]

Hobomok warned Plymouth that the troublesome settlement of Weston and Morton at Wessagusset was inciting the Indians to attack Plymouth. It was reported that the white men there planned to rob the Massachusetts tribe of their corn. One of their braves, Wituwamat, who lived near Wessagusset, had made fiery speeches against the Pilgrims in the presence of Captain Standish and before members of Cape Cod tribes. It was decided to send Captain Standish with eight armed men and Hobomok to learn firsthand about the commotion there.

On arrival at Wessagusset they found the pinnace *Swan*, which was brought over to provide supplies for the settlers, abandoned. Standish upbraided the crew for living "senseless of their own misery." The Pilgrims traded furs with the Indians and tried to size up the situation. The aggressive brave Wituwamat soon appeared, flourishing his knife, announcing that he had "killed both French and English." Another powerful brave, Pecksuot, challenged Standish: "You are but a little man, and though I be no sachem, yet I am a man of great strength and courage." All this aggravated "Captain Shrimp," who was short of stature.

Standish and his men lured these two Indians into their cottage. The captain moved toward Pecksuot, snatched the knife from his hand, and stabbed his assailant in the chest. His associates battled with Wituwamat in a hand-to-hand struggle until he fell with other braves. Some of Weston's men joined in the encounter that scattered the Indians. Standish asked Weston's colony what they wanted to do. They were afraid to stay at Wessagusset. He invited them to Plymouth, but they chose to sail for Maine on the *Swan*, hoping that they could work their way back to England on fishing boats.[18]

The Plymouth men returned home bearing the head of Wituwamat, which was placed on a spike on the top of the fort. They tried to justify their actions to the leaders of the plantation by pointing out that they had not robbed or looted, "not taking ye worth of a penny of anything that was theirs," or abused the terrified squaws. Standish ordered their release and "would not take their beaver coats from them" as much as they wanted furs with which to pay their debt in London.

This display of force, hitherto alien to the ways of Plymouth, struck terror among the Cape Cod tribes so that some "forsook their houses, running to and fro like men distracted, living in swamps and other desert places."

While the conscience of the plantation was being pricked and repercussions of the violence stirred the cottages and the meetinghouse, Pastor John Robinson spoke out in the letter that he sent on December 19, 1623 to his flock, who were still praying and waiting for him to secure passage to cross over to them:

> Concerning the killing of those poor Indians, of which
> we heard at first by report, and since by more certain

relation. Oh, how happy a thing had it been, if you had converted some before you had killed any. Besides, where blood is once begun to be shed, it is seldom staunched of a long time after. You will say they deserved it. I grant it; but upon what provocations and invitements by those heathenish Christians [Weston's men]?

Besides, you being no magistrates over them were to consider not what they deserved but what you were by necessity constrained to inflict. . . .

Upon this occasion let me be bold to exhort you seriously to consider the disposition of your Captain, whom I love, and am persuaded the Lord in great mercy and for much good hath sent you him, if you use him aright. He is a man humble and meek amongst you, and towards all in ordinary course. But now if this be merely from a humane spirit, there is cause to fear that by occasion, especially of provocation, there may be wanting that tenderness of the life of man (made after God's image) which is meet. It is also a thing more glorious, in men's eyes, than pleasing in God's or convenient for Christians, to be a terror to poor barbarous people. And indeed I am afraid lest, by these occasions, others should be drawn to affect a kind of ruffling course in the world.[19]

Myles Standish appears to have taken the rebuke from the minister he admired in good grace. At his death he left a legacy to "Mercy Robinson, who I tenderly love for her grandfather's sake."

The tragic encounter with the Massachusetts Indian tribe was out of line with the good-neighbor policy that the Pilgrims endeavored to follow. This was evidenced in their relations with the Connecticut tribe. Jonathan Brewster was head of the Pilgrim trading post at Windsor on the Connecticut River. In the spring of 1634 a devastating epidemic of smallpox broke out among the Indians in this area. Reported Governor Bradford:

> The condition of this people was so lamentable and they fell down so generally of this disease as they were in the end not able to help one another, no not to make a fire nor to fetch a little water to drink, nor any to bury the dead. And some would crawl out on all fours to get a little water, and sometimes die by the way. But of those of the English house [the Plymouth post], though at first they were afraid of the infection, yet seeing their woeful and sad condition and hearing their pitiful cries and lamentations, they had compassion of them, and daily fetched them wood and water, and made them fires, got them victuals whilst they lived; and buried them when they died. For very few of them escaped, notwithstanding they did what they could for them to the hazards of themselves.
>
> By the marvelous goodness and providence of God, not one of the English was so much as sick or in the least measure stained with this disease, though they daily did these offices for them for many weeks together. And this mercy which they showed them was kindly taken and thankfully acknowledged of all the Indians that knew or heard of the same. And their masters here did much commend and reward them for the same.[20]

Soon after the Dorchester Puritans from the Bay had seized the Pilgrim land at Windsor, the Bay Colony reported that they wanted Plymouth's help in checking the militant Pequot tribe in Connecticut, who were a threat to their fellow Indians and to the whites. The Pequots murdered English settlers and fought against the

Dutch and their neighbors, the Narragansetts and the Mohegans. Captain John Endecott of Salem staged a raid in 1636 in an effort to check this first serious friction with the Indians. The resort to force fomented ill will. Bradford reminded Governor Winthrop that the Bay had only recently acquiesced in the seizure of Pilgrim land at Windsor, and asked why they had plunged into war without first asking the advice of Plymouth.[21] Winthrop tried to pacify Bradford, and Plymouth reluctantly agreed to furnish a few troops. However, before they could sail in 1637 for Connecticut the Bay militia and Indian allies had staged a massacre of the Pequots near the mouth of the Mystic River. Over 700 Pequots were killed or captured. The survivors and their families were assigned to the Indian allies: the Narragansetts, Mohegans, and Niantics. The Pequots never recovered from the destruction. Plymouth was not implicated in this conflict that spread fear through New England and presaged the Armageddon of King Philip's War in 1675.

John Winthrop stated that during the Pequot War neighboring Indians who fought the Pequots cut off and sent in the heads and hands of their enemies. This appears to have been a common practice and was repeated during King Philip's War.[22]

The Pilgrim policy was to purchase land from the natives. They did not buy the site for Plymouth Plantation from the Patuxets because only one was living after the epidemic that swept away thousands along the New England coast before the *Mayflower* arrived. The surviving Patuxet, Squanto, might have reaped some compensation besides his rewarding friendship, but he died in 1622. Most of the land in Plymouth Colony was bought from the tribes.[23] Massasoit offered them land. The Pilgrims insisted on paying the Indian owners. In an effort to protect the natives from exploitation, the General Court ordered in 1643 that no one could purchase land without court approval:

> Whereas it is holden very unlawful and of dangerous consequence and it hath beene the constant custome from our first beginning That no person or persons haue or euer did purchase Rent or hire any lands herbage wood or timber of the Natiues but by the Majestrates consent. It is therefore enacted by the Court that if any person or persons do hereafter purchase rent or hyre . . . without the consent and assent of the Court euery such person or persons shall forfait fiue pounds for euery acree.[24]

The records indicate that the Pilgrims did not intend to dispossess the Indians, although their royal patent of 1629 gave them title to the land. They tried to buy it. At the beginning there was a sincere effort to play fairly and to check exploitation. The first registry of deeds in the New World was set up to handle land transactions. Deeds were filed with an official of the colony. Full recognition of the Indians' title was required. A body of trustworthy men was chosen to handle sales. Indians were invited to register their land along with the English.

Josiah Winslow, the son of Edward, wrote in 1676:

> I think I can clearly say that before these present troubles broke out, the English did not possess one foot of land in this colony but was fairly obtained by honest purchase of the Indian proprietors. Nay, because some of our people are of covetous disposition, and the Indians, in their straits are easily prevailed with to part with their lands, we first made a law that none should purchase or receive as gift any land of the Indians without the knowledge and allowance of the Court. . . . And if at any time they had brought

complaints before us, they have had justice impartial and speedy, so that our own people have frequently complained that we erred on the other hand in showing them overmuch favor.[25]

Plymouth set up laws to protect the rights of the native people. Captain William Macomber was fined forty shillings and given a public whipping for "abusing two old Indians." In 1665 a settler was fined and placed in the stocks for trying to collect a debt from an Indian by entering his home, seizing property and a child in an effort to force payment.[26] Joseph Bartlett was in court on March 5, 1667 "for breaking the King's peace in striking of an Indian named Sampson [and was] sentenced to pay a fine of 00/03/04."[27] Plymouth Colony records of September 25, 1639 state:

Treaty with Vssamequin and Mooanam, his son, came into the Court in their own psons, and desired that the ancient league and confederacy formerly made with this government, wherein he acknowledgeth himself subject to the King of England, and his successors, may stand and remain inviolable. . . .[28]

Plymouth Colony records of March 1, 1645 read:

Whereas complaint is made that some of the neighboring Indians of the town of Rehoboth have sustained great damage in their corn by the horses and other cattle of the said town, that some fences may be made and repaired as ought to be for preventing future damage in that behalf.[29]

It was illegal to sell alcohol to the Indians and to sell them fire arms. The Pilgrims tried to preserve order by regulating the use of liquor and guns.

The court treated English offenders against the Indians

as severely as it treated Indians who wronged white people. Dramatic evidence of this practice is found in the murder trial of Arthur Peach, Thomas Jackson, and Richard Stinnings. In 1638 four young indentured workers ran away from the plantation, breaking the terms of their agreement, and set out for the Dutch colony. While camping between the Bay and the country of the Narragansett Indians, one of that tribe passed, a trader who had cloth and beads with him. While they drank and smoked with him they planned to kill and rob him. Arthur Peach stabbed him with a rapier and stole from him five fathom of wampum and three coats of cloth.[30]

The Indians talked with Roger Williams, who was nearby in the Narragansett country, expressing fear that the English would fall upon them and that they "were ready to rise in arms." Williams "pacified them and told them they should see justice done upon the offenders." He took a physician to see the wounded Indian, who told them who had stabbed and robbed him. He died soon after. The offenders were brought to Plymouth and tried by a jury. "They all in the end freely confessed all that the Indian accused them of."[31]

Governor Bradford explained that "some of the rude and ignorant sort murmered that any English should be put to death for the Indians." The court upheld the tradition of English justice: "And so, upon the forementioned evidence, were cast by the jury and condemned, and executed for the same, September 4." The Plymouth court orders add: "Peach, Jackson & Stinnings had sentence of death pronounced vist, to be taken . . . to the place of execution, and there to be hanged by the neck vntil their bodyes were dead, wch was executed vpon them accordingly."[32]

Obviously four English offenders would have been hanged if Daniel Cross had not made his escape, and four lives taken for the killing of one Indian named Penowan-yanguis. A motion picture called *The Peach Gang* was produced at Plymouth under the auspices of the National Endowment for the Humanities, to be telecast nationally for the public schools. The film ends with the trial, without any reference to the sentence or the executions, so the viewer does not know that justice prevailed. When the producers were confronted with objection to this omission, they replied that school children could consult Bradford's *Journal* and find the outcome for themselves, knowing that this seventeenth-century classic is available only in city and university libraries. Moreover, how many American youth have the initiative to pursue such research to discover a purposely deleted but all-important fact in this story? The producers contended that it was their mission to provoke thought regarding ethnic conflict and not to be concerned about presenting the complete story.

Moreover, in this film Roger Williams appears at the trial in Plymouth as a friend and defender of the rights of the Indians. In the course of his remarks he mentioned being banished from Plymouth Colony. This again twists the facts. Williams left Plymouth voluntarily for Salem, and it was in the Bay Colony that he was brought to court and ordered to depart from their bounds. He was liked in Plymouth and supported by the people in his efforts to settle in Rhode Island.

Edward Winslow, a friend of Massasoit and frequent visitor to his domain, wrote:

We found the Indians very faithful in their Covenant of Peace with us; [and] very loving and ready to pleasure us. We often go to them; and they come to us. Some of us have been fifty miles by land in the country with them [i.e., to Sowans in Pokanoket] the occasions and relations whereof you shall understand by our general and more full Declaration (aforesaid) of such things as are worth noting.

Yea, it hath pleased God so to possess the Indians with a fear of us, and love unto us, that not only the greatest king amongst them, called Massasoyt; but also all the Princes and people round about us, have either made suit unto us, or been glad of any occasion to make peace with us; so that seven of them at once have sent their messengers to us to that end. Yea, an isle at sea, which we never saw [Capawack, now called Martha's Vineyard] hath also, together with the former, yielded willingly to be under the protection [of], and subject to, our sovereign Lord King James. So that there is now great peace amongst the Indians themselves, which was not formerly; neither would have been but for us; and we, for our parts, walk as peaceably and safely in the wood as in the highways on England. We entertain them familiarly in our houses; and they, as friendly, bestowing their venison on us.[33]

Winslow and Bradford developed a rapport with the Indians. Roger Williams was also drawn to his native neighbors; he studied their culture and language and visited their bark huts where they cooked over an open fire that roasted them and blinded them with smoke. He preached to them and won their confidence. Sachem Canonicus was his friend and other Indians trusted him. Yet Williams was conscious of their hostility, and following the Pequot War of 1637 he urged Governor John Winthrop to treat the Indians fairly, while at the same time warning him to "deal with them wisely as with wolves endowed with mens' brains." Williams did much to promote understanding and arbitrated between the natives and the newcomers. He wrote: "There is a favour of *civility* and courtesie even among these wild Americans, both amongst themselves and towards strangers."[34]

In 1651 Richard Bourne, a merchant of Sandwich, and Thomas Tupper, a farmer of the same village, worked among the Nausets, trying to tell them about Christianity. In 1646 John Eliot started his missionary labors and was soon preaching in the native tongue.

The efforts of Mayhew and Eliot won a few Christian followers among the tribes. Some natives had become convinced of the sincerity of the settlers, as Edward Winslow observed: "Our conversation amongst ourselves, and with our demeanor towards them, as well in peace, as in such warres they had unavoidably drawn upon themselves; whereby they had such experience of the justice, prudence, valour, temperance, and righteousness of the English, as did not onley remove their firmer jealousies and feares concerning us, and convict them of their owne uneven walking; but begat a good opinion of our persons, and cause them to affect our Laws and Government."[35]

In 1662 the accounts of The Acts of the Commissioners of the United Colonies lists payments to Indian teachers and helpers. There were eight Indian teachers on Martha's Vineyard, two in Plymouth Colony, and six in the Massachusetts Bay Colony.[36]

When John Cotton came from Boston to serve the Plymouth church, he started a program of evangelism among the Indians. John Eliot, the apostle to the Indians, backed his efforts. Philip, son of Massasoit, resented the efforts of the whites. He had heard Cotton preach at least once in Plymouth. He was suspicious of this outreach of the English, who were not only taking the land but seeking to undermine native culture. Cotton indicated in his *Journal* that other sachems as well were hostile to his gestures: "I went to Josiah [Indian sachem of Matakeset] to preach to the Indians but because many of his Indians would forsake him and he would lose much tribute he would not hearken."[37] Philip demonstrated his hostility to John Eliot when he grabbed hold of a button on the missionary's jacket and said that he cared no more for the Christian religion than for that button.[38]

The expansion of Pilgrim land and the growth of the colony with its influx of English settlers aggravated the Indians. The white concept of land use was alien to that of the Indians. The English wanted deeds, bounds, titles, fences, and farms set apart for dwellings, crops, and animals. All this was unknown to the open-country practice of the native people. The two theories were in continuous conflict. The whites believed that their king had the right to grant them land in the New World that he claimed, while the Indians asked how a foreign ruler who had never seen this continent could parcel out the land that they had roamed for generations?

The whites believed they had purchased the land through the exchange of tools, cloth, and merchandise. The land was plentiful and the Indians were eager to trade it for necessities like axes, hatchets, shovels, and hoes, which were important to survival in the wilderness. Implements were scarce, hard to get, and of great value. It must be remembered that the sellers wanted to dispose of the land as much as the buyers wanted it, and were satisfied with useful articles that they prized more than pounds and shillings. Indians accepted the trade as fair, not foreseeing that more and more buyers would appear and the ancestral lands would soon be taken over. Massasoit once sold 130 square miles of land for seven coats, nine hatchets, eight hoes, twenty knives, four mooseskins, and ten and one-half yards of cotton. Philip, his son, sold a four-mile piece in Taunton in 1672 for £190.[39]

Although the Pilgrims endeavored to control land by law and set up safeguards to regulate its use, increasing

confrontations developed over purchase rights, encroach-
ments on hunting areas, the irritation of fences, and domes-
ticated animals running wild.

Pilgrim-Indian relations were peaceful during the first
years of Plymouth and goodwill prevailed. Like William
Penn and his followers in Pennsylvania, the Pilgrims made
an effort to deal fairly with their neighbors. The tragedy
of conflict was fanned by mistakes and misunderstandings
after the leadership of Massasoit passed, along with that
of Brewster, Bradford, and Winslow. The conflict was
due in part to the land lust of the English. However, most
historians recognize other factors that led to armed violence. Philip's father had upheld an alliance with the
Pilgrims as a buffer against his enemies, the Narragansetts.
In the course of fifty years the influence of Plymouth
Colony grew dominant in his area. Indian culture became
subordinate to the laws and practices of the white race.
In his resentment against this influence Philip found some
Indian allies. However, a number of tribes who were
hostile to Philip took sides with the English. The confrontation was a war of causes not of race against race, writes
Alden T. Vaughan. Philip was not a messiah who was
leading a "Pan Indian crusade for freedom from white
encroachment."[40]

The Pilgrims had no military tradition. They did not
seek to impose their ways on the Indians and had no desire
to conquer their neighbors, only to live in peace with
them. The first leaders of the colony endeavored to promote friendly relations. There was a basic religious idealism
at Plymouth which provided them with a troublesome
conscience and prodded them to follow Christian ethics.

Their successors were caught in a vicious net of ever-
increasing distrust as the trend toward violence developed.
Plymouth could have cooperated with the peaceable
Wampanoags, but they were drawn into relations with

other tribes by their association with the English settlements that spread in Massachusetts, Rhode Island, and Connecticut.[41]

After fifty-five years of peace between the Pilgrims and Wampanoags, King Philip's War broke out. The conflict fanned out like wildfire through the New England colonies and raged up and down the Connecticut River valley with raids and burnings. Old ties of friendship were forgotten as vengeance took over. Descendants of former good neighbors staged the Eel River Massacre in Plymouth, close to the spot where Pilgrims and Wampanoags formulated their treaty of peace in 1621. Eleven women and children were killed. Each outburst led to attempts at retaliation and the conflict flared into a devastating encounter.

In the spring of 1676 Philip was shot in his stronghold to the west along with many of his warriors. Benjamin Church tried to save Philip's two lieutenants, but the request was refused in the confusion. Some of the captives were sold into slavery, including Philip's son, and shipped to the West Indies.

King Philip had failed to appreciate the old friendship between his people and the Pilgrims. Likewise, Josiah Winslow, who was governor from 1673 to 1680, lacked his father's genius for dealing with people. He was not able to carry on the tradition of a person-to-person relationship as his predecessors had. Before the outbreak of the war, when Josiah Winslow was chief military commander, he had ordered Massasoit's oldest son, Alexander, to come to Plymouth and discuss a reported plot that was being hatched against the English. Alexander made the trip under protest. While staying at Winslow's house in Marshfield he fell ill. He died on his way home and Winslow was blamed for his death. Josiah Winslow disliked military life and was not an effective commander during the war. The cruelties that were perpetrated on the Indians within the fort and on the survivors in the final battle have been blamed in some measure on his judgment.

Selling war prisoners was justified by some white men since Plymouth Colony had no facilities for holding captives. This course was in accord with the Old Testament code of justice, "an eye for an eye and a tooth for a tooth." Offenders who broke the treaty had to suffer the consequences. However, there were protests against this treatment of Indians. Thomas Walley wrote a condemnation to John Cotton, and Captain Benjamin Church made a plea for more humane policies. Certain Indian offenders were sentenced to domestic slavery, which was similar to indentured servitude, with the chance for release. Masters were obligated to provide shelter, clothing, food, and education.

The war caused a "searching of conscience" in Plymouth and in all New England. John Cotton urged his church to renew its covenant with God. He told his congregation that they had been "haughty in spirit, in countenance, in garb, & fashion. . . . Stubborn and rebellious against God & disobedient to their parents." It was a dire time that summoned people to consider evils that threatened their existence because they had strayed from God's will.[42]

Many were troubled by the bloodshed of the war. Josiah Winslow wrote to John Winthrop, Jr.: "We doubt not but you haue heard how it hath pleased God to exercise us under very afflictive dispensations improveing our neighbor Indians to scourge and chasten us . . . our punishment tis less, far less, then our iniquiteys haue deserved."[43]

John Cotton recorded words of humiliation and repentance for his Plymouth flock: "Whereas the Holy and Righteous God hath many wayes in yeares lately past changed the course of his favourable dispensations towards us and manifested sad signes of his displeasure against us, wee desire to be deeply humbled in his sight under his mighty hand."[44]

The once friendly Wampanoags were practically wiped out by this tragic holocaust, their huts burned, their lands seized, their people decimated. Almost every household in Plymouth Colony lost a father, husband, son, or close relative, a house, barn, cattle, and horses. The losses were overwhelming. The colony's debt was set at £27,000, over $1,000,000 in contemporary currency. The harmonious outlook of the colonists was clouded by internal strains and intercolonial quarrels. The hope of building Zion in the wilderness was undermined.[45]

The confidence developed through over fifty years of cooperation by leaders like Carver, Brewster, Bradford, Winslow, and Williams was shattered. Captain Roger Williams' house was burned by the Indians he had sought to understand and defend. He lost his furniture, clothing, books, and manuscripts, and set to work at age seventy-three to rebuild.[46]

The epic of the American continent might have been free from the exploitation and carnage had some champion of world order, an Indian or a white, like Hugo Grotius, delivered an effective warning to the contenders. This advocate of the rule of law might have sold natives and settlers on the wisdom of obeying the mandate of nature which made clear that the soil of America was not the sole property of the Caucasians who had, they thought, "discovered" it, nor did it "belong" to the Indian tribes who had squatted on it for generations, nor was it made for the sole "benefit" of the aborigines who preceded these contingents by centuries any more than it was for the deer, buffalo, bear, ducks, and geese.

CHAPTER 11

No Witches in Plymouth

Do not carry things as if the Word of God either came
from you or unto you alone.

—John Robinson[1]

The Puritans of Salem have been pommeled for their
witchcraft frenzy. This ugly tale of bigotry formed a
blotch on human reason and tolerance. But Salem's blunder,
with the total of nineteen hangings, was minor compared
with the hysteria in Great Britain and Europe. The Witchcraft Delusion of 1692 was not an isolated tragedy but one
lesser incident in the annals of superstition that raged
through the "civilized world." There were few in the
seventeenth century anywhere who saw through its sham
or dared to take a stand against it. In those days, witchcraft
was labeled a crime by the Bible, the church, science,
medicine, and law.

This unhealthy agglomeration of myth, ignorance, and
terror cannot be laid at the door of the Puritans. King
James I wrote his *Daemonnologie* in 1597 and took the
lead in prosecuting sorcerers in Scotland. Sir Matthew

Hale, chief baron of the exchequer, stated in 1664: "That there were such creatures as *Witches* he made no doubt at all; For *First*, the Scriptures had affirmed so much. *Secondly*, The wisdom of all Nations had provided Laws against such Persons."[2] Sir Thomas Browne, who wrote *Religio Medici*, testified before an English court "that the Devil did work upon the Bodies of Men and Women, to stir up, and excite such humours super-abounding in their Bodies to a great excess."[3]

Seventeenth-century New Englanders believed in witchcraft not because they were Puritans or Pilgrims but because they were people of their time. The book of Exodus laid down the law: "Thou shalt not suffer a witch to live [Exod. 22:18, KJV]." What chance did a hapless soul accused of black magic have against the holy scriptures?

Massachusetts settlers followed the laws against witches set up during the reigns of Henry VI, Henry VIII, Elizabeth I, and James I. Witchcraft had been made a capital crime based on the old Mosaic law.

Massachusetts had pious scholars like Cotton Mather who believed that the devil and witches were real and close at hand. He wrote:

> Wherefore the Devil is now making one Attempt more upon us; an Attempt more Difficult, more Surprising, more snarl'd with unintelligible Circumstances than any that we have hitherto Encountered. . . . An Army of Devils is horribly broke in upon the place which is the center, and after a sort, the First-born of our English Settlements: and the Houses of the Good People there are fill'd with the doleful shrieks of their Children and Servants, Tormented by Invisible Hands, with Tortures altogether preternatural.[4]

The devil was portrayed by Mather as "a short and a Black Man . . . no taller than an ordinary Walking-Staff, who wore a High-Crowned Hat, with strait Hair, and had one Cloven-Foot." Satan had sent witches "as a particular Defiance unto *my* poor Endeavours to bring the Souls of men unto Heaven."[5]

Samuel Sewall, often marked as the villain in the Salem tragedy, was born in England in 1652. He came to Massachusetts at the age of nine and studied under President Chauncy during his years at Harvard from 1667 to 1671. He was given a good foundation in Hebrew and Greek and no doubt in the ethics of the Cambridge reformers, interspersed with reports of the president's former adventures in Plymouth Colony. He entered business and the law and became judge of the Supreme Court in the fateful year of 1692.

As accusations piled up in Salem, Governor Phips called a court to try those charged with witchcraft. By September 22, 1692 twenty-seven suspects had been tried, all of whom denied being witches. All twenty-seven had been sentenced to die; nineteen had been hanged and one pressed to death. Judge Sewall presided. He condemned the accused and delivered the verdicts.

The terror of what was happening spread, as did revulsion against the orgy. Robert Calef, a Boston merchant, was brave enough to attack Cotton Mather and other engineers of this folly. His book, *More Wonders of the Invisible World*, helped arouse opposition. Mather denounced Calef's book as "a firebrand thrown by a mad man," and Increase Mather ordered it burned in Harvard College yard.

Thomas Brattle, a Boston merchant friend of Calef, also dared to lift his voice against the madness around him. This Harvard graduate, only twenty-four years of age, later became treasurer of his alma mater. Brattle wrote: "What will be the issue of these troubles, God only knows. I am afraid that ages will not wear off that reproach and those stains which these things will leave behind them upon our land. I pray God pity us, forgive us, and appear mercifully for us in this our mount of distress."[6]

Consequently, resentment grew. People revolted against the reign of madness. Two judges resigned from the court. The wife of Governor Phips was accused of being a witch, along with Samuel Willard of Harvard. Governor Phips ordered the court suspended to help halt the spreading epidemic of suspicion and fear. Some of the jurors and witnesses publicly repented, and some of the clergy raised their voices in protest, calling for a day of prayer and fasting.

Judge Sewall wrote his statement of contrition. Samuel Willard was Sewall's pastor at the Old South Church in Boston, a vice-president of Harvard, and acting president while Increase Mather was abroad. Willard read Judge Sewall's confession to the congregation on the fast day as the judge stood in contrition, stating that he "desires to take the Blame and shame of it. Asking pardon of men. And especially desiring prayers that God, who has an Unlimited Authority, would pardon that sin and all other sins."[7] Perhaps the judge recalled in these testing days some of the wisdom he had gleaned during his classes with President Chauncy as he studied the Hebrew Old Testament and the Greek New Testament. Something in his religious heritage caused him to face up to his failures and to make a public confession to his peers. He later tried to make further atonement by writing the first anti-slavery booklet in America, *The Selling of Joseph*, in 1700. He befriended the Indians, defended their rights, and served as secretary and treasurer of the Missionary Society to the American Indians.

Another repentance followed when twelve members of the witch-trial jury issued a statement in which they admitted that they had failed "to withstand the mysterious delusions of the Powers of Darkness, and Prince of the Air."[8]

Even Cotton Mather on the fast day prepared articles of confession that he brought before his congregation. One of them stated: "Wicked Sorceries have been practiced in the Land, and yet in the Troubles from the Divels, thereby brought in among us, those Errors, on both Hands, were committed, which wee have cause to beewayl with much Abasement of Soul before the Lord."[9]

Cotton Mather, who accepted demonology and black magic and took a hand in condemning witches, had the courage to champion the pioneering efforts at vaccination against smallpox. He also was openminded toward the new astronomy and embraced the Copernican concept of the world in contradiction to the Ptolemaic system. The people, including most of the scholars, were ignorant of modern science. The cosmic concepts of the Pilgrims were limited to the scientific outlook of their time, but they were independent people. Their intellectual leaders like John Robinson, William Bradford, and Edward Winslow appear free in their writings from naive acceptance of the uncritical beliefs that prevailed. They emerge as rational thinkers.

The witch scandal in Massachusetts makes for heart-rending reading. Some twenty-six victims were claimed in the Bay in a century. In England during the seventeenth century the number ran into hundreds. The witch-finder general, Matthew Hopkins, led at least two hundred to the gallows between 1645 and 1647. In Scotland between 1580 and 1680 it is believed that 3,400 were executed. Mannhart estimated that at least half a million were victims of execution in Europe from the fourteenth to the seventeenth century.[10]

Only rough estimates are possible, but the suggested figure of some 300,000 executions and burnings in

Europe and the British Isles during the century of the Salem Village outbreak is perhaps an understatement. Against the towering figures, the nineteen deaths on the scaffold and under heavy stones in New England in 1692 might seem a small total in proportion to the shame these deaths have spread over our colonial story.[11]

George Kittredge stated: "In prosecuting witches, our forefathers acted like other men of the seventeenth century. In repentance and making public confession, they acted like themselves. Their fault was the fault of their time; their merit was their own."[12]

The public repentance and recantation of judge and jurors in Massachusetts have had no parallel in the history of witchcraft. Francis Hutchinson wrote in 1718 in detail of the recantation of Judge Samuel Sewall and the jurors and mentioned that the towns shaken by the trials had regained their quiet.[13]

Ironically, in an era when scorn is hurled against the Salem witch-hunters, millions of Americans lean heavily on astrologers and fortune-tellers and devour books on black magic and exorcism. A Gallup poll of 1957 indicated that 61 percent of those who responded believed in a personal devil.[14]

Human life is still exploited by religious sects who kidnap children to use as human sacrifices, fanatics who defy poisonous snakes to prove that they are protected by superhuman powers, exorcists who expel demons from harassed beings, astrologers who plot life decisions for trusting clients, fakirs who entice people through their phobias and insecurities into cults built on falsehood and quackery.

With the twentieth-century advances in technology, society has not achieved control over the superstition that ran rife in the seventeenth century, wreaking its havoc on humanity. This failure reminds us that the problem of evil persists and how difficult it is to root it out of society.

The Pilgrims may have bungled their stance at tolerance in coping with the Quakers, but they did themselves proud in handling the malaise of witchcraft. This threat was a more clear-cut issue. Here was a deplorable hangover from the Middle Ages, a nightmare from the days of the Inquisition, a defiance of law and order, a resort to cruelty and violence. They made a stand for reason and enlightenment.

Plymouth had joined the other colonies in passing firm laws against witchcraft. Even the most tolerant settlements, including the Dutch, the Rhode Island liberals, the Episcopalians, the Marylanders, and the Quakers enacted stringent statutes against witches. Plymouth also had such a law on the books. However, much to its credit, this law was never enforced. The colony set up a blockade of common sense that kept the contagion of panic from creeping into its midst.

There were only two accusations and two trials in Plymouth records, and in both cases the accused were exonerated and the accusers soundly scored. The first threat arose in 1661, presenting all the ingredients for a Salem-type flare-up of gossip and hysteria, charge and counter-charge. Dinah Sylvester of Scituate brought a complaint of witchcraft against her neighbor, Mrs. William Holmes, insisting that she had seen her in conversation with the devil, who assumed the form of a bear. Fortunately for Plymouth, Governor Thomas Prence, who was known as a conservative, rose to the challenge and called the accuser and the accused before the General Court for a decision.

Mrs. Holmes of Marshfield was the wife of a lieutenant in Myles Standish's military. Lieutenant Holmes sued for slander and the case came before Governor Prence on

May 7, 1661. The governor's Board of Assistants included John Alden, William Bradford, Jr., William Colgare, Thomas Southworth, and Josiah Winslow, sound persons who resisted the witch-hunting mentality. The board gave Dinah Sylvester and her charges a sharp scrutiny:

> "What evidence have you to support your charge?" she was asked.
> "She appeared to me as a witch," she answered.
> "In what shape?"
> "In the shape of a bear."
> "How far away was the bear?"
> "About a stone's throw from the path."
> "What manner of tail did the bear have?"
> "I could not tell as the head was towards me. . . ."
> But the plot was too shallow, and whatever there was of Deviltry in it was thrown upon the one who made the Attempt.[15]

After Dinah's accusations had been aired, the court acquitted Mrs. Holmes. Dinah Sylvester was found guilty of slander. She was ordered to be publicly whipped and to pay Mrs. Holmes five pounds or to openly confess her slander and repay Holmes all costs and charges. She made a public confession two days later on May 9:

> To the honored Court assembled; whereas I haue bin convicted in matter of defamation concerning Goodwife Holmes, I doe freely acknowlidg I haue wronged my naighbour, and haue sinned aginst God in soe doing; though I had entertained hard thoughts against the woman; for it had bine my dewty to declare my grouns, if I had any, vnto some majestrate in a way of God, and not to haue devoulged my thoughts to others, to the woman's defamation. Therefore I doe acknowlidg my sin in it, and doe humbly begg this

honored Court to forgive mee, and all other Christian people that be offended att it, and doe promise, by the healp of God to do soe noe more; and although I doe not remember all that the witnesses doe testify, yett I doe rather mistrust my owne memory and submitt to the evidences.

Dinah Siluester[16]

Some four years after the death of Governor Prence, when Josiah Winslow was governor, in the year 1677, a second charge of witchcraft was made against Mary Ingham, wife of Thomas Ingham of Scituate, who was accused of bewitching Mehitabel, the daughter of Walter Woodworth. The case was heard before a jury of twelve, with the governor presiding.

Mary Ingham: thou art indicted by the name of Mary Ingham, the wife of Thomas Ingham of the towne of Scittuate, in the jurisduction of New Plimoth, for that thou, haveing not the feare of God before thyne eyes, hast, by the help of the divill in a way of witchcraft or sorcery, maliciously procured much hurt, mis-chieffe, and paine unto the body of Mehittable Wood-worth of Scittuate aforesaid, and some others, and particularly causing her, the sd Mehittable to fall into violent fitts, and causing greate paine unto severall ptes of her body at severall times soe as she the sd Mehittable Woodworth hath bin almost bereaved of her senses, and hath greatly languished to her much suffering thereby, and the procuring of great greiffe, sorrow, and charge to her parents; all of which thou has procured and done against the law of God, & to his great dishonor and contrary to our sovereign lord the kinge, his crowne & dignities.

The sd Mary Ingham did putt herselfe on the tryal of God and the country, and was cleared of this indictment in process of law, by a jury of 12 men whose names follow:

Thomas Huckins, John Wadsworth, John Howland (second), Abram Jackson, Benaiah Pratt, John Black, Mark Snow, Joseph Bartlett, John Richmond, James Talbot, John Foster, Seth Poe.

The jury brought in the verdict "not guilty and soe the said prisoner was cleared as above said." Mary Ingham was thus fully acquitted, her accuser was silenced, and the specter of witch-hunting was forever laid to rest in Plymouth.[17]

Why did Plymouth escape the witch hysteria of the Bay Colony? There is no doubt that the nucleus of intellectual acumen of John Robinson left a stamp on Plymouth. His followers, especially Brewster, Bradford, and Winslow, guided the colony for years and their influence was lasting. Theirs was a softer Calvinism. They leaned toward reason.

CHAPTER 12

Master Roger Williams

While I plead the cause of truth and innocency against the bloody doctrine of persecution for the cause of conscience, I judge it not unfit to give alarm to myself and all men to prepare to be persecuted or hunted for cause of conscience.

—Roger Williams (1644)[1]

The Pilgrims found it difficult to secure a minister who could measure up to John Robinson, their founder-mentor, who for several months had helped form their 1606 Scrooby congregation and had led them ably for twelve years in Amsterdam and Leyden. It was disappointing that he could not come over on the *Mayflower*, but it was the decision of the Green Gate congregation that Elder William Brewster should lead the first contingency to the New World. The pastor should stay in Leyden to care for the majority of the flock and to help prepare the balance for migration. He would cross over as soon as possible on one of the subsequent ships.

But it developed that the London Merchant Adventurers, who had loaned funds to finance the new settlement, thought otherwise. They kept holding back on approving Robinson's crossing because they feared King James I would be upset to learn that the controversial author was in New England spreading his liberal doctrines. The Plymouth settlers prayed fervently that Pastor Robinson would arrive soon, and they expected him on every vessel that sailed into Plymouth harbor. They waited for five years, getting along without their devoted leader, making the best of their lot, the lay members carrying on the work of the church. Robinson was seized by illness and died suddenly on March 1, 1625. Myles Standish, when he returned from his futile trip to London to raise funds, brought a letter with him from the church in Leyden announcing the grave loss of the spiritual guide who was head of a church that spanned the Atlantic, part in Leyden, part in Plymouth.

Plymouth offered a precarious post for a first-class clergyman. The colony was small, struggling, and remote. It afforded an escape for someone who wanted to run away from a bad situation in England. Some of the London Merchant Adventurers sent over such a man on the *Fortune* in 1624, along with three heifers and a bull, "the first beginning of any cattle in ye land." The animals were welcomed and the dominie, John Lyford, was treated courteously. He, however, behaved obsequiously before the settlers. "He saluted them with reverence and humility." When he asked to be made a member of the church, he was received. He spoke then of his "former disorderly walking and his being entangled with many corruptions."[2]

It was soon evident that he and John Oldham, "a mad jack in his moods" who had come on the *Anne* in 1623, were intent on undermining the colony. They wrote letters to England "full of slanderous and false accusations." They quarreled with the other settlers and set up their own public meeting on the Lord's Day. Lyford endeavored to reestablish the Church of England by christening a child with the sign of the cross.

Governor Bradford called a meeting of the court. When confronted, Lyford "burst out into tears, and confessed he feared he was a reprobate." The court sentenced him to be expelled. Oldham was to go immediately, although "his wife and family had liberty to stay all winter or longer till he could make provision to remove them comfortably." Lyford had the liberty to stay six months. "He confessed his sin publicly in the church with tears more largely than before." But he continued to write his letters to England in his efforts to sabotage the plantation.[3]

During the unpleasant wrangling, Lyford's wife confessed he had deceived her by denying that he had a bastard child before she married him, and that he had intercourse with their household maid. He had been dismissed from his parish in Ireland after he seduced the fiancée of a youth in his parish when he was supposed to be engaged in premarital counseling with her. Lyford departed from Plymouth for Nantasket where he joined Oldham. He later sailed for Virginia, "where he shortly after died."

Mad Jack Oldham was given a warm farewell as the settlers ran him through the hot oven with their paddles and hearty fists "with a bob upon the bumme." He made off for Nantasket and was killed by the Indians in 1635.

Ralph Smith was ordained as the first pastor of the Plymouth church before the close of 1629. The parish had been without a minister for nine years. Elder Brewster and his deacons managed to carry on the worship and teaching, proving that they had been well trained by Robinson in Leyden, where laymen were given responsibility. Some of the Plymouth people found Smith "sojourning with some straggling settlers that lived at Nantasket." He and his family were eager to find a roof over their heads. He had studied at Christ's College, Cambridge, was a Separatist, and looked on Plymouth with favor. Bradford described him as "a grave man. He was accordingly kindly entertained and housed, and so remained for sundry years. Yet he proved but a poor help to them in that being of very weak parts."[4]

In 1636 Smith departed from Plymouth for the Bay Colony "partly by his own willingness as thinking it too heavy a burden, and partly at the desire and by the persuasion of others."[5] Possibly the most exciting event of Smith's ministry was the period of Roger Williams' stay in Plymouth, when he served with Smith from 1631 to 1634 as teacher of the church. It was the practice of the Plymouth church to have a minister and a teacher, when they were fortunate enough to secure two leaders and were able to finance their presence. If Smith's preaching was commonplace, they had Williams to enliven the hours in the meetinghouse and keep the villagers on their toes, wrestling with biblical exegesis, the rights of the Indians, the authority of the magistrates and the way of salvation.

Roger Williams was the son of a well-to-do London Merchant tailor. He worked for Sir Edward Coke, chief justice, taking shorthand notes in the Star Chamber. After studying at Pembroke College, Cambridge, he served as chaplain in Essex among Puritans whose thoughts turned him to New England.

He arrived in Boston on the *Lyon*, together with his wife, in February 1631. A day of thanksgiving was declared since the ship brought two hundred tons of food for the hungry colony. The twenty-seven-year-old minister was warmly welcomed and offered the post of teacher in the First Church in Boston; the Rev. John Wilson was returning to England on a visit. It was the opportunity of a lifetime that the magistrates extended the youthful Roger, but he bluntly refused. He "durst not officiate to an unseparated people."[6] The people of the congregation were offended when he rebuked them and when he refused to have communion with them because they had not made an open break with the Church of England. He also shocked them when he stated that the magistrates had no right to punish swearing, breaking the sabbath, and other offenses against the first four commandments. The arrogance of the newcomer was shocking.

Salem learned of the arrival of this new minister. They had lost their teacher, John Higginson, by death. Without hearing the full story of Roger's bout with the First Church of Boston, Salem called him and he accepted. The orthodox reported the fact to Governor John Winthrop, who wrote Governor Endecott of Salem, warning the people about Williams' "dangerous opinions." In spite of a shaky start, the young preacher won friends and continued to expound his insistence on separation and restriction of the magistrate's authority. He ran into opposition, and, after a short stay in Salem, decided that Plymouth was the place for him.

The first colony was still no metropolis in 1631. The settlers were pleased to hear that a scholar who had turned down Boston and Salem chose to cast his lot with them. Williams had learned considerable, while in England, about John Robinson and the Pilgrim venture in Leyden and in New England. The reports that he gleaned during his weeks in Massachusetts convinced him that Plymouthians were Separatists and kindred rebels. Upon his arrival in Plymouth, "he was friendly entertained according to their poor ability, and exercised his gifts amongst them and after some time was admitted a member of the church."[7]

Shortly after Williams had been installed in his new post, Governor John Winthrop and John Wilson, pastor of the

First Church in Boston, paid a visit to Plymouth where they were "kindly entertained and feasted every day in several houses." Governor Winthrop described the order of worship they followed and the participation of a number present in the service: Roger Williams, Ralph Smith, William Bradford, William Brewster, Samuel Fuller, and two or three other members.

The record shows not only how Williams took part in the afternoon service, where laity participated with the clergy in dialogue, but also the simple form of worship followed by the Pilgrims. The young pastor must have felt on trial since Winthrop and other dignitaries of Boston had sent out a warning regarding his heresies. However, he came through that test and settled down to the daily chores of clearing land, chopping wood, planting, and harvesting. He wrote that he won his food "by as hard *digging* as most *diggers* in Old or New England have been put to."[8] Some of the warnings from the Bay were substantiated by the newcomer's thesis that the land belonged to the Indians and the king of England had no right to take it from them, by any patent of his, and emphasis on rigid separation from the Church of England. He came to Plymouth assuming that they were a Separatist people, but he was dismayed by their friendliness with the Church of England, and rebuked them for following Robinson's advice and visiting the mother church when they were back in their homeland. He insisted that it was wrong to remain in a church that did not censure members who fraternized with the Established Church.

Williams challenged the authority of the magistrates, stating that Plymouth should not require the oath of fidelity to their commonwealth of any who were unregenerate because the oath was invoked in the name of God and was therefore a type of religious communion with others who took it.

Cotton Mather wrote that "there was a whole country in America like to be set on fire by the rapid motion of a windmill in the head of one particular man."[9] The Plymouth congregation was accustomed to independent thinking, but these concepts led a number to agree that "God had put a windmill in Roger Williams' head." In spite of his personal popularity, Williams' contentions led to discontent on both sides and his request for dismission to the church in Salem, where he still had friends, "was granted, with some caution to them concerning him and what care they ought to have of him." Elder Brewster agreed that it might be best for Plymouth. William Bradford summed up the stay of this stormy petrel, writing that he "was a man godly and zealous, having many precious parts but very unsettled in judgment. . . . And his teaching well approved, for the benefit whereof I still bless God and am thankful to him even for his sharpest admonitions and reproofs so far as they agreed with truth."[10]

Bradford apparently admired Williams and wrote some time after his departure from Plymouth: "He is to be pitied and prayed for; and so I shall leave the matter and desire the Lord to show him his errors and reduce him into the way of truth and give him a settled judgement and constancy in the same, for I hope he belongs to the Lord and that He will show him mercy."[11] Edward Winslow was another friend of Williams. He called him "the sweetest soul I ever knew." Dr. Samuel Fuller wrote in his will: "Whatsoever Mr. Roger Williams is indebted upon my books for physic, I freely give him." He also left two acres of land on Strawberry Hill to Williams' son, "if Mr. Williams refuse to accept of them as formerly he hath done."[12]

Nathaniel Morton, secretary of the colony and Bradford's nephew, wrote in *New-Englands Memoriall* (1669) about the controversies that Roger Williams generated:

He proceeded more vigorously to vent many dangerous opinions, as amongst many others these were some;
that it was not lawful for an unregenerate man to
pray, nor to take an oath, and in special, not the oath
of fidelity to the civil government; nor was it lawful
for a godly man to have communion, either in family
prayer, or in an oath, with such as they judged unregenerate; and therefore he himself refused the oath
of fidelity, and taught others so to do; also, that it was
not lawful so much as to hear the godly ministers of
England, when any occasionally went thither, and
therefore he admonished any church members that
had done so as for heinous sin; also he spake dangerous words against the patent, which was the foundation of the government of the Massachusetts colony;
also he affirmed, that the magistrates had nothing to
do in matters of the first table, but only the second;
and that there should be a general and unlimited toleration of all religions, and for any man to be punished
for any matters of his conscience, was persecution.[13]

Roger Williams stirred things up in Plymouth, but they
were ready for some real mental food. They were accustomed to the best intellectual diet in England and Holland,
familiar with the learned phraseology of Cambridge and
skilled in the intricacies of theological disputation. Williams
was admired in Plymouth for his outspoken courage. He
had the same fortitude that led the Pilgrims to take a
stand against James I and to plan their moves to Holland
and to New England. They liked his spunkiness, and he
liked the Plymouth stance.

In his exposure to the wilderness, Williams was drawn
to the Indians and their culture. To supplement his meager
salary, he traded with them and studied their speech. He
was by nature a linguist, and he learned to talk with them,

preached to them, and planned a book on a key to their language. He passed many hours visiting with them in their "filthy smoke holes." He sensed their feelings about the white intruders who were moving in around them, and he soon denied the rights of the English to appropriate Indian land.

Williams had an affinity with the natives, and many of them became his friends and kept their pledge of peace with him. He was later treated as a son by Canonicus, chieftain of the Narragansetts. Canonicus sent for him when he was dying, asking that Master Williams might close his eyes. His faithful white friend walked many miles to be with the chief and he wrote that "he was bound in cloth of my own gift."[14]

During his short stay in Salem, Williams further expanded his radical doctrines about the invalidity of the royal patent and his agitation against the oath of loyalty and his challenge to the authority of the magistrates. He found scant comfort among his parishioners, and was distressed over the impurities of the church and decided that no church could achieve purity in this world. He had expressed his conviction by separation from the mother church and by denouncing her, by withdrawal from the churches of the Bay, and by refusing to share communion with the governor, convinced that he could partake with no Christian except his own wife. Governor Winthrop of the Bay wrote in his *Journal* in October 1635:

> Mr. Williams was again convented, and the ministers in the bay being desired to be present, he was charged with the said two letters, that to the churches, complaining of the magistrates for injustice, extreme oppression, etc., and other to his own church, to persuade them to renounce communion with all the churches in the bay, as full of anti-christian pollution,

etc. . . . And he, at his return home, refused communion with his own church, who openly disclaimed
his errors, and wrote an humble submission to the
magistrates, acknowledging their fault in joining.[15]

Williams refused, however, to discontinue his agitation.
Realizing that exile to England was forthcoming, he fled
to Rhode Island during the winter of 1636, the year that
Harvard College was founded. He started to build in
Seekonk, writing:

> I received a letter from my ancient friend, Mr.
> Winslow, then Governor of Plymouth, professing his
> own and others' love and respect to me, yet lovingly
> advising me, since I was fallen into the edge of their
> bounds and they were loath to displease the Bay, to
> remove but to the other side of the water, and then,
> he said, I had the country free before me and might
> be as free as themselves, and we should be loving
> neighbors together.

Later Williams referred to assurances from William
Bradford that "I should not be molested and tossed up
and down again while they had breath in their bodies. . . .
That great and pious soul, Mr. Winslow, melted, and
kindly visited me at Providence, and put a piece of gold
into the hands of my wife for our supply."[16]

Plymouth remained friendly with Williams, keeping up
communications and conferring with him on problems
with the Indians. He was not exiled from the colony and
was free to visit them at any time. Years after his expulsion
from the Bay, he volunteered to come to Plymouth to
debate with theologians. Thomas Prence was then governor. Williams had heard that Prence and certain zealots
were planning to suppress toleration in Rhode Island. The
conservative Prence replied that Williams' services were

not to be forgotten and that the reports that Plymouth intended to interfere with his policies of tolerance were "foul and false." Prence actually praised the Providence experiment. "If you judge it advantageous to your Colony's interest, and what you account the only way of worship among you, who can hinder you to maintain the discussion of those propositions in any of our towns, and at what times you please?"[17]

The first resident Englishman to collect furs in the Narragansett area, Williams had an eye to business as well as theology, building a trading post at Wickford Harbor on Narragansett Bay. He operated this business for fifteen years, in addition to his religious labors and political contributions as the leader of Providence Plantation. He owned a canoe, a shallop, and a pinnace, and kept contact between Providence and his post.[18]

Roger Williams had trouble with the sectarians who moved into his new colony. Samuel Gorton, a religious maverick, called himself "Professor of Mysteries and De Primo." He said that sermons were "Lies, tales and false-hoods," churches were "devised platforms," and communion was "vanity and a spell."

During the time Gorton stayed in Plymouth he boarded with Pastor Ralph Smith and his family. When he became a problem Smith tried to get rid of him. Gorton claimed in public that Mrs. Smith enjoyed his prayers more than her husband's. At length, Gorton had to be brought before the court, where he addressed the magistrate as "Satan," and cried, "Come down from Jehoshuah's right hand."[19] When Gorton was ordered to leave Plymouth, he moved to Williams' new colony. The founder of Rhode Island testified that Gorton "maddened poor Providence" and tried his patience.

Anne Hutchinson and her "antinomian controversy"

associates, who were pushed out of Boston because of their unconventional views, also settled in Rhode Island. So did William Coddington, who proved to be a traitor to the colony. Then the Quakers came. Although opposed by Williams, they were not persecuted. The extremists who moved into Rhode Island found it difficult to live together, but their conflicts eventually led to progress along the road to religious tolerance.

When the Quakers invaded the colonies in 1656, the Bay ruled "by the prudent care of that government" that doors should be closed to these iconoclasts. Rhode Island permitted them to enter as long as they would subject themselves to all the duties required of them in the colony. Roger Williams favored admitting the Friends but not abetting them. He could not accept their doctrines and staunchly defended his own against them. In 1672 he challenged George Fox to a debate. Fox had left the area, but three of his disciples took on the redoubtable Williams: John Burnyeat, William Edmondson, and John Stubbs. The founder, now almost seventy, rowed his dory from Providence to Newport, some thirty miles, and the next morning faced a crowded meetinghouse, speaking from 9:00 A.M. to 6:00 P.M. He was interrupted and heckled. Hearers shouted, "Old man, old man," but he held out against them. The interchanges were full of recrimination. He is reported to have called George Fox an old cow with a kettle on her head.[20]

Williams objected to Quakerism on much the same basis as did the Pilgrims. He disliked their scorn of church meeting places and learned ministers. Their concepts were not based on scripture. He distrusted guidance of the "inner light," the arrogant assumption that people were part of God. It was blasphemy to assert that Quakers were equal in power and glory with God and to affirm that

Jesus Christ had come again to reveal the way to them. For these reasons Williams wrote his fiery *George Fox Digg'd Out of His Burrowes*.

What Roger Williams brought with him to Plymouth and what he gleaned in the company of that congregation was carried to the Providence Colony. He learned much during his exile, just as the Pilgrims had advanced to broader views during their exile in Holland. In his days at Plymouth he felt that there was too much fraternization between the regenerates and the unregenerates and that there were few saints with whom he could share the sacrament of communion. Although he rebuked the Plymouthians for visiting the Church of England and listening to their ministers, for following John Robinson's advice and enjoying private communion with the mother church, he continued to grow in his outreach toward fellowship as expressed in the Providence covenant of 1640: "We agree, as formerly hath been the liberties of the town so still, to hold forth liberty of Conscience."[21]

He had been part of the Pilgrim company of exiles who were searching for the right to worship according to conscience. When he was sentenced by the Bay Colony, he realized what it was to be on his own, as the Pilgrims had been for ten years. He discovered what a formidable task it was to embrace the ideal of liberty as he contended with Gorton, Hutchinson, Coddington, Harris, the Bay people, the Connecticut people, the Indians, and the Quakers. His achievements along the uphill way to tolerance are expressed by the monument which marks the spring near the spot where he landed in 1636 with his handful of supporters: "Liberty is reserved for the inhabitants to fetch water at this spring forever."

On March 25, 1671 Roger Williams wrote to John Cotton, his successor in Plymouth, reflecting on his stormy career:

I have now much above fifty years humbly and earnestly begged of God to make me as vile as a dead dog in my own eyes so that I might not fear what men should falsely say or cruelly do against me; and I have had long experience of his merciful answer to me in men's false charges and cruelties against me to this hour. . . .

God knows what gains and preferments I have refused in universities, city, country, and court, in old England and something in New England, to keep my soul undefiled in this point and not to act with a doubting conscience. God was pleased to show me much of this in old England and in New, being unanimously chosen teacher at Boston (before your dear father came, divers years). I conscientiously refused and withdrew to Plymouth, because I durst not officiate to an unseparated people, as, upon examination and conference, I found them to be. At Plymouth, I spake on the Lord's days and weekdays, and wrought hard at the hoe for my bread (and so afterward at Salem) until I found them both professing to be a separated people in New England (not admitting the most godly to communion without a covenant) and yet communicating with the parishes in old England by their members repairing on frequent occasions thither.[22]

In spite of his contacts with Plymouth Separatists of the Robinsonian type, Williams clung to his rigid position, while moving on to complete religious tolerance. However, when pacifists and idealists protested against the plan to organize a militia for the protection of Providence, he wrote a letter to the town of Providence, speaking to them as their president:

There goes many a ship to sea, with many hundred souls in one ship, whose weal and woe is common, and is a true picture of a commonwealth or a human combination or society. It hath fallen out sometimes that both Papists and Protestants, Jews and Turks, may be embarked in one ship, upon which supposal I affirm that all the liberty of conscience that ever I pleaded for turns upon these two hinges: that none of the Papists, Protestants, Jews, or Turks be forced to come to the ship's prayers or worship, if they practice any. I further add that I never denied that, notwithstanding this liberty, the commander of this ship ought to command the ship's course, yea, and also command that justice, peace, and sobriety be kept and practiced, both among the seamen and all the passengers.[23]

Roger Williams' figure was chosen to represent Calvinism in America in the Reformation Monument in Geneva, along with Calvin, Farel, Beza, and Knox.

In 1936, three hundred years after Williams left the Bay in order to avoid deportation to England, the General Court of Massachusetts approved a resolution: "Resolved, that, in so far as it is constitutionally competent for the general court to revoke the sentence of expulsion passed against Roger Williams by the general court of Massachusetts Bay Colony in the year sixteen hundred and thirty-five, the same is hereby revoked."[24]

CHAPTER 13

Pastors Charles Chauncy and John Cotton, Jr.

God hath wonderfully erected schools of learning that there might be continually some comfortable supply and succession in the ministry. Is it not so, O ye people of God in New England! Let me testify against you in the Lord's name, for great unthankfulness. . . . Many make wicked returns of these blessings, and pull down schools of learning, or deny or withhold maintenance from them; as good as to say, "Raze them, raze them to the foundations!" How exceeding hateful unto the Lord is this unthankfulness!

—Charles Chauncy[1]

Writers sometimes dwell on the paucity of intellectual stimulation in Plymouth Colony. But much excitement was generated in the colony by the arrival of "the learned Mr. Chauncy," who came in 1638, having held the post of Greek lecturer at Trinity College, Cambridge. The settlement buzzed with pride to learn that Charles Chauncy was considered to be one of the greatest Hebrew scholars in the Western world. He had been condemned by the authorities of the Church of England for heresy in 1629 and thrown into prison by Archbishop Laud in 1634. Here was an intellectual like their own John Robinson, who delivered learned sermons and upheld the tradition of the quest for "more truth and light" which they had begun in Gainsborough, Babworth, and Scrooby and carried on during their years in Amsterdam and Leyden.

Born in Hertfordshire in 1589, Chauncy studied at Trinity College, Cambridge and then taught Hebrew and Greek there. He served as minister at Marston and at Ware and was soon in trouble because of his criticisms of the Established Church. Confronted by the authorities of Cambridge University and Archbishop Laud, Chauncy had three times submitted to censure, recanted, and, haunted by conscience, retracted his apology. These submissions under ecclesiastical pressure troubled him and he referred in his will to them "with mourning and abhorrence." As an innovator he was prone to pursue novel concepts. His motto, from Ecclesiastes 1:18, KJV, found in several of his books, reads: "He that increaseth knowledge increaseth sorrow."[2]

Hoping to escape fines and jail, Chauncy made his way to Plymouth a few weeks before the earthquake of 1638. He knew of John Robinson and the tradition of learning in the Leyden-Plymouth church and he may have admired the independent spirit of the Pilgrims demonstrated by their record of eighteen years in Massachusetts. At any rate, the eminent scholar chose Plymouth and came as co-minister with John Rayner. Chauncy had heard of his predecessor in Plymouth, Roger Williams, who had emerged as one of the luminaries in New England and the founder of the new colony of Providence.

Charles Chauncy lived up to the erudite preaching of John Robinson and Roger Williams, and Plymouth was proud of his knowledge. His wife, Catherine, was the daughter of Robert Eyre, a barrister of Salisbury, England. Her maternal grandfather was John Still, bishop of Bath and Wells. This gentlewoman brought a few family treasures from that beautiful section of England to her house in Plymouth, where she and her husband and children lived for three years. Grandfather Still presented Catherine with a set of directives for the holy life to follow in rearing her family. She succeeded in measuring up to his admonitions as the mother of eight children. Her epitaph, written at the close of an adventurous life, stated:

> In faith she was a Puritan.
> Active and constant she was here,
> In heaven above ye palm she weares.[3]

Increase Mather claims that Chauncy was "an exceeding plain preacher, frequently saying, 'It is the glory of art to conceal the art'; and yet a more *learned* and a more *lively* preacher has rarely been heard." In 1656 a book of twenty-six of his sermons was published. They are full of Hebrew, Greek, Latin, and biblical quotations which, when he delivered them, may have been interspersed with some of those "plain" words and timely applications. At any rate, the people of Plymouth profited by his knowledge and devotion.

The congregation soon learned that their preacher was a strong-willed man who was apt to champion novel doctrines that he believed were justified by scripture. He surprised them by coming out for immersion as the one and only form of baptism, a departure from the prevailing practice of sprinkling. He held firmly that baptism "ought only to be by dipping, and putting the whole body under water, and that sprinkling was unlawful"[4] and he clung to this conviction in spite of the opinion of his flock.

The church yielded that immersion or dipping was lawful, but in this cold country not so convenient.

But they could not, nor durst not yield to him in this, that sprinkling (which all the churches of Christ do for the most part use at this day) was unlawful and an human invention, as the same was pressed. But they were willing to yield to him as far as they could, and to the utmost, and were contented to suffer him to practice as he was persuaded.

But how was this to be done without splitting the parish into pro and con factions? It was a theological hot chestnut, one that had puzzled many Christian predecessors and could cause a furor even in the twentieth century in many a meetinghouse. The crisis was handled with tact and rare common sense that form a challenge to doctrinal wranglers. It was decided to leave it to the people, to let those who wanted immersion to use Chauncy and those who preferred christening to use Rayner, for at this point the church was blessed with a pastor and a teacher. It was a generous compromise that evidenced a tolerant outlook.

And when he came to minister that ordinance he might do it to any that did desire it in that way, provided he could peaceably suffer Mr. Rayner and such as desired to have theirs otherwise baptized by him by sprinkling or pouring on of water upon them, so as there might be no disturbance in the church hereabout. But he could not yield hereunto. Upon which the church procured some other ministers to dispute the point with him publicly, as Mr. Ralph Partridge of Duxbury, who did it sundry times, very ably and sufficiently; as also some other ministers within this government. But he was not satisfied. So the church sent to many other churches to crave their help and advice in this matter, and with his will and consent sent them his arguments written under his own hand.[5]

Churches in Boston, the Bay, Connecticut, and New Haven joined in a lively exchange. Many "able and sufficient answers" came from "learned ministers who all concluded against him. But himself was not satisfied therewith."

The master of Hebrew and Greek also insisted that communion should be celebrated only in the evening, but he was not able to convince his Pilgrim congregation, who wanted a more flexible practice.

In spite of these disagreements, the Pilgrims wished to keep Chauncy in their meetinghouse, but he was drawn to nearby Scituate. Bradford suggested that Chauncy become headmaster of an academy to be founded on Jones River in Kingston, but Edward Winslow pointed out that "they must still retain his errors, etc. with his gifts." The project failed and Plymouth did not launch a rival to Harvard College.

John Winthrop called Chauncy "a great scholar, and a godly man." Referring to the Plymouth pastor's debates with New England clergy over baptism, Governor Winthrop wrote: "Yet he would not give over his opinion; and the church at Plymouth, (though they could not agree to call him to the office, yet) being much taken with his able parts, they were very loath to part with him."[6]

Like his predecessor, the rugged individualist Roger Williams, the controversial Chauncy had his friends in Plymouth. However, in 1641, he moved to Scituate, where he persisted in promulgating his unpopular doctrines. Some of his congregation seceded. Governor Winthrop reported that while Chauncy was conducting the baptism of his twins by total immersion the excitement caused one of the children to swoon. A tense mother, who was waiting with her child to be immersed, grabbed hold of the pastor and "near pulled him into the water."

In the midst of his theological conflicts in 1654, Chauncy decided to book passage to England. He had been invited by his former parish in Ware to return. Perhaps he was hoping to get back to England and to teaching his favorite subjects, Hebrew and Greek. While in Boston, making arrangements to send his family home, he was approached by overseers of Harvard College about becoming president.

Henry Dunster, the first president, had been dismissed because of his unconventional views on baptism. He had refused to have one of his children baptized. The news that he had become an antipaedobaptist shook the college. He was tried by the court at Cambridge on July 30, 1654 for interrupting a baptismal service to expound his views. He was sentenced to public admonition by a magistrate in the meetinghouse on the next lecture date.[7] The corporation treated him considerately, but he lost his post and returned to Scituate, where Chauncy had been preaching. Here Dunster found friends like the Plymouth Colony liberals James Cudworth and William Vassall, and served as a minister without being ordained.[8]

Meanwhile, Chauncy was accepted as the second president of Harvard at a salary of £100 a year, after agreeing "that he forbear to disseminate or publish any Tenets concerning the necessity of immersion in Baptism and Celebration of the Lords Supper at Evening."[9] The new president plunged into his responsibilities with vigor, upholding the standards of Harvard. He was intent on training Christian leaders for the churches of the New World. During Dunster's fourteen years at Harvard, 45 out of 74 graduates became ministers. During Chauncy's seventeen years there were 66 out of 122 who entered the ministry. He taught that "true prophets of the Lord" must have their hearts made new by grace. Neither their own study nor the teaching of others was sufficient for their education. They must "be much in prayer unto the Lord: daily and duly to draw near unto the Lord, to beg of him the spirit of wisdom."[10]

President Chauncy admonished his students:

Let scholars mainly intend, labour and study for this; to be prophets and Nazarites: and therefore let speaking to edification, exhortation, and comfort be aimed at in all your studies; and behave your selves as being set apart in peculiar manner for the Lord. To use the "vessels of the temple" to quaff and carouse in, was a Babylonian practice. You should have less to do with the world and worldly delights, and be less cumbered than others with the affairs of this life.[11]

He advised one young cleric that "being once in office" he should "catechise every Lord's day in the afternoon, so as to go through the catechism once a year."[12]

This teacher of students for the ministry proved thorough and demanding. He maintained the Cambridge tradition of scholarship as he taught the future "faithful shepherds" who spread out into the ever-growing villages of New England to interpret the word of God to the people. The former Plymouth minister helped Harvard fulfill its original mission, which was to provide spiritual leaders for New England, creating a learned ministry who bore the "mark of holiness upon their foreheads."[13]

He stated in his inaugural address: "Although you can easily find a more learned President than myself, and better qualified in many respects for this duty and station, you could not have found one more affectionate towards you or more zealous of your good."[14]

President Chauncy was well liked in Cambridge and apparently talked on themes other than immersion and communion in the evenings when he gave his monthly lecture in the meetinghouse. When he had been there for a year or two, the church "kept a whole day of Thanksgiving to God, for the mercy which they enjoyed in *his* being there."

He was a learned lecturer like Robinson, but he was an

ascetic compared with the practical and genial Leyden leader. Cotton Mather described Chauncy's daily routine at Harvard College. He must have followed this rigid schedule to some extent in Plymouth also: "He rose very early, about *four a clock*, both Winter and Summer, and he set the Scholars an example of diligence, hardly to be followed." Following "near an hour in secret prayer," he attended morning devotions in the college hall. Here he expounded a chapter from the Old Testament, read by a student out of Hebrew into Latin. He then returned home to lead his family in prayers and catechize his children and servants. At 11:00 A.M., while the students were eating, and at 4:00 P.M., he retired for a time of personal meditation. During evening devotions in the college hall and in his home he read from the New Testament and prayed. When the 9:00 P.M. bell rang to end the day, "he retired for another hour of *secret prayer* before the Lord." The president preached a sermon every other Sunday to the students in the Cambridge meetinghouse.[15]

Cotton Mather entered Harvard soon after Chauncy's death. He wrote of the dedicated leader:

> How *learnedly* he now conveyed all the Liberal Arts
> unto those that sat at his feet; how *wittily* he mod-
> erated their Disputations, and other Exercises; how
> *Constantly* he expounded the Scriptures to them in
> the College Hall; how *fluently* he expressed himself
> unto them, with Latin of a *Terentian* phrase, in all his
> Discourses; and how *carefully* he inspected their Man-
> ners, and was above all things concerned for them . . .
> will never be forgotten by many of our most *worthy*
> *men*, and who were made *such* men, by their Educa-
> tion under him.[16]

With all this erudition he advised his students to work in country parishes and to be plain preachers. "Shoot not over the heads of your hearers like unskilled archers," he counseled. "Neither use any *dark Latin Words*, or any derived thence, which poor people can't understand, without explaining of them, so that the poorest and simplest people may understand all." He admonished: "Preach the Necessity of Union and Communion with Christ, Faith, and the Fruits thereof, Love and Good Works, and Sanctification."[17]

The president found it impossible to live on his salary. He had a wife, six sons (twin sons graduated from Harvard in 1651, one in 1657, and three in 1661), two daughters, and three servants to support. He stated that he had "no other means of farm or rents which the former President had," no ground "to keep any cattle upon, so that neither milk, butter nor cheese can be had but by the penny," and "that the greatness and multitude of College busynesses doeth require the whole man and one free from other distractions."[18]

The court had previously granted Chauncy five hundred acres of land near Marlborough, but it was distant from Cambridge and possibly too wild to be rented. He also supplemented his income with fees that he collected as a physician. It was common for the clergy in this period to study medicine and carry on some practice in the art of healing. A court order in 1647 stated that Francis Crooker may marry Mary Grant of Barnstable, if "Mr. Chauncy and some other approved physician" will certify that his is "not the famming sickness."[19]

The Plymouth Colony records of March 7, 1648 mention "a bill exhibited unto the Court by Mr. Charles Chauncy, complaining of the neglect of payment of the charges of Roger Cooke, for the diet in the time of sickness, and for his funeral expenses which is required of the town of Marshfield."[20] A court order dated March 2, 1647 refers to Mr. Chauncy as an "approved phisition."

Due to scarcity of medical people, pastors ministered to the sick as best they could, using their knowledge of medications as well as their ability as counselors and spiritual comforters. While in Plymouth, Chauncy may have discussed medicine with Dr. Samuel Fuller, with Edward Winslow, who doctored Massasoit when he was seriously ill, or with Myles Standish, who owned a collection of medical books. Increase Mather commented "that until two hundred years ago, *physick* in England was no profession distinct from *divinity*; and accordingly princes had the same persons to be their *physicians* and their *confessors.*"[21]

The bookish Chauncy, the man of prayer, rose to prophetic heights in one of his commencement addresses as he talked in plain words to the people of New England, upbraiding them for their neglect of learning and their failure to contribute to Harvard and to their educational institutions.

> God hath wonderfully erected schools of learning, and means of education for our children, that there might be continually some comfortable supply and succession in the ministry. Is it not so, O ye people of God in New England! But then let me testify against you in the Lord's name, for great unthankfulness to the Lord for so great a mercy. The great blessing of a painful ministry is not regarded by covetous earth worms; neither do the schools of learning, that afford oil to the lamps, come into their thoughts, to praise the Lord for them.
>
> Or, some little good they apprehend in it, to have a minister to spend the Sabbath, and to baptize their children, and keep them out of harm's way, or teach them to write and read, and case accounts; but they despise the *angel's bread*, and count it *light stuff* in comparison of other things, yea, there be many in

the country that account it their happiness to live in the vast howling wilderness, without any ministry or schools, or means of education for their posterity; that have much liberty, they think, by this *want*. Surely their practice about their children is little better than the merciless and unnatural profaneness of the Israelites (that sacrificed their sons and their daughters unto devils!). And many make wicked returns of these blessings, and fearfully abuse them, and seek what they can to weary our ministers, and pull down schools of learning, or, which is all one, deny or withhold maintenance from them; as good as to say, "Raze them, raze them to the foundations!" But how exceeding hateful unto the Lord is this unthankfulness! Do you thus require the Lord, ye foolish people and unwise?[22]

Chauncy died on February 19, 1671 in his eighty-second year. His six sons followed in the path of their father as ministers and physicians. Increase Mather said:

Chauncy, whom we may properly style Charles the Great, was a venerable old man, most accomplished in the fundamental principles of science and in the use of language, most expert in the art of instruction, and devoted himself with exemplary and unfailing diligence to the instruction of the prophets. The death of so great a man left the college crippled and well nigh crushed.[23]

So Plymouth Colony could boast of three eminent divines on its roster of fame: John Robinson, Roger Williams, and Charles Chauncy. They were Cambridge scholars, able preachers, and stimulating thinkers. From the records Robinson appears to have been more even-natured, normal in outlook, a leader who won and held the loyalty of his people. He was less of a Don Quixote than Roger Williams, who found very few who could share his high standards of Christian discipleship. He was not an ascetic like Chauncy in his devotional life, or as prone to defend tangential tenets of theology. Robinson was equally strong in his convictions, willing to pioneer as a reformer, yet capable of emphasizing Christian ethics in daily living and the value of fellowship. If Robinson had made it to the New World, he might have labored with Williams and Chauncy and augmented the contribution of Plymouth to New England thought.

Looking back nearly 350 years, it is obvious that Americans have much to admire in men like Robinson, Williams, and Chauncy, who had the courage to engage in independent thinking and uphold learning.

After the departure of Ralph Smith, John Rayner, a well-to-do graduate of Magdalene, Cambridge, came to the Plymouth church in 1636 and remained until 1654. He was "an able and godly man, and of meek and humble spirit, sound in the truth and every way unreproveable in his life and conversation. Whom after some time of trial they chose for their teacher, the fruits of whose labours they enjoyed many years with much comfort, in peace and good agreement."

About the same time, John Norton arrived as associate minister from Peterhouse College, Cambridge. "He stayed about a year and was well liked of them and much desired of them, but he was invited to Ipswich, where were many rich and able men and sundry of his acquaintences."[24] Plymouthians had their ups and downs with the clergy, but they were not a contentious lot. The parish was proud of its tradition of individual thinking. They held to their convictions, as they listened to their preachers, and were quite tolerant for their time.

After John Rayner left Plymouth in 1655 for Dover,

Massachusetts, there was a period of over ten years when the church had no minister. Elder Thomas Cushman, who assumed the post of the venerable Brewster, carried on with the aid of the magistrates. Nathaniel Morton wrote that not a Sunday passed without two gatherings in the meetinghouse. Services were conducted by Cushman or by visiting ministers. Once again the lay people filled the breach and kept the church alive.

During this period one member raised questions about the ordinances of the church. Some lay members tried to handle the controversy, but ran into snags. The clerk, Morton, wrote amid this entanglement with theology: "As in the proverbe it is ezier for a Child yea a foole to Cast Stones into a well then for a wise man to Gett them out; In which Respect it had ben better to haue qvelled and stiffled such qvestions Rather: then to haue disputed them."[25]

In the fall of 1666 John Cotton, Jr. was invited to leave his labors among the Indians and come to Plymouth, but it took him a year to make the transfer. A graduate of Harvard in 1654, he was short in stature, ruddy-cheeked, and an eloquent preacher. This son of the famous divine had been involved in some alleged youthful indiscretions and had been temporarily dismissed from his father's church. He had redeemed himself by entering the ministry, and had served as a missionary among the Wampanoag Indians under Thomas Mayhew on Martha's Vineyard. In later years he assisted in preparing an edition of John Eliot's Indian Bible. He continued his interest in the Indian language and in preaching to the Indians.

After checking on him, Plymouth was evidently convinced of his piety. His sister was married to Increase Mather, which must have carried some weight. Young Cotton brought with him the prestige of Harvard and Boston and two of its first families, the Cottons and the

Mathers. When he was ordained in Plymouth, Elder Thomas Cushman gave the charge and John Howland joined in the laying on of hands. Cotton's salary at the time of his settlement was set at £50, but it was soon raised to £80, to be paid one third in wheat or butter, an equal amount in rye, barley, or peas, and the remainder in Indian corn. This income was "so to continue till God in his Providence shall so impoverish the town that they should be necessitated to abridge the same."

In 1668 the church warmed up to Cotton and agreed to take care of his wife and children in case of his death. He was paid more salary than the £50 given to the governor. His gifts and valuable contacts in the Bay made him a desirable choice for Plymouth. Exchanging pulpits with Increase Mather and Cotton Mather brought his parish into contact with the foremost minds of Boston.[26]

Increase Mather served as president of Harvard from 1685 to 1701. John Cotton, Jr. had contact with his brother-in-law there. Cotton Mather, a son of Increase, born in 1663, was ordained in the North Church and preached there with his father. He upheld the witch-hunters and wrote *Memorable Providence Relating to Witchcraft* in 1689. One wonders what John Cotton, Jr. thought about the work of his nephew. He was in Plymouth until 1697 amid the furor of Salem's hysteria. One of the Cotton boys from Plymouth lived with Cotton Mather while he studied at Harvard.

With his associations at Harvard and Boston, John Cotton, Jr. should have been well informed on what the intellectuals were thinking in the metropolis to the north. As one of the new generation of Harvard-trained men, he initiated closer association between the churches of Plymouth and the Bay as together they evolved the Congregational Way on the soil of New England. He led the church for nearly thirty years, vindicating the prophecy of John Robinson made in 1620: "There will be little difference between the unconformable [the nonseparating Puritan] ministers and you when you come to the practice of the ordinances out of the Kingdom." He had urged his followers "by all means to endeavor to close with the godly part of the Kingdom of England and rather study union rather than division."[27]

Cotton guided Plymouth into the fellowship of the Bay as they were politically absorbed in 1692, thus bringing to harmonious termination the separate existence of the first colony. As "a man of strong parts and good abilities to preach the word of God," Cotton built a new meeting-house with a cupola and a bell. In an effort to launch a spiritual revival, he reintroduced the catechism that John Robinson and William Brewster had published at their Pilgrim Press in Leyden, based on the teachings of William Perkins.

His long service to Plymouth was marred by an alleged scandal that involved him with young women in the parish. Judge Samuel Sewall was brought in from Boston to try to solve the problem. It was decided that John Cotton should "make an orderly secession from the Church." The unfortunate controversy, which may have been exaggerated by critics and gossips in the town, led to his departure for a post in Charleston, South Carolina in 1698, where he died the following year.

Pilgrim ministers were held in respect like the Puritan clergy. They were part of the remarkable brain trust that engineered the Reformation in England and laid the foundations of New England, men of education, who owned libraries, could write and handle words, and possessed ability in public speaking and dealing with human nature. Although church and state were kept separate, the ministers were occasionally informal advisers on thorny issues and were "on the side" drawn into discussion of colony problems. They were looked up to as the pacesetters in intellectual and spiritual affairs. Ichabod Wiswall was sent from the Duxbury church to England to negotiate with the crown in 1690, while Increase Mather was there representing the Bay. The clergy spearheaded special days of thanksgiving and humiliation and served as "faithful shepherds" of their people. In spite of their vicissitudes, the Pilgrims did well during the brief life of their colony, where nearly twenty years were passed under their own lay leadership. They were fortunate to possess such laymen as William Brewster and Thomas Cushman, and such ministers as John Robinson, Roger Williams, Charles Chauncy, and John Cotton, Jr., who could hold their own among the most celebrated of the Bay and of England.

CHAPTER 14

The Sermon

It is the first duty of man to inform his conscience aright; and then to follow the direction that it gives.

—John Robinson[1]

The Pilgrims' reverence for the Bible led to a similar respect for the teaching of the scriptures. Therefore, the sermon evolved as the paramount aspect of worship. Teaching content was more important than ritual. The word of God was central, and listening to its exposition was the climax of the service. Worship was basically an intellectual exercise. The sermon was not to be a homily, as in the Church of England, but a well-prepared exegesis of scripture that people could understand and that was related to their daily living.

John Robinson attacked the ministers of the Established Church for superficial scholarship, slovenly preparation, and indifferent delivery. These practices implied that "the ability to preach was not necessarily required of all." It made the clergy dependent and weak. He waged a campaign against unworthy ministers, those incompetent, unscholarly, undedicated persons who had been placed by king and bishop in some living because "he can give an account of his faith in Latin, or hath been brought up in a bishop's house, though he have been his porter or horse-keeper. . . . Aptness and ability to teach is not necessarily required in the English ministry."[2]

He disagreed vigorously with the prevailing concept that "preaching is no necessary annexum or appurtenance unto orders." As a Cambridge scholar he stood with Puritan leaders in demanding a learned ministry made up of persons who took their jobs seriously, studied the Bible in its original tongues, and expounded its meaning conscientiously as teachers of their people. Pastor Robinson said, "In preaching, we must ever make the Scriptures our text and ground work, and must speak according to them."[3] To this diligent study of the Bible must be added an effort to relate to people and to expound the word in a direct and comprehensible manner without Latin and Greek phrases, without show and pretense. Too many preachers "are men pleasurers, flattering the mighty with vain and plausible words."[4] Robinson and his people were advocates of the prophetic emphasis in worship, not the priestly. Meditation was secondary to the message of the prophet. The prayer book encouraged priestly religion. Minister and people grew to depend on familiar phrases rather than the words of the prophet who summoned them to an ethical response.

Too often the formal, liturgical service was an escape from reality. The aim of the Pilgrim was to keep service and action in view and to find guidance for the duties of life. This ethical emphasis gave strength to preaching and made the Puritan sermons outstanding. Homilies could not be adequate substitutes for the scholarly sermon that possessed solid content relevant to life. The sermon had a strong ethical emphasis, stressing in prayers and preaching that the Christian Way was one of discipline. The church was a communion of people who had "separated" from the world, "gathered" around the code for Christian living. Its roots were firmly planted in the moral law of God. Moral obedience was demanded of all who came into the church. Members must prove themselves worthy to take the sacrament of communion. Periods of humiliation were set apart in time of crisis to turn the minds of the people toward repentance and obedience.[5]

Sermons were treated with respect in this era and people flocked to hear eminent Puritan divines. Vast quantities of sermons were published and read. "It is hardly possible to exaggerate the importance of the sermon in the seventeenth century world."[6]

The Pilgrims condemned the Anglican clergy for mouthing phrases, for dullness and lethargy, for lack of directness, for ignoring the needs of their people, and for insincerity. They were dubbed "dumb dogs" because they leaned on the prayer book for their prayers and on casual performances for what should have been carefully prepared sermons. Readings from the bede book were not true prayers. Borrowed talks were "shoddy substitutes" for expositions of the word. In the early church, they insisted that "ministers were preachers, not bare readers." Thomas Cartwright of Cambridge, a pioneer Puritan reformer, stated: "As the fire stirred giveth more heat, so the Word, as it were, blown by preaching, flameth more in the hearts than when it is read."[7]

John Robinson wrote his sermons carefully, judging by the excerpts that are found in his *Essays*. They are intellectual in style, practical and ethical in emphasis as some of the title indicate: Equability and Perseverance in Well Doing, Authority and Reason, Knowledge and Ignorance, Wisdom and Folly, Discretion, Thought, Speech and Silence, Books and Writing, Labour and Idleness, The Use and Abuse of Things, Riches and Poverty, Sobriety, Patience, Peace, Envy, Slander, Flattery, Conscience, Prayer, Zeal, Fear, Hypocrisy, Anger, Humility and Meekness, Modesty, and Marriage. No doubt William Brewster, William Bradford, Edward Winslow, and Samuel Fuller, who preached in the early days at Plymouth, followed Robinson's style. They all could write well. The Pilgrim preacher upheld the scholarly tradition, not extemporaneous techniques. He thought of himself as the teacher of the people.

Robinson outlined the form of worship that was employed by his friend Richard Clyfton in the church at Amsterdam, where the Pilgrims worshiped at times during their first year in Holland. It was the order they used in Leyden and, according to the visit Governor John Winthrop paid to Plymouth, it was much the same in the New World.

1. Prayer and giving of thanks by the pastor or teacher.
2. The Scriptures were read, two or three chapters, as time serves, with a brief explanation of their meaning.
3. The Pastor or teacher then takes some passage of Scripture, and expounds and enforces it.
4. The Sacraments are administered.
5. Some of the Psalms of David are sung by the whole congregation, both before and after the exercise of the Word.
6. Collection is then made as each one is able for the support of the officers and the poor.[8]

William Perkins and John Robinson agreed that sermons were different from metaphysical disputations and lectures on divinity. They should be delivered in understandable English, not in the verbiage of academia, and preachers should concentrate on the application of the scriptures to human life and need. Their authority was the

Bible, and they should turn the thoughts of their auditors to the scriptures, training them to verify everything for themselves.

One difficulty with the Church of England was the regimentation, the overemphasis upon forms, on "conformity and subscription," the controls of ecclesiastical law, while "the preaching of the Word is no such necessary or essential duty, but a work casual, accessory and supererogatory, which may be done or undone, as the minister is able, or willing, without any such absolute necessity."[9] The obligation to wear a surplice was a case in point. This outward dressing up of Christianity was wrong. Vestments were not essential to the gospel, to its ethics, or to a human being's accessibility to God. The Pilgrims considered vestments superfluous, meaningless in the quest for God, and objectionable to free minds because they were compulsory. They were symbols of allegiance. Pastor Robinson preached in a dignified costume of the period: probably wearing the ruff of the university scholar, a wool or cotton jacket with silver buttons, a leather belt, knickers of similar material, long stockings, and sturdy shoes with buckles.

Due to his background as a Cambridge don, he obviously conducted the service with order and decorum. There was freedom from set forms, but the service proceeded with propriety with the use of the psalms, well-thought-out prayers, and a learned sermon. His preaching, like that of Brewster, Williams, and Chauncy, reflected the Puritan tradition: directness bred by freedom from trammels of ritual regulation and domination, opening of the long-locked books of the Bible, and exposition of their truths in a forthright manner and in words the people could grasp.

Male church members not only had the right to vote in church meetings, to choose their own officers and ministers and operate the church, but they also had the right to join in public discussion of the Bible, religion, and church affairs. Although women did not vote, they had a voice in the life of the church, as stated in Chapter 5 on the Pilgrim family. The Pilgrims encouraged discussion of the sermon, not mere passive listening as in the Established Church. Robinson said that following the preaching of a learned minister the congregation should participate after a gifted member had opened up the subject for comment. The elders should exhort those who had the gift of public speaking and were qualified to give their ideas for the edification of the congregation.[10]

One of Robinson's important books was *The Peoples' Plea for the Exercise of Prophecy*.[11] Lay people were part of the church in fact as well as in theory. Prophecy did not mean speaking with tongues, which was "vain and ridiculous," without real content and value. True prophecy was not an exercise in emotionalism, pentecostal mumblings, and excesses. Prophecy was a sane and profitable exercise whereby lay members stood up in meetings and gave constructive ideas for the "edification, exhortation and comfort of the church."[12]

Those who had received spiritual gifts were to use them in prophesying, as Paul proposed. Those who participated were those who had proved themselves. Their "gifts and abilities should be known in some measure before they once be thought of as officers; and there is none other use, or trial of those gifts, but in prophesying." The capacity to teach should be developed. Lay leaders were discovered through "discussing and debating, carrying and contriving of church affairs."[13]

It was required in the Leyden congregation that

such as have bent their thoughts towards the ministry, should beforehand use their gifts publicly in the church. The order of prophecy should be observed according to Paul's institution; and that into this fellowship, to wit of prophets, should be admitted not only the ministers but also the teachers, and of the elders and deacons, and even of the very common people, if there were any which would confer their gifts received of the Lord to the common benefit of the church.[14]

Pastor Robinson explained that there were seven reasons he favored "the exercise of prophecy":

> That such as are to be taken into the ministry of the church, may both become and appear apt to teach;
> that the doctrine of the church may be preserved pure from the infection of error;
> that things doubtful arising in teaching may be cleared, things obscure opened, things erroneous convinced;
> for the edification of the church and conversion of them that believe not; and, finally,
> lest by the excluding the commonalty and multitude from church affairs, the people of God be divided, and charity lessened, and familiarity and good-will be extinguished between the order of ministers and people.[15]

The Sunday afternoon service was devoted to this type of dialogue. When Governor John Winthrop made his visit to Plymouth in 1632, taking the Rev. John Wilson, minister of the First Church in Boston, with him, they worshiped in the meetinghouse. Winthrop's report of what happened gives an idea of how the lay members participated with Roger Williams, the teacher, and with Ralph Smith, the minister. It sounds something like the modern dialogue-discussion technique.

> On the Lord's Day there was a sacrament, which they did partake in; and, in the afternoon, Mr. Roger Williams (according to their custom) propounded a ques-

tion, to which the pastor, Mr. Smith, spake briefly; then Mr. Williams prophesied; and after the governor of Plymouth spoke to the question; after him the elder; then some two or three more of the congregation. Then the elder spoke to it. When that was ended, the deacon, Mr. Fuller, put the congregation in mind of their duty of contribution; whereupon the governor and all the rest went down to the deacon's seat, and put into the box, and then returned.[16]

The sermon was of central importance. It was the gateway into the church. Interpreting the word, expounding the Bible, and presenting its truths were the ways to bring people into the faith. Baptism was not the main entrance, nor any other ritual process. The only method for the development of true Christians was training through the preaching of the word.

The Pilgrims saw the sermon not as preaching for conversion, that is, proselytizing to draw converts from other persuasions, but rather as the offering of spiritual nurture to their own communion. John Robinson said, "It is the pastor's work to feed them that are already begotten, converted, and prepared: and therefore the apostle Paul comprehends the whole pastor's and elder's duty under the feeding of the flock."[17]

Robinson wrote to one of his critics, Bernard, that he and his people were not intent on trying to convert others, that they could "not stand [as] ministers to an unconverted people nor dispense unto them the holy things of God."[18] They were content to defend their faith but were not driven by the usual Christian complex that impelled believers to evangelize the world. This attitude kept them from the fanatic fringes so troublesome in religion. They at least escaped the label of "Christian imperialists," who in later generations dressed the scantily clad but healthy and handsome Hawaiians in Mother Hubbards, demanded the abolition of China's ancestral scrolls, and boasted of their slogan "the evangelization of the world in one generation."

But the policy was perilous from the standpoint of self-preservation. Who was to recruit the newcomers? Perhaps they believed that living an exemplary Christian life was the best possible way to draw others to the faith, and that the rational, teaching approach was the best method for providing new members. The church did survive the passing of the Leyden Pilgrims and their children, and it did filter out into the countryside and nation. It endured in the concept of what little people can accomplish in history, in the value of the individual, in the spirit of initiative, in faith in a power greater than the human self.

Archbishop Grindal said to Queen Elizabeth in 1576 that preaching was "the only means and instrument of the salvation of mankind."[19] He was rebuked by the queen, but the decades that followed proved the wisdom of his statement. Charles I told his son, knowing full well the reform generated by the Puritan preachers, "People are governed by the pulpit more than the sword in times of peace."[20]

Vast quantities of Puritan sermons were printed between 1550 and 1660. It was estimated by Godfrey Davies that at least 340,000 sermons were preached in England and Wales from the turn of the century to the Revolution.[21]

The content of Puritan preaching was different from that of the establishment, and so was the manner of delivery. Preachers turned to the common people since the hierarchy would not listen to them. They spoke directly to their listeners, summoning them to the new life that they could discover through the Bible and a living faith built on its truths. The people called their preaching "spiritual," in contrast to the witty sermonizing of the traditional priests. Their forthrightness and sincerity, bred by their deep personal experience, impressed their listeners. Their message came from the heart, in contrast to much of the empty traditionalism of the parish priests.

The Puritans were said to preach "the Word of Wisdom," while the Anglicans spoke "the Wisdom of Words." Puritanism tended to reshape and revitalize the homiletical life of the church and to move the people. Sermons were popular and important. As they were printed, they tended to create a reading public.

The well-rooted scholarship of the Puritans gave dignity to their appeal and a challenge to incompetent royal appointees who held livings. Henry Hallam testified after Elizabeth I had silenced many reforming clergy through her restrictive orders: "The Puritans formed so much the more learned and diligent part of the clergy, that a great scarcity of preachers was experienced throughout this reign [Elizabeth's], in consequence of the silencing of so many of the former."[22]

The Pilgrims were nurtured in the high tradition of scholarly and relevant preaching represented by John Robinson. These preachers were a unique alliance, a spiritual association, emanating largely from the halls of Cambridge, including such illustrious names as Thomas Cartwright, William Perkins, Paul Baynes, Laurence Chaderton, Arthur Hildersham, John Dod, Richard Sibbes, William Gouge, John Preston, John Cotton, and John Robinson. These scholarly teachers championed more than a system of church organization, more than a theology. Puritanism "was a new way of life," wrote William Haller, a literary man who grasped the spiritual essence of the movement, "overrunning all the divisions which from time to time seamed its surface and threatening in each of its manifestations to disrupt the existing society."[23]

These physicians of the soul challenged the minds and fired the imaginations of the English people through their preaching as they summoned them to face the limitations and corruptions of their church and also to reexamine their religion in light of the Bible and early Christianity, and so restructure their thinking and living.

The influence of Puritan preaching is evidenced in the writings of Pilgrims like Robinson, Bradford, and Winslow. They reflect not only knowledge of the Bible and Christian history, but also a dignity of style comparable to that of their Geneva Bibles. Like John Milton and John Bunyan, and many of the writers of the era, they were profoundly influenced by Puritan thinking, which helped shape the literary taste and form of expression in England.

CHAPTER 15

Prayer

He always thought it were better for ministers to pray oftener and divide their prayers, than be long and tedious in the same, except upon solemn and special occasions. . . . His reason was that the heart and spirits of all, especially the weak, could hardly continue to stand bent as it were so long towards God as they ought to do in that duty, without flagging and falling off.

—William Bradford on Elder William Brewster[1]

Pilgrim decisions were made only after prayer. The Pilgrims prayed at their underground meetings in England, as they planned their escape to Holland, and as they contemplated the crossing to America. Before setting out from Leyden for the seaport of Delfshaven, some twenty-four miles distant, on their horse-drawn barges, "they had a day of solemn humiliation" spent in their meetinghouse in meditation. After their passage through the canals among quiet meadows, grazing cattle, turning windmills, and villages with their church steeples, they carried the possessions of the emigrating delegation aboard the *Speedwell*. They had purchased this small Dutch vessel, which was to sail to Southampton and accompany the waiting *Mayflower*.

The departing company, surrounded by their friends, gathered on the quay in front of the fifteenth-century "Old Church," which since that time has been known as the Pilgrim Fathers' Church. They may have gone inside for the parting message of Pastor Robinson and for his farewell prayer. They spoke for the last time to many Leyden associates who were planning to cross over on subsequent ships, after the vanguard had made it to the New World. There were words of admonition and blessing and last fond farewells. "The rest of the time was spent in pouring out prayers to the Lord with great fervency."[2]

The Mayflower Compact, drawn up and signed in the cabin of the *Mayflower* before landing in Provincetown in November 1620, begins with the phrase "In the Name of God Amen." It was framed by people of deep religious faith. The brief document was a pledge "for the Glory of God and advancement of the Christian faith."[3]

Following the sixty-six-day voyage of the *Mayflower* to "a good Harbor, and brought safe to land, they fell upon their knees and blessed the God of Heaven who had brought them over the vast and furious ocean, and delivered them from all the perils and miseries thereof, again to set their feet on the firm and stable earth, their proper element."[4] During their preliminary exploration of Cape Cod, the party of men resorted to prayer "about five o'clock in the morning" as they prepared for breakfast and their day's journey.[5] Enroute from Provincetown to Plymouth, the explorers in the shallop took refuge in a heavy storm on Clark's Island near Plymouth harbor. They were wet and freezing that Saturday night as they huddled together. Bradford wrote:

> With much ado they got fire (all things being so wet): and the rest were glad to come to them, for after midnight the wind shifted to the northwest and it froze hard.
>
> But though this had been a day and night of trouble and danger unto them, yet God gave them a morning of comfort and refreshing (as usually He doth to His children) for the next day was a fair, sunshining day, and they found themselves to be on an island secure from the Indians, where they might dry their stuff, fix their pieces and rest themselves; and gave God thanks for His mercies in their manifold deliverances. And this being the last day of the week, they prepared there to keep the Sabbath.[6]

This first worship service on the shore of New England is believed to have taken place in the shelter of the great rock that stands on the small island. Here ten passengers of the *Mayflower* and six members of its crew attended to the words of Governor John Carver, possibly assisted by the youthful William Bradford and Edward Winslow, grateful for their temporary haven in a hostile sea on the edge of an unknown new world. While exploring the Plymouth area from the *Mayflower*, there was a prayer service: "So in the morning, after we had called on God for direction, we came to this resolution: to go presently ashore again, and to take a better view of two places, which we thought most fitting for us."[7]

In the fall of 1621 the settlers gathered in their first harvest, stacking the corn after the custom of the Indians and taking stock of their winter vegetables. They had seen harvest festivals in England and Holland and decided to hold a thanksgiving celebration. It was natural for them to feel grateful for the food the good earth had provided after their anxious planting. They felt pride in the cottages that dotted the enclosure within the cedar stockade, and the stores of grain and vegetables they had gleaned from the fields, which they had laboriously planted. Although there is no record of formal religious worship during this commemoration, there were spiritual overtones in the midst of the feasting and good cheer. The Pilgrims were a praying people, who gave first credit to the Almighty for their preservation and protection.

Moreover, the state of their frail hamlet, their scanty stores, and the precarious holding in the wilderness were ever-present reminders of hardship. The first New England thanksgiving was noteworthy because it was an expression of confidence in divine guidance, determination to persevere, and an open-door hospitality that welcomed ninety Indians to share the feast of venison, turkey, lobsters, clams, fish, pumpkins, greens, nuts, dried fruits, and homemade wine. There must have been prayer in the cottages as the day dawned and heads of households offered their petitions to the Almighty, and there may have been a blessing by Elder Brewster before the festivities began.

The thanksgiving celebration in the fall of 1621 did not indicate that the Pilgrims were now on easy street. The *Anne* and the *Little James* crept into the harbor in the summer of 1623, bringing some ninety more settlers, who were shocked at the destitution of the colonists: "For they were in a very low condition; many were ragged in apparel and some little better than half naked. . . . The best dish they could present their friends with was lobster or a piece of fish without bread or anything else but a cup of fair spring water."[8]

As "starvation time" continued, a severe drought occurred during May, June, and July of 1623. For six weeks no rain fell. The corn, wheat, barley, peas, beans, pumpkins, and squash drooped, wilted, and dried up on the parched earth. The settlers hoped and prayed for even a mild shower that might salvage some of their crops, but the hot sun continued to beat down on the dusty soil. Realizing that it was too late to plant a second crop, even if seed were available, the people took stock of their desperate condition. Without a harvest, they might all perish. Edward Winslow wrote a graphic account of this crisis and of the second thanksgiving that followed:

> These, and the like considerations moved not only every good man privately to enter into examination with his own estate [condition] between God and his conscience; and so to humiliation before him: but also more solemnly to humble ourselves together before the Lord by fasting and prayer.
>
> To that end, a Day was appointed by public authority, and set apart from all other employments: hoping that the same God which had stirred us up hereunto, would be moved hereby in mercy to look down upon us, and grant the request of our dejected souls; if our continuance there, might any way stand with his glory and our good. But, O the mercy of our God! who was as ready to hear as we to ask. For though in the morning, when we assembled together, the heavens were as clear, and the drought as like[ly] to continue, as ever it was: yet our Exercise [public worship] continuing some eight or nine hours, before our departure, the weather was overcast, [and] the clouds gathered together on all sides. And, on the next morning, [they] distilled such soft, sweet, and moderate showers of rain, continuing some fourteen days, and mixed with such seasonable weather; as it was hard to say, Whether our withered corn, or [our] drooping affections, were most quickened or revived. Such was the bounty and goodness of our God.[9]

Hobomok and other Indians, who were as deeply concerned as the white people, gathered around the meetinghouse and prayed to the Great Spirit. Winslow records that they

> admired [wondered at] the goodness of our God towards us that wrought so great a change in so short a time. . . .
>
> So that, having these many signs of God's favour and acceptation, we thought it would be great ingratitude, if secretly we should smother up the same, or content ourselves with private thanksgiving for that which by private prayer could not be obtained. And therefore another Solemn Day was set apart and appointed for that end: wherein we returned glory honour and praise, with all thankfulness to our good God, which dealt so graciously with us; whose name (for these, and all other his mercies towards his Church and chosen ones), by them, be blessed and praised, now and evermore. Amen.[10]

The records of Plymouth Colony show that periodically there were times of tribulation and times of rejoicing when days of humiliation or praise were set aside. On March 8, 1651 "the Court have desired that a public day of thanksgiving throughout the colony may be observed therein to give thanks to God for the great victories granted to the army in the behalf of the Parliament and Commonwealth of England."[11] Days of self-examination, humiliation, and exultation were held in the old Fort Meeting House until the first regular church building was erected. It was a simple wooden structure built on what is now the town square at the top of Leyden Street. Like other Congregational churches, it was used for community purposes, for gatherings of the General Court, for assemblies of the freemen, and for town meetings.

Prayer was a far deeper matter than reading glibly from the prayer book. The Pilgrims agreed with Robinson:

> We cannot but mislike that custom in use by which the Pastor is wont to repeat and read out of a prayer-book certain forms, for his and the Church's prayer. . . . In prayer we do pour out matter, to wit the holy conceptions of the mind, from within to without, that is, from the heart of God; on the contrary, in reading, we do receive and admit matter from without to within; that is, from the book into the heart. Let him that prayeth do that which he doth, not another thing, not a divers thing. Let the whole man, and all that he is, both in soul and body, be bent upon God, with whom he converseth.[12]

Robinson criticized the concept of prayer as a form of magic which led to blind dependence upon the Divine: "For us to ask anything at the hands of the Lord which withal we do not offer ourselves ready instruments to effect and bring to pass, is to tempt God's power and to abuse his Goodness." He considered it unwise for people to neglect the help of physicians when they were sick and count on God only to cure their pain and carry them through.[13]

The Pilgrims believed in free prayer rather than in the "stinted forms" of the mother church. They tried to carry on the tradition of early Christian worship. They insisted that reading prayers provided for the clergy a "quenching of the spirit," for "the Spirit also helpeth our infirmities: for we know not what we should pray for as we ought [Rom. 8:26, KJV]." Commenting on this verse, Robinson wrote: "Yes, Paul, with your leave, right well; for we have in our prayer-book what we ought to pray, word for word, whether the Spirit be present or not."[14]

Robinson pointed out that there was no imposed liturgy for the first three hundred years of the church. He quoted Tertullian in support of extemporary prayer: "We pray, saith he, without any to prompt us, because we pray from the heart."[15] The Pilgrims rejected all "devised, printed and stinted prayers, read out of your human service-book"[16] because they quenched the spirit of prayer and "deprive the church and minister of that liberty of the spirit of prayer, which God would have them use."[17]

In the early meetinghouse in Plymouth the men kept their hats on but uncovered their heads during prayer. Bradford stated that the Dutch Reformed people prayed with their heads covered, but "we pray uncovered." As to the posture of prayer, the Pilgrims stood and did not kneel.

The Pilgrims insisted that God had "nowhere commanded or required in his Word, which is the only rule for worship, any human writings to be used in his church to worship him by, much less to be read by stint." As to the use of the Lord's Prayer, they denied "it to be Christ's meaning to bind them to these very words." Robinson pointed out that the two gospels that record this prayer, Matthew and Luke, did not use the same words. "The use of a certain form of words was no part of Christ's intentment."[18] "The Lord's Prayer was only a pattern to be followed. Christ did not stint his followers to this form of words."[19] The Lord's Prayer was not a justification for set forms of prayers nor was it a liturgical formula. It was not in any way a sanction for the prayer book.

Pilgrim prayers, like Puritan prayers, were long compared with contemporary custom. Elder William Brewster, who must have done a lot of praying during the first nine years at Plymouth as he conducted worship, possessed a common-sense attitude and opposed long-winded praying. He made a point that must have won him many friends when he spoke for moderation.

He always thought it were better for minsters to pray oftener and divide their prayers, than be long and tedious in the same, except upon solemn and special occasions as in days of humiliation and the like. His reason was that the heart and spirits of all, especially the weak, could hardly continue to stand bent as it were so long towards God as they ought to do in that duty, without flagging and falling off.[20]

During the first winter, services were held aboard the *Mayflower*. One of the earliest religious meetings on shore was in the Common House, after it was erected in March 1621. As soon as the Fort Meeting House was built, the people worshiped there on the first floor, with the cannon brought over on the *Mayflower* set on the deck above. It was not until 1648 that a separate meetinghouse was dedicated. It was a modest building with windows, providing more of God's sunlight than the shadowy fort. The people sat on benches facing the minister or teacher, who stood at the front. The leader announced the psalms to be sung, gave the prayers, read the scriptures, and preached a sermon. The minister prayed with head uncovered as the people stood uncovered, also with their eyes closed.[21]

It must be borne in mind that the Pilgrims were rebelling against a state church which had tight controls on every phase of worship, the slightest deviation from which was a punishable offense. To preach or pray from one's own mind and heart was a new freedom. They discarded the use of the organ, the cross, and other church symbols, because they were tokens of oppression by kings and bishops. Consequently, the Pilgrims harped on "borrowed sermons" and "stinted prayers." It did not mean they favored impromptu sermons and prayers but rather personally prepared and sincere ones.

The Congregational church has returned to more beauty and form in recent years. The chancel, altar, cross, and organ are common. However, a prayer book is not used. The preaching of the word is still central and simplicity of worship prevails.

CHAPTER 16

Music

They that stayed at Leyden feasted us that were to go [to the New World], at the pastor's house; where we refreshed ourselves, after tears, with singing of psalms, making joyful melody in our hearts, as well as with the voice, there being many of our congregation very expert in music; and indeed it was the sweetest melody that ever mine ears heard.

—Edward Winslow[1]

The Pilgrims, like the Puritans, did not use the organ in their worship services. It was not that they disliked organs or that they were against music, but because they did not consider them essential in their quest for reality in worship. It is assumed that they enjoyed listening to the pipe organ in the Pieterskerk in Leyden. Their Green Gate conclave was just across a narrow street from this great Dutch Reformed church that had formerly been a Roman Catholic edifice. The Reformed Church did not use the organ during the Sunday gatherings, but it did respect it. Its people attended concerts given by the city organ master. The Pilgrims heard the melodic sound reverberating through the huge brick sanctuary and must have often gone inside to listen.

John Calvin did not approve of instrumental music in the church, although he encouraged psalm-singing. He believed that worshipers would attend more to the externals and miss the true purpose of worship, but he did not object to the organ outside the church.[2] The Pilgrims obviously followed the same pattern in Holland when a pipe organ was available and close at hand.

They loved their congregational singing and joined lustily in the psalms. This exercise formed a wholesome emotional outlet for them as they met secretly in England and in their Dutch haven. Thus they found sanctuary from anxiety over their precarious lot, daily labor, financial burdens, and uncertain future. While the Dutch sang from their Geneva psalter in the nave of the high-vaulted St. Peter's, the Pilgrims chanted their own psalms, mingling their voices in tunes that Henry Ainsworth borrowed from the French and the Dutch.

Calvin believed that church music should be confined to the psalms. Hymns should be drawn from the Bible. This was the practice of the Pilgrims. They accepted with the English Puritans the belief of Calvin that human beings were corrupt, since they were children of original sin. This sinfulness made it difficult for them to determine how they should worship God. Fortunately God had made the way clear in the Bible, and people should turn there and learn how they could "glorify God and enjoy him forever."[3]

In barren surroundings the Pilgrims were capable of worshiping God because their minds transcended the need for altar, cross, candles, flowers, statues of the saints, and stained glass that portrayed the drama of Christianity. As Paul Baynes, Cambridge mentor of Robinson and many of the Puritan reformers, expressed it: "In the eloquent silence of God's presence, he required not the melting strains of music; in the piercing blaze of God's truth, he desired not the imagery of symbolic forms."[4]

The Pilgrims accepted the teaching of Calvin that only those forms of Christian worship justified by the Bible should be employed, rather than Luther's teaching that rites of worship not prohibited or condemned in scripture were agreeable. The liturgy of Calvin was barren compared with that of Luther, who countenanced vestments, ritual, and music that appealed to the five senses. Calvin believed that the decalogue ruling against graven images meant vestments and ceremonies too.[5]

Throughout the sixteenth and seventeenth centuries, English Protestants based their congregational singing on metrical versions of the psalms. The first complete psalter in English was that of Sternhold and Hopkins in 1562. In 1612 Henry Ainsworth, friend of the Pilgrims from Amsterdam, published *The Book of Psalmes: Englished both in Prose and Metre*, a book of 342 pages. The psalms were presented with commentary and an exposition on the principles of tune selection. Side by side with the prose translations were metrical arrangements adapting the translation in "singing notes."[6] Some forty tunes were set forth. Ainsworth selected songs that had been current in Elizabethan England and also among the French and the Dutch. He wrote of his selections:

> Tunes for the Psalms I find none set of God; so that each people is to use the most grave, decent and comfortable manner of singing that they know. . . . The singing-notes, therefore I have most taken from our former Englished Psalms, when they will fit the measure of the verse. And for the other long verses I have also taken the gravest and easiest tunes of the French and Dutch Psalms.[7]

For many years after they left Leyden, the Pilgrims clung to the psalter of Ainsworth in Plymouth, preferring it to the later *Bay Psalm Book*. A typical favorite was Psalm 23:

> Jehovah feedeth me, I shall not lack;
> In grassy folds He down doth make me lie;
> He gently leads me quiet waters by.
> He doth return my soul, for His name sake
> In paths of justice leads me quietly.[8]

Popular psalms used in Leyden and Plymouth included:

PSALM 86

Bow down Thine ear, Jehovah, answer me:

For I am poor, afflicted, and needy.
Keep thou my soul, for merciful am I;

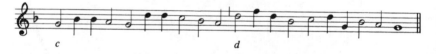

My God, Thy servant save, that trusts in Thee.

In day of my straight tribulation
I call on Thee; for Thou wilt answer me.
Among the gods, not any is like Thee
O Lord, and like unto Thy works are none.

Unto Thy servant give Thy strength, and save
Thine handmaid's son. A sign for good show me;

And let mine haters see and shamed be
That I from Thee, Lord, help and comfort have.[9]

PSALM 100

Shout to Jehovah, all the earth;

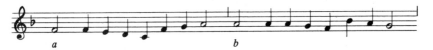

Serve ye Jehovah with gladness.

Before Him come with singing mirth,
Know that Jehovah He God is.

It's He that made us, and not we,
His folk, and sheep of His feeding.
Oh, with confession enter ye
His gates, His courtyards with praising.

Confess to Him, Bless ye His name,
Because Jehovah He good is;
His mercy ever is the same,
And His faith unto all ages.[10]

PSALM 136

Confess to Jehovah thankfully,

For He is good, for His mercy
Continueth for ever.

To God of gods confess do ye
Because His bountiful mercy

Continueth for ever.

Unto the Lord of lords confess,

Because His merciful kindness
Continueth for ever.

To Him that doth Himself only
Things wondrous great, for His mercy
Continueth for ever.[11]

Ainsworth's psalms have been considered untuneful and staid, but their theological content is superior to the gospel hymns of the nineteenth century. Since they were based on the psalms of the Bible they have a universal and timeless appeal. They have dignity and are intellectually acceptable to discriminating minds.

The *Bay Psalm Book* was published in 1640, and in 1650 *The New England Psalm-Book*, which contained a preface on the lawfulness of singing in church worship, came out. The latter offered improvements on Ainsworth, but the Plymouth people held loyally to their first love. The popular hymnbook passed through eighteen English editions and twenty-two Scottish editions.[12]

During the ministry of John Cotton, who was serving the Plymouth church in 1680, there was considerable discussion as to whether a psalm should be read before it was sung. The minister was asked to preach on the issue. He favored reading the psalms. The church members met, discussed the matter, and voted to go along with their pastor's suggestion.

Psalm-singing was popular among the masses of England. Bishop Jewell wrote to Peter Martyr about hearing six thousand people in London singing together at Paul's Cross. England was a musical country and led the world at this period of history in composition and publication in this field of art. Large quantities of songbooks came off the printing presses. One hundred twenty-five editions on what to sing and how to play instruments were published between 1560 and 1600.

The English madrigals were the delight of Europe. Much of England's poetry was written to be sung. The country abounded in musicals that were held in court, castles, palaces, manor houses, and parlors. Singing was a feature of English life.[13] In most communities town musicians were fostered by the magistrates, and they played at many public gatherings. The people enjoyed singing madrigals, catches and rounds during work and leisure, and psalms during their private and public devotions.[14]

The English Reformation stimulated the development of music. The breakup of the monastic choirs pushed musicians into new channels of expression. Composers moved away from the stylized forms of the mass. Concepts had to be presented in new rhythm and a new tongue rather than in the old Latin. The Reformation emphasized the tongue of the people along with simplicity and directness. "The result was a splendid epoch in music, such as we have never known before or since, compared only to the drama with which it was contemporary."[15]

Henry VIII composed music. Queen Mary and Queen Elizabeth I played the virginal. Charles I played the bass viol. John Milton was an accomplished musician like his father. John Bunyan made his own flute while he was in prison. Robert Browne, the avid Separatist, was a flutist and taught music to his congregation. His son, Timothy, played the viol for the singing of psalms. Music flourished under Oliver Cromwell and the Puritans.[16]

Edward Winslow wrote about the farewell gathering before the *Speedwell* set out from Holland to join the *Mayflower* in England:

> And when the ship was ready to carry us away, the brethren that stayed having again solemnly sought the Lord with us and for us, and we further engaging ourselves mutually as before, they, I say, that stayed at Leyden feasted us that were to go, at our pastor's house, being large; where we refreshed ourselves, after tears, with singing of psalms, making joyful melody in our hearts, as well as with the voice, there being many of our congregation very expert in music; and indeed it was the sweetest melody that ever mine ears heard.[17]

Undoubtedly some of the Pilgrims played instruments in England, Holland, and Plymouth. Music was an essential part of the heritage they brought with them across the ocean. They knew the madrigals and ballads that were popular in the homeland and sang them as they cooked and washed, cut timber, planted corn, and fed the cattle.

Percy Scholes researched Puritan and Pilgrim music and was convinced that the Pilgrims were not against music or art and beauty. Their inventories list a few musical instruments. There was one "treble viall" mentioned. Plymouth used drums to call people to the meetinghouse and to public assemblies. The drum was required by law in every town in the colony. It is believed that horns and trumpets may also have been in existence, and there is some indication that jew's harps were used as a means of barter with the Indians. Judge Samuel Sewall, who traveled through the Bay and also in Plymouth Colony, mentions "my wife's virginal," and refers to trumpets, dinner music, and certain musical programs that he attended.[18]

Elnathan Chauncy, one of the sons of Charles Chauncy, president of Harvard after his departure from the Plymouth church, kept a journal while he was a student at Harvard. He made frequent mention of music and dancing, which indicates that they were not frowned upon by his contemporaries. An examination of young Chauncy's copybook showed "no trace of the sullenness and severity so often alleged against our Puritan ancestors."[19]

Increase Mather commended music for its "great efficacy against melancholy." John Cotton of Boston said in 1647 that although he did not favor the use of musical instruments in the worship of the church, they could be used in the home for psalm-singing. Puritans used the parable of the prodigal son to justify music in the home.[20]

There were some in the colony who found psalm-singing in the meetinghouse a bit monotonous. One was Robert Bartlett, who came from Sussex, England. Perhaps he was seized by nostalgic memories of the choir in the eleventh-century Norman church in Stopham that he had heard as a lad. He was an outspoken chap and was finally brought before the court for his polemics. On May 1, 1660

> att this court, Robert Bartlett appeered, being summoned to answer for speakeing contemptuously of the ordinance of singing of psalms, and was convict of the fact and did in part acknowledg his euill therein, promising that hee hoped it should bee a warning to him; on which the Court sharply admonished him, and required him that unto such as hee had soe opprobriously spoken of the said ordinance he should acknowledg his falt, which hee engaged to do as hee should bee minded of them, and soe hee was discharged.[21]

When Isaac de Rasieres visited Plymouth from New Amsterdam in 1627, he described the march of the villagers on Sunday to their meetinghouse:

> They assemble by beat of drum, each with his musket or firelock, in front of the captain's door; they have their cloaks on, and place themselves in order, three abreast, and are led by a sargeant without beat of drum.[22]

The Dutch ambassador from the New York settlement was impressed with the spirit of the plantation. He painted a lively picture of the hamlet, the rat-a-tat-tat of the drummer in his formal costume, sounding his summons through the tranquil air of a summer morning, calling young and old to slip into their Sunday best, hurry out into the village street, and form a line for the march to the top of the hill. Governor, elder, and captain led the march, side by side, the chief magistrate's robe billowing in the breeze, the preacher in his cape, Bible and sermon notes in hand, and the military leader with his sword and cane. It was another bright and happy moment for those who had managed to finish their breakfast, a summons to lay aside ax and hoe, churn and washtub, to rest and to worship. Some carried muskets, others Bibles and their Ainsworth psalters, and others parcels of tidbits to serve as snacks for the children during the lengthy stay in the meetinghouse.

Psalm-singing proved a boon to the settlers, a blessed release from their doubts and sorrows. Even without the organ, which they once enjoyed in England, and although they were without a choirmaster, there was dignity and glory in their mingled voices. They flung out their praise to the oak and pine of the forest, over Town Brook and the ever-watchful ocean. The old tunes of England, Holland, and France framed in the matchless idiom of the Hebrew psalms held deep meaning for the founders of the plantation, words of comfort and assurance that played a sustaining role in the life of the Old Colony of New Plymouth.

CHAPTER 17

The Sacraments

Our [church] practice being wholly grounded on the written Word, without any addition or human invention known to us, taking our pattern from the primitive churches.

—Edward Winslow[1]

The Pilgrims accepted only two sacraments: The Lord's Supper and baptism. Their practice rested upon the apostolic example.

Communion was simple, strictly in accord with the New Testament. It was a solemn and sacred service administered in utmost seriousness. The Pilgrims did not sanction the use of responses like "the tossing to and fro of tennis balls." This repetition of liturgy had little content or value to them.

A comparison is given between the Anglican communion practices and those of the primitive church (as advocated by the Pilgrims): They (the Anglicans) use "wafer cakes," we (the Puritans and Pilgrims) use "common bread." They "borrow from the papists," while we use only "Christ's words of institution." They take communion "with custom," we "with conscience." We receive it sitting, they kneeling. They minister the sacrament "pompously, with singing, piping, surplices and cope wearing," we "minister the sacrament plainly."[2]

Communion was celebrated without kneeling, since kneeling was considered unapostolic, contrary to the precepts of the Reformation and to the custom of the primitive church. The Pilgrims agreed that the truly reformed churches ruled out kneeling: "All the churches in France, Flanders, Hungary, Poland, Berne, Zurich, Savoy and Scotland."[3] They quoted Bullinger and Beza in support of their position.

The minister served the deacons and the deacons passed the bread and the wine to the congregation. The ethical emphasis was strong in the Pilgrim communion. Only those who endeavored to follow faithfully the Christian Way were considered worthy to partake. Communion was regarded as a pledge of God's promise. Its commemoration strengthened the unity and fellowship of the church, offering spiritual nourishment to the faithful, while emphasizing their communion with Christ as members of "one mystical body."[4]

The sacrament was to be administered only by an ordained minister. During Pastor Robinson's protracted delay in making the crossing from Leyden to Plymouth, his congregation in New England sorely missed the Lord's Supper. They requested Elder Brewster to write to Leyden and ask their spiritual leader if he could commission Brewster to serve communion to them. In spite of Robinson's close ties with and high esteem for Brewster, he said no. He held to his standard that ordained persons only, who were properly trained at the university and set apart for the work of the church, should officiate.

As they sought permission for their move to America,

Robinson and Brewster wrote in 1617 to the authorities in England:

> Touching the ecclesiastical ministry, namely of pastors for teaching, elders for ruling, and deacons for distributing the church's contribution, as also for the two sacraments, baptism and the Lord's Supper, we do wholly and in all parts agree with the French Reformed Churches, according to their public confession of faith.[5]

Robinson and Brewster also wrote of some minor differences between the Pilgrim congregation in Leyden and the Reformed churches there:

1 At first, their ministers do pray with their heads covered; ours uncovered.
2 We choose none for Governing Elders but such as are able to teach; which ability they do not require.
3 Their elders and deacons are annual, or at most for two or three years; ours perpetual.
4 Our elders do administer their office in admonitions and excommunications for public scandals, publicly and before the congregation; theirs more privately and in their consistories.
5 We do administer baptism only to such infants as whereof the one parent at the least is of some church, which some of their churches do not observe; though in it our practice accords with their public confession and the judgment of the most learned amongst them.

Other differences worthy mentioning we know none in these points.[6]

Baptism, the second sacrament, was also to be administered by ordained ministers. Robinson and the Pilgrims rejected private baptism and baptism by women, such as midwives, although infant baptism was accepted as worthwhile. Godparents were not used in the sacrament because the prime responsibility for the child was on the parents, who were the sole sponsors. Interrogatives directed toward the child were considered improper.

The Pilgrims did not require people who joined their church to be rebaptized. They accepted the baptism performed by the Church of England and even the Church of Rome. Robinson said, "We retain our outward washing without repetition."[7] This was contrary to the idea of the Anabaptists in Holland who rebaptized their members. After he had lived in Holland for a time, John Smyth, formerly of Gainsborough, who had helped form the early Pilgrim meetings in England, came to the conclusion that baptism was the way to form a church.[8] He repudiated the baptism he had received in the Church of England, rebaptized himself and his associates, Thomas Helwys and John Murton, and they rebaptized their candidates for membership.[9]

Robinson said they were so much enamored of their own baptism that they despised other ministers'. They were wrong in saying that "there cannot be a church of unbaptised Christians." Even though administered by an apostate church, baptism had meaning, and when followed by baptism of the spirit it need not be repeated. The church was not gathered around baptism but around the preaching of God's word. The Pilgrims had many arguments with Smyth, Helwys, and Murton concerning baptism. Robinson wrote voluminously in defense of his views, but he warned in all of his controversial books that "disputations in religion are sometimes necessary, but always dangerous."

Baptism was practiced by sprinkling, although Plymouth also permitted immersion during the ministry of Charles

Chauncy. Usually the rite was simple, involving dipping a few drops of water from an ordinary bowl. The sign of the cross was ruled out in baptism since it had no defense in the Bible and therefore should be "thrust clean out of the church." Insistence upon crossing was considered an attempt to institute another sacrament, which was unjustifiable popish superstition.

Robinson said that one purpose of baptism was to initiate the parties into the church of Christ. Upholding his concept of the church, he said that "the covenant must be before the church, and the church before the sacrament,"[10] so that infants "might be born into the church, and men of years received into it, and both the one and the other be baptized afterwards." Baptism should "follow upon" admission into the church. The sacrament came after the church covenant.[11]

He taught that there was distinction between external and internal baptism:

> There is an outward baptism by water, and an inward baptism by the Spirit: which though they ought not to be severed, in their time, by God's appointment, yet many times are by men's default: that the outward baptism in the name of the Father, Son and Holy Ghost administered in an apostate church, is false baptism in the administration, and yet in itself, and own nature, a spiritual ordinance, though abused; and whose spiritual uses cannot be had without repentance: by which repentance, and the after baptism of the Spirit it is sanctified, and not to be repeated.[12]

Baptism was a symbol of God's gesture toward humanity, a means "by which [God] can both declare and effect his goodness toward infants."[13] It was a seal of God's promise and its benefits were limited to the faithful.

John Robinson believed that the "Lord's visible covenant," rather than the word and the sacraments, formed the "essential property of the visible church." He wrote: "And as the Word and sacraments may be sacrilegiously usurped by them which are no church of Christ, nor have any right at all unto them, so may the true church of Christ be for a time without them, though never without spiritual right to them."[14]

It was the custom of the Leyden Pilgrims to administer baptism to children, one of whose parents was a member of the congregation. This practice was continued in Plymouth. Churches in Plymouth Colony were distressed by the decline in religious interest, but they were not in favor of the Half-Way Covenant of 1662 and did not accept it for some time. This effort was considered essential by others who believed that it would help check the decline of church membership in New England.

Marriage was not considered a sacrament. It was a civil rather than a religious ceremony and was the responsibility of the state, a civil contract, not the affair of the church. Robinson wrote of marriage:

> Considering how popish superstition hath so far prevailed, that marriage in the Romish church hath got a room amongst the sacraments, truly and properly so called, and by Christ the Lord instituted; the celebration, and consecration whereof the patrons, and consorts of that superstition will have so tied to the priests' fingers, that by the decree of Evaristus the First, they account the marriage no better than incestuous, which the priest consecrates not; it the more concerns the reverend brethren, and pastors of the reformed churches to see unto it, that by their practice they neither do, nor seem to advantage this popish error. . . .[15]

We cannot assent to the received opinion and practise answerable in the reformed churches, by which the pastors thereof do celebrate marriage publicly, and by virtue of their office . . . neither ought the pastor's office to be stretched to any other acts than those of religion, and such as are peculiar to Christians: amongst which marriage, common to Gentiles as well as to them, hath no place.[16]

The Puritan reformers objected to the Church of England marriage service. They criticized the part where the bridegroom said, "With my body I thee Worship," as an overemphasis upon the physical and misuse of the term worship, which should be applied only to God. The wedding ring was considered a relic of the Roman Church, and since it had no basis in early Christianity it was not used.

The election and ordination of ministers was considered a significant ceremony. Robinson had been ordained by the Church of England when he was at Cambridge University, and he was reordained by his congregation in Holland. The first pastor to be ordained in Plymouth was Ralph Smith in 1629.

The first Puritan church created in Massachusetts was in the Salem settlement in the summer of 1629. John Endecott, the governor, made friendly overtures to Plymouth, and Bradford and a delegation were invited to come to Salem for the ordination of Samuel Skelton as pastor and Francis Higginson as teacher. The Salem governor

set apart a solemn day of humiliation for the choice of a pastor and teacher. The former part of the day being spent in prayer and teaching, the latter part about the election, which was after this manner. The persons thought on (who had been ministers in England) were demanded concerning their calling, the one an inward calling when the Lord moved the heart of a man to take that calling upon him and fitted him with gifts for the same; the second was an outward calling which was from the people, when a company of believers are joined together in covenant to walk together in all the ways of God. And every member (being men) is to have a free voice in the choice of their officers, etc. . . .

So these two servants of God, clearing all things by their answers, and being thus fitted, we saw no reason but we might freely give our voices for their election after this trial. So Mr. Skelton was chosen pastor and Mr. Higginson to be teacher. And they accepting the choice, Mr. Higginson with three or four of the gravest members of the church had their hands on Mr. Skelton, using prayer therewith. This being done, there was imposition of hands on Mr. Higginson also.[17]

It is believed that the ordination of Robinson in Holland and Smith in Plymouth was similar to the Salem procedure. Governor John Winthrop described an ordination in Boston:

Nov. 22, 1632. A fast was held by the congregation at Boston, and Mr. Wilson (formerly their teacher) was chosen pastor, and Oliver a ruling elder, and both were ordained by imposition of hands, first by the teacher and the two deacons (in the name of the congregation) upon the elder, and then by the elder and the deacons upon the pastor.[18]

Confirmation was not a sacrament. It was seen as superfluous, because baptism was the beginning of the Christian life. The Lord's Supper marked its confirmation.

While "set prayers" and "set homilies" were rejected,

the Pilgrims did make use of a formal catechism for teaching and preparing people for membership. Robinson liked the catechism that had been prepared by his professor, William Perkins at Cambridge. He and William Brewster published an edition of this work at their Pilgrim Press in Leyden, and it was used in Plymouth for many years.

The Pilgrims rejected the excesses that had accumulated around funerals and the trauma and mystery of death. They ruled out prayers for the dead along with anniversary masses and memorial services to help take the departed soul through purgatory and into the vast labyrinth of superstitious mythology.

There was no graveside service. Friends gathered about their minister and walked to the grave, where they stood in a silent committal.

> Their dead are buried with graue decensie, without either reading, praier or singing, being accompanied by their friends and the neborhoode to the graue in a comly sorte.
>
> Their ministers goe in graue and desente apparell, and so minister, without retaining any relikes of popish ornaments.[19]

John Robinson said to those who defended the traditions of funerals that although they denied belief in purgatory,

> yet how well your practice suits with it; Your absolving of men dying excommunicate, after they be dead, and before they may have Christian burial: your Christian burial in holy ground, if the party will be at the charges; your ringing of hallowed bells for the soul; your singing the corpse to the grave from the church stile; your praying over, or for the dead.[20]

In 1697 Captain Jonathan Alden, a son of Pilgrim John, was laid to rest in Duxbury with a military escort and an address by Pastor Wiswall, but no religious exercises were recorded. In 1685 Pastor Wilson of Medfield gave a prayer with an assembled group before going to the grave of Pastor Adams of Roxbury, but the practice was not widespread until the middle of the eighteenth century. As late as 1774, when Joseph Howland (the great-grandson of Pilgrim John) was buried in Newport, two ministers, Drs. Hopkins and Styles, walked in the procession, but no service was held, "it not being the practice then, as now, for a prayer or address to be offered at a funeral."[21]

Holy days were eliminated because they were entangled with non-Christian tradition. There was one holy day, the sabbath, and that was all that was needed. Many of the church days in England had been secularized so that they were barren of spiritual meaning. They had become occasions for drinking ale and wine, for revelry and dissipation. These days were a travesty on the Christian faith.

While in Holland the Pilgrims were shocked by the commercialization of the holy days, and this was mentioned as one of the reasons they felt they should depart from Holland. The Dutch did not uphold John Calvin's respect for the sabbath. They made it a day of feasting and merrymaking, especially for youth. Bradford commented on "the great licentiousness of youth in that country."[22]

The Pilgrims tried to keep Sunday as a day of religion. It was not that they were ascetics; they loved good food, beer, wine, and companionship. But it was central to their philosophy that they should spend Sunday thinking foremost of God, the Bible, and their church.

CHAPTER 18

Ties with Calvinism

We seek enlightenment from others who see further into the matter, for we are always prepared to give way modestly to those who teach better things.

—John Robinson[1]

It is a glorious character of every true disciple of Christ Jesus to be never too old to learn.

—Roger Williams[2]

The Pilgrims were Calvinists in many of their religious views, but they were followers of William Perkins and the Cambridge University reformers who sparked the Reformation in England more than Calvin, who had passed from the scene in 1564. They did not accept Calvin's rigid supervision of the morals, dress, and habits of the people, nor did they seek legalistic conformity or persecution of dissenters such as the Geneva theocrat displayed toward Servetus, who was executed for heresy, or Castellio, who was harassed for his liberal interpretation of the Song of Solomon, or Perrin, who was jailed for dancing with his wife, or Gruet, who was tortured and beheaded for criticizing Calvin's theology.

While the Pilgrims did not share Calvin's ascetic ideas, they were influenced by his emphasis upon learning and enlightenment and Bible study as the key to faith and conduct, and by his concept of the role of the individual. In spite of his constant harping on original sin, the absolute sovereignty of God, and predestination, Calvin managed to generate initiative and a creative urge in the Christian believer. People were fired with a sense of significance and the obligation to make something of their lives and to contribute to society. Twenty-seven collections of Calvin's sermons had appeared in England by 1592.

Other continental reformers seem to have influenced the Pilgrims as much as Calvin: Zwingli, Beza, Bullinger, Pareus, Zanchi, Piscator, Bucer, and the British disciples, who displayed more moderation. In spite of his capacity for intolerance, Calvin was capable of a humane spirit at times, such as when he displayed hospitality toward the English refugees. He expressed concern for the oppressed Christian leaders in England and tried to intercede for them. He welcomed the Waldensian refugees who were driven out of Italy in 1545 and raised funds to help them. Beza, Farel, and Bullinger joined in this effort.

Geneva accepted many refugees, granting them a haven and citizenship if they wished it. Calvin revealed an ecumenical outlook when he tried to make an agreement with the Lutherans and offered friendship to Archbishop Cranmer, stating that he would cross ten seas if he could be of service.

Bullinger welcomed the English refugees who fled to Europe under the tyranny of Queen Mary from 1553 to 1558. He and the people of Zurich befriended leaders like

Bishop John Jewell of Salisbury, Bishop John Parkhurst of Norwich, and Archbishop Edmund Grindal, who remembered this kindness when they returned to their homeland. Theodore Beza wrote to Grindal on June 5, 1566:

> There is a report brought unto us, and the same is confyrmed by certaine mennes letters both out of Fraunce and out of Germany, that in your countrie, many Ministers of gods words (who otherwise wer faultlesse as well in life as in doctrine) were put out of offyce by the queenes maiestie, even with the consent of you Bishops, because they refused to subscribe to some certain Ceremonies. . . . I wrote agayne to those freendes of mine, That the church of God did perswade it selfe farre other wise, bothe of the queenes maiestie, and also of so many learned and religious bishops.[3]

Bishop John Hooper lived for eight years in Zurich and was a friend and admirer of Bullinger. Bullinger corresponded with a number of English churchmen and his writings were read in England.

John Knox was a disciple of Calvin and considered during his residence in Geneva that it was "a perfect school of Christ." The Pilgrims were familiar with his role in the Geneva story and his encounters with Queen Mary of Scotland. They knew King James I feared the Scottish presbytery as a foe of monarchy. They read Knox's *Geneva Liturgy* of 1556 and the *Geneva Psalter* of 1564.

Thomas Cartwright fled from Cambridge University to live in Ireland, then in Geneva, and for several years in the Netherlands. Sixteenth- and seventeenth-century Puritans were familiar with the thinkers of the Continent. These refugee scholars helped develop the freedom-seekers, the people of the opposition, the radicals of England's Reformation. In the 1640s John Milton paid tribute to these pioneers, "the true Protestant divines of England, our fathers in the faith we hold."[4]

The persecutions under James I and Charles I impelled these people to depart from their country just as they had under "Bloody" Mary Tudor, when over eight hundred of her foremost scholars escaped to the Continent. In the 1630s, however, there were twenty thousand or more who set out for the New World. They were caught up in what Calvin called a state of "unsettledness" that motivated them to seek a better country. Thomas Shepard wrote: "I saw the Lord departed from England . . . and I saw the hearts of most of the godly set and bent that way [toward the New World], and I did think I should feel many miseries if I stayed behind."[5]

While bishop of London and archbishop of Canterbury, Laud promoted the policy of repression against the Puritans and many took ship for New England, seeking in the footsteps of the Pilgrims for freedom to worship as they saw fit. After the Long Parliament changed this policy in the 1640s, immigration fell off. This was evidence that the religious motive was important among the colonizers.

The Pilgrims owed much to Calvin, but they also studied Augustine and the church fathers, who moderated the rigid system of the Genevan.[6] Samuel Eliot Morison pointed out that the founders of New England were by no means strict Calvinists and that the first true New England Calvinist was Jonathan Edwards.[7]

As distasteful as certain traits of Calvin's character were, and as abhorrent as some of his deeds were, his pen and personality proved a major force in shaping the thought of the Western world. While today many revolt against his dogmatism, there are still those who uphold his ironclad precepts. Numerous aspects of Pilgrim religion and ethics relate to "that somewhat amorphous theological pantechnicon known as Calvinism," to use the words of B.R. White.[8] This warehouse of accumulated tradition that has gathered around the Genevan touches a number of planks in the Pilgrim platform of faith and order.

The Pilgrims shared Calvin's belief in a sovereign God, with its concomitants—original sin, predestination, and the doctrine of the elect. Calvin's theology was well structured, the product of a systematic, legal mind. His clear-cut concepts appealed to English scholars and to the laity who wanted to break away from the cumbersone restrictions of their church.

One major influence was the centrality of the Bible as the prime rule for thought and action. "He who knows how to use the Scripture properly, is in want of nothing for salvation or for a holy life." The concept of the Bible as the guidebook for living led to daily concentration on its pages and encouraged literacy and respect for learning.

Calvinism strengthened the English love of music in the church. John Calvin compiled a *Book of Music* in 1539. He advocated the use of psalms in the church. Singing was a form of prayer. He wrote, "And in truth we know by experience that singing has great force and vigor to move and inflame the hearts of men to invoke and praise God with more vehement and ardent zeal."[9]

Calvin's work ethic emphasized the dignity of labor. Each person was called to toil with the hands and make a contribution to society. This doctrine, coupled with the mission to serve God in the world, gave significance to the individual and incited everyone to think independently and to engage in the struggle for reform and progress.

Calvin helped develop an aggressive faith among the Pilgrims, the Puritans, the Covenanters of Scotland, and the Sea Beggars of Holland—an assertion of human rights and a resistance to oppression. The Calvinist faith contributed to the establishment of the Dutch Republic and to the flowering of a wealthy nation that established trade relations with the outside world. Compared with other countries, Holland was a land of relative political and religious freedom when the Pilgrims arrived there.

The Calvinistic doctrine of predestination did not lead Christians to passive dependence upon the will of the Almighty, but rather fired them with zeal to share with God in the battle against evil. Opposed by a hostile society, the believers identified with God and were inspired to contend. Such a system of determinism might breed irresponsibility, but instead it seemed to make the individual conscious of personal responsibility and led to an identification with God. "His will was God's will, his plan God's plan, his enemies God's enemies, and his eventual success was certain because his work was God's work and could not fail."[10]

The Calvinist did not withdraw to the contemplative life but believed that "it is certainly the duty of a Christian man to ascend higher than merely to seek and secure the salvation of his own soul." "Zeal to show forth the glory of God" should be the prime motive of every person's existence.[11]

The Pilgrims embraced Calvin's imagery of the perpetual combat of the saint with the forces of evil. The Genevan believed that God permitted the devil "to exercise the faithful in fighting, attack them in ambuscades, harass them with incursions, throw them into confusion, terrify them."[12] The Pilgrims considered that they were soldiers of God, whose mission was to contend against Satan. They were caught in the battle between good and evil, fighting as warriors against sin in a mighty cosmic contest. They were always in danger and must ever be on guard against the attacks of Satan.[13]

In the sermon that Deacon Robert Cushman gave in Plymouth in 1621 he charged his fellow-settlers to maintain their calling as contenders against all opposition. He spoke of some of the Virginia colonists who in England had appeared to be "religious, zealous and conscionable," but amid the tribulations of Jamestown had "lost even the sap of grace, and edge of goodness; and are become mere worldlings."[14]

Michael Walzer wrote: "The Calvinist saint seems to me the first of those self-disciplined agents of social and political reconstruction who have appeared so frequently in modern history."[15]

Calvinism developed into a powerful reform movement in Holland, and the Pilgrims were exposed to it as they lived among the Dutch. William of Orange became a Calvinist in 1573. Numerous Walloon and Huguenot refugees fled to Holland as King Philip II of Spain waged war from 1566 to 1577. The Reformed faith encouraged resistance to Philip as his ruthless representative, Alva, sought to wipe out the Protestants. Following his assassination in 1574, William was followed by his son, Maurice, who in 1609, the year after the Pilgrims arrived, concluded a twelve-year treaty of peace with Spain. This led to the final establishment of the Dutch Republic.

Professor Jacob Arminius of Leyden University died in 1609. He was the founder of Arminianism, or the Remonstrant faith, which was an effort to liberate Calvinism from its dogmatism. Arminius was succeeded by Simon Episcopius at Leyden University. He invited John Robinson to debate with him publicly since Robinson was a Cambridge disciple of William Perkins. The defenders of Calvinism at the university issued a Counter-Remonstrance. Feeling ran high in the city, which was traditionally tolerant. The learned Episcopius was chased through the streets by a blacksmith with a red-hot iron. Magistrates who opposed the Remonstrants drove ministers from their pulpits. Civil disorder was threatening.

Jan van Olden Barneveldt, the advocate of Holland, supported the Remonstrants. King Maurice developed political differences with his advocate, turned against him and the Remonstrants, and gave support to the Calvinists. Maurice called for the Synod of Dort in 1619 to try to settle the conflict. He put Olden Barneveldt in jail along with Hugo Grotius, the distinguished legal scholar.

Episcopius made an able defense of his views at Dort. One of the English delegates, John Hales, was so impressed that he said he must "bid John Calvin goodnight." The Anglicans embraced some of the ideas of Episcopius and Arminius, while the Puritans and Pilgrims clung to predestinarian Calvin.

But Episcopius and the Remonstrants had a rough time before the synod, which was attended by delegates from Holland and England, including William Ames, theologian and friend of the Pilgrims. John Robinson did not go and played no part in the intolerant proceedings. It was suggested that he write a book on the conclave and in 1624 he published *A Defense of the Doctrine Propounded by the Synod of Dort.*

The religious implications of the synod were overshadowed by political considerations. Maurice wanted a monarchy, while Olden Barneveldt advocated a republican form of government. Maurice felt it was expedient to eliminate the advocate and had him beheaded. Grotius escaped from his confinement in a trunk and fled to Paris, where he continued to write his books on international law and religion.

The synod ruled against Episcopius. His followers were exiled, but at the death of Maurice in 1625 they were permitted to return, to establish Remonstrant churches, and to worship freely. The regression from the path of tolerance was short-lived, but it formed a blemish on the record of the Netherlands.

Robinson and some of his Leyden band must have read *On Reconciling the Dissensions Among Christians*, written by Jacob Arminius in 1600, in which conferences to promote unity among the divisions of Christendom were proposed. The Pilgrims were moving in the same direction, practicing interchange with their neighbors on the Continent. They shared the outlook of the Remonstrants in their yearning for fellowship and goodwill.

The Pilgrims knew what persecution meant. They were moved by the barbaric treatment that had been meted out by their queen to Barrowe, Greenwood, and Penry, reformers whom they admired for their courage. They knew first-hand the terror of vengeance that was wreaked on people who dared question the absolutism of church and crown. They must have felt with Castellio that "to burn a heretic is not to defend a doctrine, but to kill a man."

In an age of mass burnings and butchery perpetrated in the name of the Prince of Peace, the Pilgrims displayed forbearance and moved forward toward liberality. Many contemporaries in positions of responsibility in this time of agitation and cruelty were more harsh.

Robinson was a defender of his professor, William Perkins, and was deeply influenced by his friends William Ames and Paul Baynes, eminent defenders of English Calvinism. During the period that he was writing his book on the Synod of Dort, he spoke with Ames and read the writings of Baynes. He had conferred with Baynes in Cambridge before he made his break with the Church of England. During his lectures before the Green Gate congregation, Robinson must have mentioned the dramatic struggle then in process in Holland between the Calvinists and the Remonstrants. He was deeply involved in trying to evaluate his position and that of the Cambridge men. He undoubtedly talked with Brewster, Carver, Bradford,

Winslow, Fuller, Cushman, and other lay people who were concerned about this mighty theological argument in which their own pastor had been publicly involved since his debates with Episcopius in the halls of Leyden University.

He was reenforced in his conviction as he read from Paul Baynes, who ruled out "any dispositions of reason in men" as their basis of election, as he ascribed the salvation of all people to the "mere gracious pleasure" of the Almighty. "Let us ever hold that the choice and purpose of calling to the heavenly inheritance, is merely from [God's] will, because he wills, without respect to the works or condition of his creatures: framing mankind to diverse ends, with as much freedom, as the Potter doth his clay."[16]

While he upheld the theology propounded by the Synod of Dort, Robinson stated that this parley had not spoken the last word: "As for men, how uncharitable they are. . . . How injurious in relating their own misinformed collections for their opinions! . . . As if the Word of God came out from them, or to them alone."[17]

Robinson agreed with William Ames and the Cambridge scholars on the basic principles of Calvinism and concluded his book with these words: "Glory be to God, and good men!" He recognized the good people of his era, and especially those who welcomed wider vistas. He would have included Remonstrants like Arminius, Episcopius, and Grotius.

In spite of his advocacy of association with all people of goodwill and his yearning for more truth, Robinson adhered to a limited concept of atonement. He held that the death of Jesus was sufficient for all if it had so pleased God to ordain it. However, this act was not for the whole world but rather for those whom God had chosen.[18]

Robinson believed in the sovereignty of God as opposed to complete freedom of the will: "God hath not only foreseen and determined the issues and events of His works, but hath also decreed and purposed the works themselves before the foundation of the world."[19]

Men and women, according to the Pilgrim pastor, lived in a state of sin due to the transgressions of their ancient ancestors. Adam made his mistake through free choice, God having decreed the conditions under which that choice was made. Descendants of this first sinner were born with a disposition to sin. To alter this pattern, the gift of supernatural grace was needed. Such an atonement was possible only through the grace of God in the work of Jesus. This redemption was not universal, however, but limited to the elect. Since this was the prevailing concept of the time, Robinson and the Pilgrims accepted it, although they often broke through to broader concepts.

In dealing with the Bible and theology, Robinson tried to apply reason and common sense, saying that reason lifted human beings above all earthly creatures and made them second to God.[20] Beyond reason was the ultimate mystery of an infinite being which exceeded all human bounds. Only the grace of a sovereign God was the source of salvation.

The plodding, tortuous advance through the jungles of theology toward historic accuracy and ecumenical vistas should render readers humble as they reflect on the failure to surpass Pilgrim ideology and in some cases even to equal their outreach to larger truth and wider kinship.

John Robinson was a pragmatic leader. He was wary of entanglements with those belonging to fringe sects like the Anabaptists Smyth, Helwys, and Murton, with quarrelsome Separatists like Johnson, and with the Remonstrants, who were the new lights in Holland. He no doubt sensed that a break with the English Calvinist position would entangle him and his followers in conflicts that would impede the unity of his movement and plans for their removal and settlement in some other part of the world.

The irenic views of Arminius and Episcopius, who were intent on tempering the harshness of orthodoxy, must have appealed to Robinson, Brewster, Bradford, and Pilgrims who leaned toward tolerance. But the sovereignty of God and God's plans for the elect were so dominant in their thinking that they did not wish to venture a breach with this basic thesis in their philosophy of religion.

The Independents who followed individualism too far fell into disputation and dissolution. Those who clung to the Calvinist precept that grace was limited to the elect proved more successful amid the melee of argumentation. John Robinson may have been wise in rejecting the continental liberalism of Arminius and Episcopius and holding to the tried and true principles that had brought his followers together and proved effective in building his well-unified and purposeful company.

Outside the vast city hall in Rotterdam there are two statues that the Dutch erected to two victims of the brutal treatment extended to Hugo Grotius and Jan van Olden Barneveldt during the dark period when regression from tolerance prevailed and politics and prejudice strangled truth. These two, who dared to protest the dogmatics of Calvinism, now stand beside the council chambers of Europe's greatest seaport as reminders of the folly of bigotry.

A group of Calvin's followers also felt the compunction of repentance for the failures of their leader in Geneva, and they set up in 1903 an expiatory monument near the spot where Servetus was martyred.

Visitors to the great brick church of St. Peter's in Leyden, set within fifty feet of the spot where the Green Gate Pilgrim community stood, view the final meeting place of two eminent theologians, John Robinson and Jacob Arminius, in the two aisles back of the chancel. On the sides of the opposing walls are tablets in memory of these reformers who contended in the quest for "more light and truth" over election and grace and who were united as one voice in their appeal for Christian alliance.

John Robinson's magnanimous nature brought him into conflict with Calvin's rigidities, even though Robinson did not embrace the position of the Remonstrants. He comes through as an unorthodox disciple of John Calvin. His personality appears incompatible with dogmatic assertiveness. He was no autocrat who laid down an ironclad regimen or a punctilious canon of directives to regulate behavior. He was a warm, congenial person, fond of his wife, family, and friends, and blessed with a cheerful disposition.

Robinson shunned the dictatorial role. His writings reveal the gift of common sense. Because he was humble in his search for truth, reaching out toward new revelation, he was free from arrogance and bigotry. His irenic spirit led him to emphasize fellowship and to seek harmony in place of disputation. Brewster, Bradford, Winslow, and other Pilgrims reflected these qualities. The Congregational Way they followed affirmed their belief that "God had more truth and light yet to break forth from his holy Word."

CHAPTER 19

Pilgrims and Puritans

There will be little difference between the unconformable [the nonseparating Puritan] ministers and
you when you come to the practice of the ordinances
out of the Kingdom. . . . By all means endeavor to
close with the godly part of the Kingdom of England
and rather study union rather than division.

—John Robinson[1]

The label Puritan was first used around the year 1590.
It was considered an odious name among opponents of
church reformers.[2] Although part of the Puritan movement, the Pilgrims were a special group. Their independent
origin in England was one factor that made them unique.
A spontaneous and unsponsored company that came into
being in the villages of Lincolnshire, Nottinghamshire, and
Yorkshire, they were strong characters of considerable initiative—yeomen, farmers, artisans, and merchants. Not the
typical church constituents, willing to accept the usual
formalism, the Pilgrims were instead sturdy independents
without the labels of the establishment. So they possessed a

freshness and directness that kept them from the dogmatism of the ecclesiastical world. They had not built up the usual patterns of belief or the traditional "thou shalt not" codes and were willing to experiment and try new ways.

The Pilgrims had walked lonely paths in England long before they faced disputants like Roger Williams, Puritan extremists who would accept only church members as voters, Baptists who insisted on immersion, or Quakers who defied authority. They knew what it was to have to assemble secretly. Because they dared to break with the mother church, they had endured the scrutiny of spies, the hostility of neighbors, the condemnation of church and state, fines, and imprisonment. They felt more compassion for unpopular causes than some of their Puritan neighbors.

The second factor that made the Pilgrims unique was the time spent in exile in Holland, which also encouraged their independence. There they were forced to stand on their own feet. Living on the Continent also widened their horizons, and they began to think of Christianity in terms broader than the English parish and the English nation. They were among the first English Protestants to practice intercommunion with the Christians of Europe. Liberal Leyden stretched their outlook toward tolerance.

The third factor in the Pilgrims' uniqueness was the years of testing in the New World, which bred a certain maturity that the Puritans did not possess when they came ten years later. The Pilgrims had made it all alone in New England. When a new crisis confronted them they were a little better equipped to cope with it.

The Pilgrims had passed through stormy waters of disputation. They learned something through their encounters with the dissidents in the Church of the Ancient Brethren in Amsterdam; with John Smyth, who plunged into one religious adventure after another; with Richard Clyfton, who was caught up in controversy; with Francis Johnson, a bold Separatist, always embroiled in dispute; with George Johnson, his belligerent brother and his associate, Deacon Studley; and with the experimenters in baptism, Thomas Helwys and John Murton.

The group that clung to John Robinson after departure from England and gravitated toward him and his Leyden congregation of more liberal refugees lifted their sights to a higher plane of emphasis on broader concepts. They had been jounced about by persecution and expatriation. Any acrimonious pride and other rigidities had been tempered, and they were less straitlaced than some of their contemporaries.

With the passing of James I in 1625, the Puritans were praying that their new king would be more tolerant. They were quickly disappointed in Charles I and turned their thoughts to the New World as their only hope. They had been watching the Plymouth experiment, where English settlers proved that they could survive in New England. The first expedition was led by Governor John Endecott, who sailed to Salem in 1628. He was followed in June 1630 by John Winthrop, who was to serve as governor of the Massachusetts Bay Colony. He arrived in Salem with a fleet of vessels, bearing men, women, children, cattle, goats, and ample supplies of food and drink. Some seventeen ships brought his contingency. Nearly 1,000 new settlers landed that year, spreading out to form villages in the Boston area. The Puritan influx was underway. Francis Higginson, another Cambridge man, spoke as the armada departed from England: "We do not go to New England as Separatists from the Church of England, though we cannot but separate from the corruptions in it, but we go to practice the positive part of church reformation, and propagate the gospel in America."[3]

The newcomers were welcomed by the Plymouth settlers and found that they were kindred spirits. When the

Abigail's passengers disembarked, many were suffering from scurvy and fever. Endecott appealed to Dr. Samuel Fuller, who went to doctor them. He was the center of conversation about the Plymouth church and government and the Pilgrims' experiences in England, Holland, and Massachusetts. On May 11, 1629 Endecott wrote in appreciation to Governor Bradford:

> God's People are all marked with one and the same mark and sealed with one and the same seal, and have for the main, one and the same heart guided by one and the same spirit of truth. And where this is there can be no discord, nay here must needs be sweet harmony. And the same request [with you] I make unto the Lord that we may, as Christian brethren, be united by a heavenly and unfeigned love, bending all our hearts and forces in furthering a work beyond our strength, with reverence and fear, fastening our eyes always on Him that only is able to direct and prosper our ways.
>
> I acknowledge myself much bound to you for your kind love and care in sending Mr. Fuller among us, and rejoice much that I am by him satisfied touching your judgments of the outward form of God's worship. It is, as far as I can gather, no other than is warranted by the evidence of truth. And the same which I have professed and maintained ever since the Lord in mercy revealed himself unto me. Being far from the common report that hath been spread of you touching that particular. But God's children must not look for less here below, and it is the great mercy of God that He strengthen them to go through with it.[4]

William Bradford had heard that Endecott was coming and "some others with him, to make some preparation for the rest . . . I had occasion to write him, though unknown by face, or any other way, but as I had heard of his worth."[5]

The Salem settlers learned that the Pilgrims were not a conclave of heretics to be shunned, but warmhearted neighbors in the wilderness. They did not live up to their reputation as dangerous radicals who were on the blacklist of James I and Charles I. The Puritans had heard that the Pilgrim church was rigidly Separatist and were surprised to find that the Pilgrims were followers of Robinson's moderation and that being involved with them would not hazard their standing with the king.

Representatives of the Plymouth church were invited to attend the forming of the Salem church in July 1629. Bradford, Brewster, and others set sail in their shallop, but were delayed by head winds. They did not arrive to hear the covenant repeated: "In the presence of God to walke together in all His blessed Word of truth." They did make it in time "to give them the Right Hand of Fellowship" and to congratulate the minister and teacher.[6]

On July 26, 1630 Samuel Fuller, Edward Winslow, and Isaac Allerton were visiting in Salem. They wrote to Plymouth, stating that a letter had come from Governor Winthrop of Boston to the Salem people reporting a serious epidemic in Charlestown. The Boston people sought the advice and support of Plymouth, proposing that a time of prayer be set aside in the crisis, "that they may humble themselves before God and seek him in his ordinances . . . solemnly to enter into covenant with the Lord to walk in his ways." The new Boston settlements asked Plymouth also to "set apart the same day, for the same end, beseeching God as to withdraw his hand of correction, so to establish and direct them in his ways."[7]

Samuel Fuller wrote again to Bradford, on August 2, 1630 from Charlestown, indicating that he was paying early visits to the new settlers to the north:

The sad news here is, that many are sick, and many are dead, the Lord in mercy look upon them! Some are entered into a church covenant, the first were four— the Governor, Mr. John Winthrop, Mr. Johnson, Mr. Dudley, and Mr. Wilson; since that, five more are joined unto them, and others it is like will add themselves to them daily. The Lord increase them, both in number and holiness, for his mercy's sake. I here but lose time and long to be at home, I can do them no good, for I want drugs, and things fitting to work with. I propose to be at home this week (if God permit) and Mr. Johnson, and Captain Endecott will come with me; and upon their offer, I requested the Governor to bear them company, who is desirous to come, but saith he cannot be absent two hours. . . .

Here are divers honest christians that are desirous to see us, and the good persuasion they have of us; others to see whether we be so evil, as they have heard of us. We have a name of love and holiness to God and his saints; the Lord make us answerable and that it may be more than a name, or else it will do us no good.[8]

Bradford added in his *Letter Book*: "But this worthy gentleman, Mr. Johnson, was prevented of his journey, for shortly after he fell sick and died, whose loss was great and much bewailed."[9]

Dr. Fuller's letter makes clear the precarious state of the settlers and the concern of the Pilgrims for their welfare. Dr. Fuller, the roving ambassador, also visited the Dorchester settlement, doctoring the sick and discussing religion. He met there with a reluctant Puritan who argued church polity "till I was weary." John Warham insisted that "the visible church may consist of a mixed people, godly and openly ungodly." Fuller said he hoped the "Lord would give a blessing" to their disputation.[10]

Governor John Winthrop and most of his expedition were nonseparating Puritans. Before sailing from the mother country, Winthrop, like Endecott, had spoken in conciliatory rhetoric to the establishment:

> We esteem it our honor to call the Church of England our dear mother . . . ever acknowledging that such hope and part as we have obtained in the common salvation, we have received in her bosom and sucked it from her breasts. We leave it not, therefore, as loathing that milk wherewith we were nourished there; but pleasing God for the parentage and education, as members of the same body, shall always rejoice in her good.[11]

The Pilgrims likewise cherished their English heritage, but they were more realistic. They broke with the evils that flawed their national church in order to dramatize the plight of religion and advocate positive steps to right wrongs. Many of the Puritans shifted their views when they found themselves three thousand miles away from home, as they coped with the challenges of the wilderness, nursing their loved ones when plague terrorized them, fighting hunger, cold, and loneliness. It was natural for them to turn to their only neighbors, the Pilgrims, mitigating points of divergence in theology, reaching out in response to their longing for human companionship.

The Puritans in Salem, Dorchester, Charlestown, and Boston knew something of the Pilgrim adventures in England and Holland, that they were dissenters who had been imprisoned, that they had dared to publish books critical of king and bishops, and that James I had hounded them. These Puritans were followers of nonseparating reformers like William Ames, Henry Jacob, Robert Parker, William Bradshaw, Paul Baynes, Laurence Chaderton, John Cotton, Thomas Hooker, and John Davenport. Although they avoided open cleavage with the church, they did separate themselves from its malpractices and from the corruptions of the world. They leaned toward the Congregational Way of Robinson rather than the Presbyterian Way. Due to the reputation of Robinson and the achievements of Plymouth Colony, they were curious to learn more from Plymouth.

Fuller reported that John Cotton had stated that "they [the people of Boston] should take advice from them at Plymouth, and should do nothing to offend them."[12]

On July 27, 1630, as the first church in Boston was being planned, "We, of the congregation kept a fast, and chose Mr. Wilson our teacher, and Mr. Nowell an elder, and Mr. Gager and Mr. Aspinwall, deacons," wrote Governor Winthrop. "We used imposition of hands, but with the protestation by all, that it was only as a sign of election and confirmation, not of any intent that Mr. Wilson should renounce his ministry he received in England."[13]

Bradford visited Boston in November 1631. John Winthrop and Mr. Wilson, pastor of Boston, visited Plymouth on October 25, 1632.[14]

> In 1634 Bradford and Winslow, with Mr. Smith, their pastor, came to Boston by water, to confer with some of the magistrates and ministers about the case of Kennebec. There met hereabout Mr. Winthrop, Mr. Cotton, and Mr. Wilson, and after they had sought the Lord, they fell first upon some passages which they had taken some offence at, but those were soon cleared.[15]

The congregation that was organized in Charlestown on July 30, 1630 divided into three churches: Charlestown,

Watertown, and Dorchester. The Pilgrims were invited to some of these events. They did not journey about seeking to sell their type of religion but were glad to make new friends and to share in the fellowship in the Bay Colony.

Governor Bradford spoke of Governor John Winthrop, the newcomer, as "that worthy and godly gentleman," who began "the plantations there, which have since much grown and increased under his godly, able, and prudent government, and the church of God, especially, to the rejoicing of our, and the hearts of all good men."[16]

Boston and other new congregations made use of covenants similar to the Scrooby and Leyden covenants. Winthrop's planters took this pledge: "To walk in all ways according to the Rule of the Gospel, and in all sincere conformity to his Holy Ordinances and in mutual love and respect each to other, so near as God shall give us grace."[17]

The people of the Bay shied away from Plymouth for a time because of the Pilgrims' reputation as strict Separatists. John Cotton wrote Samuel Skelton of Salem, warning him that he might be listening too much to Plymouth: "I am afraid your change hath sprung from New Plimoth men, whom though I much esteem as godly and loving Christians, yet their grounds which they have received for this tenet [regarding use of a church covenant] from Mr. Robinson, do not justify me, though the man I reverence as godly and learned."[18]

Later, in 1636, John Cotton preached in Salem and publicly admitted that he had been in error regarding a church covenant and that Samuel Skelton was right in using it.[19] When the esteemed Cotton gave his approval to the Plymouth-Salem practice, the Pilgrim Way had won a staunch ally. This did not mean that Plymouth shaped the course of Congregationalism in New England. Plymouth never made such a claim. In 1644 William Rathband advanced this concept when he wrote:

Master Robinson did derive his way to his separate congregation at Leyden; a part of them did carry it over to Plymouth in New England where Master Cotton did take it up . . . [and] the most who settled their habitations in that Land [of New England] did agree to model themselves in Churches after Robinson's pattern.[20]

Edward Winslow wrote that the Bay people learned something from the Plymouth church, but said it was not true that settlers

> took Plymouth as their precedent as fast as they came. 'Tis true I confess that some of the chiefs of them advised with us (coming over to be freed from the burthensome ceremonies they imposed in England) how they should doe to fall upon a right platforme of worship, and desired to that end since God had honored us to lay the foundation of a Commonweale, and to settle a Church in it, to shew them whereupon our practice was grounded.[21]

Winslow pointed out:

> We accordingly shewed them the primitive practice for our warrant, taken out of the Acts of the Apostles and the Epistles . . . together with the commandments of Christ, and for every particular we did from the book of God. They set not the Church at Plymouth before them for example, but the Primitive Churches were and are their and our mutual patterns and examples, which are only worthy to be followed.[22]

William Bradford was conservative in assuming credit for Plymouth in setting up a model for the churches of Massachusetts:

> And whereas Mr. Baylie affirmeth that, however it was, in a few years the most who settled in the land

[New England] did agree with reverend John Cotton, that there was no agreement by a solemn or common consultation; but that it is true they did, as if they had agreed by the same spirit of truth and unity, set up, by the help of Christ, the same model of churches, one like another, and if they of Plymouth have helped any of the first comers in their theory, by hearing and describing their practices, therein the Scripture is fulfilled that the kingdom of heaven is like unto leaven which a woman took.[23]

Certain Puritans had hoped to "transport both the English State and Church to Massachusetts and there reform them at will." Thomas Shepard wrote: "Could God have expected us to remain helpless in England, protesting futilely and only find a way to have filled the Prisons . . . when a wide doore was set open of liberty otherwise?"[24]

All the settlements had people who were willing to share. This process of interchange in New England, coupled with similar experiences in England, evolved into the Congregational Way. It was worked out in various places and under varying circumstances. The first colony learned from the newcomers. The people of the Bay found that Robinson's followers were to be cultivated not shunned. John Cotton told them that Robinson "was a man of the most learned, polished, and modest spirit of that way, and withal he might have said, so piously studious and conscientiously inquisitive after the truth, that it had been truly a marvel, if such a man as he, had gone on to the end a rigid Separatist."[25]

Cotton was somewhat like John Robinson, a man of learning, mild in temper, and successful as a reformer in England. His opinions carried weight both in England and in the Bay Colony. His regard for Robinson, whose story he had learned when he was minister of the Stump Church in Boston, Lincolnshire built a bridge of friendship between the Bay and Plymouth. He wrote:

> It is very likely (and by the fruits of some of them, it is very evident) that the church of Plymouth in New England received very much light and life, by the blessing of Christ upon Mr. Robinson his ministry, whilst he lived with them in Holland: nor need we to be ashamed, to learn any truth of God from him, or them, or from any other saints of God, of far meaner gifts, than he or they had received.[26]

Cotton denied the false report that the Pilgrims had left Leyden because of dissension:

> For the church at Leyden was in peace, and free from any division, when they took up thoughts of transporting themselves into America with common consent. Themselves do declare it, that the proposition of removal, was set on foot and prosecuted by the elders upon just and weighty grounds. For (to use their own words) though they did quietly and sweetly enjoy their Christian and church liberties under the States; yet they foresaw Holland would be no place for their church, and their posterity to continue there comfortably. . . . Their departure therefore was not in a way of division among themselves, but with mutual consent, and common intendment of peaceful cohabitation.[27]

John Cotton wrote of the interplay of Plymouth on the church life of the Bay:

> Neither did the church of Plymouth incontinently leaven all the vicinity. . . .
> I do not know, that they agreed upon it by any common consultation: but it is true, they did as if they

had agreed (by the same spirit of truth and unity) set up (by the help of Christ) the same model of churches, one like to another. But whether it was after Mr. Robinson's pattern, is spoken gratis; for I believe most of them knew not what it was, if any at all. And if any did know it, the men were such as were not wont to attend to the patterns of men in matters of religion (for against that many of them had suffered in our native country) but to the pattern of the Scriptures.[28]

Congregationalism changed in the 1630s and 1640s. William Hooke wrote in 1644: "It is a truth, we saw but little in comparison of what we now do, when we left our native homes."[29] The setting was radically altered on the frontier of a vast new continent, where there was no established church or government, where settlers were on their own. The entire framework of thought assumed new proportions amid a panorama of an unlimited horizon. Some were influenced by the Congregational principles of Ames and Robinson. Most of the immigrants shared the demand for purity in the church and a zeal toward the pattern of the gathered church. "The evidence suggests that New England Congregationalism, like its English counterpart, emerged among prophetic, zealous Puritans as a form of response to the 1630s."[30]

The Congregational Way that John Cotton advocated in Boston was close to the Plymouth Way. He paid tribute to Ames, Baynes, Parker, and the nonseparators rather than to Robinson, because in the paper war he had to be cautious. He could not afford to be called a Brownist by the crown. As Robinson worked out some of his conflicts with the Puritans during his dialogues in Leyden with Ames, Parker, and Jacob, so Plymouth and the Bay smoothed out petty differences and united on basic practices. Larzer Ziff points out: "The difference between Robinson or Ames as a parent amounted, in practice, to no larger a difference than that between a Boston man and a Plymouth man."[31]

The New England churches ultimately adopted the Congregational Way. Although most of the ministers did not join the Separatists and deny that the parish churches of England were true churches, they did practice semi-Separatism. In this they followed the Plymouth Pilgrims, acknowledging "the lawfulness of communicating with the Church of England, in the Word and Prayer but not in the Sacraments and Disciplines." John Cotton here affirmed the philosophy of John Robinson.[32]

Pressures from the Presbyterians tended to bring together the Pilgrim Separatists and the Bay Nonconformists. The Bay people found that Plymouth practiced private communion with the Church of England and did not follow the hidebound exclusivism of Roger Williams, and they could see scant difference between their meetinghouse and that of the first colony.

Richard Mather advocated a united front with Plymouth in 1643. In answer to the question "Whether all and every of your churches (including Plymouth) do precisely observe the same course both in Constitution and Government of themselves?" he wrote: "For ought we know there is no material point, either in constitution or government, wherein the Churches in New England [viz. In the Bay, in the jurisdiction of Plymouth, or Connecticut, and Quilipiake (New Haven)] do not observe the same course."[33]

As William Haller wrote of the interplay of Pilgrim and Puritan,

Robinson's congregation succeeded first and so early in flinging a small detachment across the ocean, a feat of the greatest difficulty, because of the strength of its leadership and organization. But the voyage in the *Mayflower* was inspired by the ideals common not only to Separatists but to Puritans in general. It was Puritan faith and character and the Puritan dream of a godly Utopia, transfigured by the Puritan epic, which were to bear fruit in Massachusetts.[34]

The Congregational churches were in a different position in New England. They were no longer suppressed by the state. The government was sympathetic and offered them protection. They were now the dominant religious way. It was necessary to assume a more defensive posture as conserver and protector. They were not the innovators, who now were the Presbyterians, the Baptists, the Anglicans, and the Quakers. These holders of varying faiths brought a threat to the harmony of the colony. Dissension was a peril in the new enterprise they faced, and it became necessary to set standards. The Puritans of the Bay faced the same dilemma. A conference of leaders was called and the Cambridge Platform was drawn up in 1646. This document affirmed the basic concepts of the Congregational Way: the autonomy of the local church, the dependence of the churches upon one another for counsel, and the representative character of the ministry.[35]

The Pilgrims were Congregationalists, emphasizing the autonomy of the congregation and its independence from outward controls. The Presbyterian system was considered to be, as John Milton put it, "New presbyter is but old priest writ large." Oliver Cromwell was critical of the intolerance of the Presbyterians on the charge that they sought an established church with a system of synods and a unified discipline. Cromwell upheld the Congregational principle that there should be no power superior to the local church except the government.

In 1680 the churches of Massachusetts adopted the Congregational Savoy Confession that had been drawn up in England in 1658, a revision of the Westminster Confession, still holding to Calvinistic precepts but setting up a congregational church order.

Through the years Plymouth had been gradually drawn into economic and political ties with the Massachusetts, Providence, and Connecticut colonies. In December 1686 Governor Edmond Andros was sent by James II to Boston, accompanied by royal troops, to assume the post of governor of the New Dominion that was to include Plymouth. There was widespread anxiety concerning limitation of local government, the new taxes that were to be levied, and the fate of the Congregational churches under their devout Roman Catholic king.

Plymouth's governor, Thomas Hinckley, protested to Andros and to the crown. The independent spirits of Plymouth were distressed to learn that seven Anglican bishops had been brought to trial in the summer of 1688. Resentment ran high in England, and William of Orange and his English wife, Mary, spearheaded a revolution against James II. The declaration issued by William promised a restoration of New England's former status.

Plymouth was at length annexed to Massachusetts according to the new charter of October 7, 1691. Massachusetts became a royal province and Plymouth was included. The future of the commonwealth entered a new era.[36] The third generation of citizens and ministers managed to preserve the Pilgrim concept of religion and its role in New England.

In the spring of 1693 the Plymouth church gathered for a day of thanksgiving, offering gratitude that their lot was as auspicious as it was, rendering praise to the God who had guided them through seventy-three stormy years.

In spite of changes in Plymouth's boundaries and government, the Pilgrim Story endured in the saga of the secret founding in Scrooby, the Holland exile, the *Mayflower* crossing, the first winter and the Great Sickness, the treaty with the Wampanoags, the figures of Brewster, Bradford, Massasoit, and Squanto, the thanksgiving with native neighbors, the debt and its repayment, the first enduring family settlement, the first self-sustaining white colony, the first self-government, the first free enterprise system, the first great American book, and the first independent meetinghouse in the New World.

$\mathcal{N}otes$

INTRODUCTION

1. John Robinson in Edward Winslow, *Hypocrisie Unmasked* (London, 1646).
2. Hilaire Belloc, *Elizabeth, Creature of Conscience* (New York: Harper & Bros., 1942), pp. 2-3.
3. George M. Trevelyan, *English Social History* (New York: Harper & Bros., 1942), p. 100.
4. H.M.C. Mss. of the Marquis of Bath, II, 7; see Alfred L. Rowse, *The England of Elizabeth* (New York: Macmillan, 1951), p. 397.
5. *Seconde Parte of a Register* (1586), II, 157-58.
6. Thomas W. Mason, *New Light on the Pilgrim Story* (London: Congregational Union of England and Wales, 1920), p. 7.
7. In R.W. Dale, *History of English Congregationalism* (London: Hodder & Stoughton, 1907), p. 177.
8. J. H. Shakespeare, *Baptist and Congregational Pioneers* (London: National Council of Evangelical Free Churches, 1905), p. 129.
9. William Bradford, *Of Plymouth Plantation*, ed. Samuel Eliot Morison (New York: Knopf, 1952), p. 236.
10. Robert M. Bartlett, *The Pilgrim Way* (Philadelphia: United Church Press, 1971), pp. 63-77.
11. William Bradford, *Dialogue*.
12. Bradford, *Of Plymouth Plantation*, op. cit., p. 10.
13. In Adriaan J. Barnouw, *The Dutch, A Portrait Study* (New York: Columbia University Press, 1940), p. 432.
14. Bradford, *Of Plymouth Plantation*, op. cit., chap. 6.
15. Ibid., p. 36.

16. The *Mayflower* company and the arrivals on half a dozen subsequent ships were given the name Pilgrims. This is due largely to the passage in William Bradford's journal, *Of Plymouth Plantation*, as he described the departure of the *Speedwell* from Delfshaven in July 1620: "So they left that goodly and pleasant city which had been their resting place near twelve years; but they knew they were Pilgrims, and looked not much on those things [their obstacles], but lifted up their eyes to the heavens, their dearest country, and quieted their spirits [p. 47]." Bradford was taking his word Pilgrims from the Bible (Hebrews 11:13-16).

CHAPTER 1: PEOPLE OF PROVIDENCE

1. William Bradford, *Of Plymouth Plantation*, ed. Samuel Eliot Morison (New York: Knopf, 1952), p. 27.
2. Ibid., p. 11.
3. Ibid., p. 33.
4. Ibid., p. 47.
5. Ibid., p. 27.
6. Ibid., p. 25.
7. Carl Bridenbaugh, *Vexed and Troubled Englishmen, 1590-1642* (New York: Oxford University Press, 1968), pp. 95ff., 259ff. Cf. Peter Laslett, *The World We Have Lost* (New York: Charles Scribner's Sons, 1965), pp. 2-5; Mildred Campbell, *The English Yeoman in the Tudor and Stuart Age* (New York: A. M. Kelley, 1968), pp. 300-10; Christopher Hill, *Society and Puritanism in Pre-Revolutionary England* (New York: Schocken Books, 1964), chap. 13.
8. Robert Cushman, *The Danger of Self Love* (London, 1622), quoted in Alexander Young, *Chronicles of the Pilgrim Fathers* (Boston: Little, Brown & Co., 1841), p. 261.
9. Bradford, *Of Plymouth Plantation*, op. cit., p. 82.

10. Ibid., p. 63.
11. Ibid., p. 161.
12. Edward Johnson, *Wonder Working Providence* (London, 1654; Andover, 1867), p. 26.
13. Peter N. Carroll, *Puritanism and the Wilderness: The Intellectual Significance of the New England Frontier, 1629-1700* (New York: Columbia University Press, 1969), pp. 3-80.
14. Bradford, *Of Plymouth Plantation*, op. cit., p. 46.
15. John Robinson, *Works* (London: John Snow, 1851), II, 79.
16. Bradford, *Of Plymouth Plantation*, op. cit., p. 23.
17. Ibid., p. 62.
18. Ibid., p. 178.
19. William Bradford, *Letter Book* (Massachusetts Mayflower Society, 1901), pp. 36-37.
20. Bradford, *Of Plymouth Plantation*, op. cit., pp. 279-80.
21. Ibid., pp. 302-3.
22. Ibid., pp. 253-54.
23. Ibid., p. 334.
24. Ibid., pp. 328-29.
25. Ibid., p. 11.
26. Ibid., p. 236.

CHAPTER 2: AN INTELLECTUAL FAITH

1. John Robinson, *Works* (London: John Snow, 1851).
2. William Bradford, *Of Plymouth Plantation*, ed. Samuel Eliot Morison (New York: Knopf, 1952), p. 6.
3. Robinson, *Works*, op. cit., III, 103.
4. Ibid., III, 141.
5. Ibid., III, 45.
6. Bradford, *Of Plymouth Plantation*, op. cit., p. 274.
7. Robinson, *Works*, op. cit., III, 141.

8. William Bradford, *Dialogue* in Alexander Young, *Chronicles of the Pilgrim Fathers* (Boston: Little, Brown & Co., 1841).
9. Robinson, *Works*, op. cit., I, 67.
10. In Bradford, *Of Plymouth Plantation*, op. cit., p. 113.
11. Massachusetts Historical Society, October 1889, pp. 38-81.
12. *Plymouth Colony Wills and Inventories*, II, Part I, 53-59.
13. Ibid., II, 8-9.
14. Ibid.
15. Ibid.
16. Ibid.
17. *Mayflower Descendant*, II, 16, 62.
18. Ibid.
19. Ibid.
20. Bradford, *Of Plymouth Plantation*, op. cit., p. 314.
21. Perry Miller and Thomas Johnson, *The Puritans* (New York: American Literary Service, 1938), p. 11. Cf. Thomas Goddard Wright, *Literary Culture in Early New England, 1620-1730* (New Haven, Conn.: Yale University Press, 1920); Perry Miller, *The New England Mind*, Vol. II, *From Colony to Province* (Boston: Beacon Press, 1961): Vernon L. Parrington, *Main Currents in American Thought*, Vol. I, *The Colonial Mind, 1620-1800* (New York: Harcourt, Brace, 1927); Lawrence D. Geller and Peter J. Gomes, *The Books of the Pilgrims* (New York: Garland Publishing, Inc., 1975).

The Cambridge historian James B. Mullinger called Leyden "the foremost Protestant university in the seventeenth century." In addition to this citadel of learning there was a college of theology, founded in 1592, and a college for French students, established in 1606. The streets around the Green Gate community, established by the Pilgrims, were enlivened by students from the Low Countries, France, Switzerland, Germany, Poland, Russia, and England. Bradford said that the English refugees "were willing to learn and labor to the end that they might serve God in peace." In the midst of the humble jobs they were obliged to take they were exposed to the culture of the Continent and the cosmopolitan stance of Leyden.

Pastor Robinson brought his friends from the university, like John Polyander, professor of sacred theology and "the chief preacher of the city," Regent Festus Hommius, Antonius Walaeus, the Greek scholar, John Hoornbeek, Domine Teellinck, and others as visitors and speakers at the Green Gate church. This exposure stimulated respect for learning and an intellectually respectable religion.

CHAPTER 3: PEOPLE OF THE BOOK

1. In Adriaan J. Barnouw, *The Dutch, A Portrait Study* (New York: Columbia University Press, 1940), p. 432.
2. John Robinson, *Works* (London: John Snow, 1851), I, 43.
3. In Edward Arber, *The Story of the Pilgrim Fathers, 1605-1623* (London: Ward & Downey, 1897), p. 496.
4. In Champlin Burrage, *The Early English Dissenters in the Light of Recent Research, 1550-1641* (Cambridge: The University Press, 1912; reprinted, New York: Russell & Russell, 1967), pp. 11, 162.
5. William Bradford, *Of Plymouth Plantation,* ed. Samuel Eliot Morison (New York: Knopf, 1952), p. 6.
6. Edward Winslow, *A Brief Narration* in Alexander Young, *Chronicles of the Pilgrim Fathers* (Boston: Little, Brown & Co., 1841), p. 401.
7. Geoffrey F. Nuttall, *Visible Saints: The Congrega-*

tional Way, 1640-1660 (Oxford: Basil Blackwell, 1957), p. 54.

8. Robinson, *Works*, op. cit., III, pp. 40-41.
9. Ibid., I, 49.
10. Ibid., I, 54, 67.
11. Joseph Gaer and Ben Siegel, *Puritan Heritage: America's Roots in the Bible* (New York: New American Library, 1964), p. 32.
12. *Plymouth Church Records*, 1620-29, p. 132; William Bradford, *Dialogue* in Young, op. cit., pp. 442-43.
13. B.R. White, *The English Separatist Tradition: From the Marian Martyrs to the Pilgrim Fathers* (New York: Oxford University Press, 1971), pp. 1-3.
14. Carl Bridenbaugh, *Vexed and Troubled Englishmen, 1590-1642* (New York: Oxford University Press, 1968), p. 278.
15. Thomas Hobbes, *English Works*, ed. Sir William Molesworth (New York: Adler's Foreign Books, Inc., 1966), VI, 190.
16. Bridenbaugh, *Vexed and Troubled Englishmen*, op. cit., p. 276.
17. William Ames, *The Marrow of Theology*, tr. John Eusden (Philadelphia: United Church Press, 1968), p. 169. See also White, *The English Separatist Tradition*, op. cit., and Horton M. Davies, *The Worship of the English Puritans* (Philadelphia: Westminster Press, 1948).
18. Ralph Barton Perry, *Puritanism and Democracy* (New York: Vanguard Press, 1944), p. 192.

CHAPTER 4: OUTREACH TOWARD TOLERANCE

1. *Plymouth Colony Records*, III, 204, 121-26.
2. John Robinson, *Works* (London: John Snow, 1851), I, 37-38.

3. Ibid., III, 60.
4. Ibid., I, 40.
5. Ibid., III, 105.
6. Edward Winslow, *Hypocrisie Unmasked* (Providence, R.I.: The Club for Colonial Reprints, 1916), p. 93.
7. Robinson, *Works*, op. cit., III, 11.
8. Ibid., II, 59-60.
9. Ibid., I, 32.
10. William Bradford, *Of Plymouth Plantation*, ed. Samuel Eliot Morison (New York: Knopf, 1952), pp. 17-18.
11. Ibid.
12. Thomas Prince, *A Chronological History of New England* (Boston, 1736), pp. 86-90.
13. William Bradford, *Dialogue*, p. 51.
14. Ibid.
15. Edward Winslow, *A Brief Narration* in Alexander Young, *Chronicles of the Pilgrim Fathers* (Boston: Little, Brown & Co., 1841), p. 387.
16. Bradford, *Of Plymouth Plantation*, op. cit., p. 7.
17. Robinson, *Works*, op. cit., III, 400.
18. Ibid., III, 407.
19. Winslow, *Hypocrisie Unmasked* in Young, op. cit., p. 96.
20. Robinson, *Works*, op. cit., III, 155.
21. Ibid., III, 417.
22. John Cotton, *Way of the Congregational Churches Cleared* (London, 1642), p. 14.
23. Winslow, *A Brief Narration* in Young, op. cit., pp. 388-89, 337.
24. Henry M. Dexter, *The England and Holland of the Pilgrims* (Boston: Houghton Mifflin Co., 1909), pp. 650-52.

25. Robinson, *Works*, op. cit., III, 237.
26. Ibid., I, 329.
27. Ibid., III, 77-78, 97.
28. Ibid., I, 36.
29. Ibid., I, 270.
30. Winslow, *Hypocrisie Unmasked* in Young, op. cit., pp. 394-95.
31. Robinson, *Works*, op. cit., III, 63-64.
32. Ibid., III, 63.
33. Bradford, *Of Plymouth Plantation*, op. cit., pp. 171-72.
34. Winslow, *A Brief Narration* in Young, op. cit., p. 402.
35. Ibid., p. 404.
36. Ibid., pp. 404-5.
37. Ibid., p. 405.
38. *Plymouth Colony Records*, pp. 2, 147, 156.
39. *Massachusetts Historical Society Collection* (Boston, 1854), IV, 53-55.
40. Samuel Willard, *Ne Sutor ultra Crepidam, a brief Ammad version upon the New England Anabaptists* (London, 1681).
41. *Plymouth Colony Records*, II, 528.
42. Ibid., II, 64.
43. Winthrop Papers, pp. 5, 55-56.
44. Hutchinson Papers, V, 1, 173-74.
45. Samuel Groom, *A Glass for the People of New England* (London, 1676), p. 31.
46. Wales, Sig C 2, p. 157.
47. *Plymouth Colony Records*, 3, 111.
48. Ibid.
49. George Bishop, *New England Judged by the Spirit of the Lord* (London, 1667), p. 118.
50. *Plymouth Colony Records*, II, 67-68, 100.
51. Ibid., III, 124-30.

52. Ibid., III, 139.
53. William Penn, preface to George Fox, *Journal*, I, xxxiv.
54. *Plymouth Colony Records* in Roland G. Usher, *The Pilgrims and Their History* (New York: Macmillan, 1918), pp. 482-83.
55. Samuel Eliot Morison, *The Old Colony of New Plymouth* (New York: Knopf, 1956), p. 165.
56. *Plymouth Colony Records*, III, 169.
57. Ibid., III, 204, 121-26.
58. William Brigham, *The Compact with the Charter and Laws of the Colony of New Plymouth* (Boston: Dutton & Wentworth, 1836), p. 125.
59. Ibid.
60. George D. Langdon, Jr., *Pilgrim Colony: A History of New Plymouth, 1620-1691* (New Haven, Conn.: Yale University Press, 1966), p. 76.
61. *Plymouth Colony Records*, III, 8, 105. For the story of the later Quakers, see Rufus M. Jones, *The Quakers in the American Colonies* (New York: Russell & Russell, 1962), and Sidney V. James, *A People Among Peoples* (Cambridge, Mass.: Harvard University Press, 1963).
62. Bradford, *Of Plymouth Plantation*, op. cit., p. 33.
63. John Robinson, preface to *The Lawfulness of Hearing the Ministers of the Church of England* (1624) in *Works*, op. cit., III, 393.
64. Ibid.
65. Ibid.
66. Harry M. Ward, *Statism in Plymouth Colony* (Port Washington, N.Y.: Kennikat Press, 1973), p. 166.
67. Samuel H. Emery, *The Ministry of Taunton* (Boston: Jewett, 1853), p. 123. For the Quaker account of their persecutions, see George Bishop, *New England Judged by the Spirit of the Lord* (London, 1667). For Thomas

Murton's defense of what he considered unjust treatment by Plymouth Colony, see his work *New England Canaan* (Amsterdam, 1637; reprinted Boston: Prince Society, 1883). For the disputes within the Ancient Brethren Church of Amsterdam, see B. R. White. "The Story of Francis Johnson," *The English Separatist Tradition: From the Marian Martyrs to the Pilgrim Fathers* (New York: Oxford University Press, 1971), pp. 91ff.

John Robinson grew more ecumenical the longer he lived. During his last five years, while he was waiting to secure passage to Plymouth, he laid plans for the education of his son in the ministry, stating to Dutch friends that he hoped the boy would serve the Dutch churches. His wife, Bridget, survived him until 1642. After his passing she and the children, living in Leyden, joined the local Reformed church—so their friend Prof. John Hoornbeek indicated. See Albert Eckhof, *Three Unknown Documents Concerning the Pilgrim Fathers in Holland* (The Hague: Nijoff, 1920).

There is a document in the English Reformed Church of Amsterdam, written in 1628 and signed by Robinson's friends, Professors Antonius Walaeus and Festus Hommius. It mentions conversations that Robinson held with them and Domine Teellinck about the divisions that existed between the Separatist congregations in Holland and the other English communions there, "and that he had at divers times testified that he was disposed to do his utmost to remove the schism." See Henry M. Dexter, *The England and Holland of the Pilgrims* (Boston: Houghton Mifflin Co., 1909).

In 1655 the remnant of the Green Gate congregation was absorbed into the English-Scot Reformed

Church of Leyden, with which Robinson had been seeking to arrange a merger during the month preceding his death.

CHAPTER 5: THE PILGRIM FAMILY

1. John Robinson, *Works* (London: John Snow, 1851).
2. William Bradford, *Letter Book* (Massachusetts Mayflower Society, 1901).
3. *Plymouth Colony Records*, XL, 18.
4. Darrett B. Rutman, *Husbandmen of Plymouth* (Boston: Beacon Press, 1967).
5. Robinson, *Works*, op. cit., I, 240.
6. Ibid., I, 240, 239.
7. Ibid., I, 242.
8. Ibid., I, 239-40.
9. Ibid., I, 240.
10. Ibid., I, 20.
11. William Bradford, *Of Plymouth Plantation*, ed. Samuel Eliot Morison (New York: Knopf, 1952), p. 236.
12. John A. Goodwin, *The Pilgrim Republic* (Boston: Houghton Mifflin, 1888), p. 396.
13. John Demos in *William & Mary Quarterly*, 3d Ser., XXII, 202.
14. Mildred Campbell, *The English Yeoman in the Tudor and Stuart Age* (New York: A. M. Kelley, 1968), pp. 300ff.
15. *Plymouth Colony Records*, IV, 140.
16. John Demos, *The Little Commonwealth: Family Life in Plymouth Colony* (New York: Oxford University Press, 1970), pp. 85ff.
17. *Plymouth Colony Records*, IV, 40.
18. Ibid., II, 28.
19. Demos, *The Little Commonwealth*, op. cit., p. 90.
20. Roland G. Usher, *The Pilgrims and Their History* (New York: Macmillan, 1918), p. 248.

21. *Plymouth Colony Records*, II, 13.
22. *Plymouth Court Order*, I, 107.
23. *Plymouth Court Records*, July 5, 1635.
24. *Plymouth Colony Records*, Misc., 39.
25. Robinson, *Works*, op. cit., I, 236.
26. Ibid., III, 57.
27. Ibid., III, 317; cf. II, 216.
28. Bradford, *Of Plymouth Plantation*, op. cit., p. 65.
29. Ibid., p. 205.
30. Ibid., p. 373.
31. Sidney V. James, ed., *Three Visitors to Early Plymouth* (Plymouth: Plimoth Plantation, 1963), pp. 75-77, 3-18.
32. For further references on the Pilgrim family, see Bernard Bailyn, *Education in the Forming of American Society* (Chapel Hill, N.C.: University of North Carolina Press, 1960); Peter Laslett, *The World We Have Lost* (New York: Charles Scribner's Sons, 1965), pp. 89ff.; Richard Morris, *Studies in the History of American Law* (New York: Harper & Bros., 1930), chap. 3 on the "Lot of Women in Early America"; Christopher Hill, *Society and Puritanism in Pre-Revolutionary England* (New York: Schocken Books, 1964), chap. 13; Elizabeth A. Dexter, *Colonial Women of Affairs* (Boston: Houghton Mifflin, 1924); Alice M. Earle, *Child Life in Colonial Days* (New York: Macmillan, 1946).

CHAPTER 6: BEGINNINGS OF DEMOCRACY

1. John Robinson, *Works* (London: John Snow, 1851).
2. William Bradford, *Letter Book* (Massachusetts Mayflower Society, 1901).
3. Robinson, *Works*, op. cit., II, 222.
4. Ibid., II, 141.

5. John Robinson in Alexander Young, *Chronicles of the Pilgrim Fathers* (Boston: Little, Brown & Co., 1841), p. 60.
6. William Bradford, *Of Plymouth Plantation*, ed. Samuel Eliot Morison (New York: Knopf, 1952), p. 32.
7. Bradford, *Letter Book*, op. cit., p. 46.
8. Bradford, *Of Plymouth Plantation*, op. cit., p. 76.
9. Samuel Eliot Morison, *Freedom in Contemporary Society* (Boston: Little, Brown & Co., 1956), pp. 8-9.
10. Bradford, *Of Plymouth Plantation*, op. cit., p. 76.
11. John A. Goodwin, *The Pilgrim Republic* (Boston: Houghton Mifflin, 1888), p. 389.
12. Samuel Eliot Morison, *The Old Colony of New Plymouth* (New York: Knopf, 1956), pp. 152-53.
13. Edwin Powers, *Crime and Punishment in Early Massachusetts, 1620-92* (Boston: Beacon Press, 1966), p. 28.
14. In ibid., p. 16.
15. General Court, *Plymouth Colony Records*, II, 148-49.
16. *Plymouth Court Records* (1623), p. 12.
17. Roland G. Usher, *The Pilgrims and Their History* (New York: Macmillan, 1918), pp. 222ff; *Plymouth Colony Records*, I, 13, 36.
18. Robinson, *Works*, op. cit., I, 42.
19. William Bradford's copy of John Robinson's "A Justification for Separation from the Church of England."
20. Robinson, *Works*, op. cit., III, 277.
21. Usher, *The Pilgrims and Their History*, op. cit., pp. 262-63.
22. George D. Langdon in *William & Mary Quarterly*, 3d Ser., II, No. 4 (October 1963), 521.
23. Usher, *The Pilgrims and Their History*, op. cit., pp. 216-19.
24. Vernon L. Parrington, *Main Currents in American*

Thought, Vol. I, *The Colonial Mind, 1620-1800* (New York: Harcourt, Brace, 1927), pp. 22ff.

25. George Lee Haskins, *The Government of the Massachusetts Bay Colony* (New York: Macmillan, 1960).
26. Bradford, *Of Plymouth Plantation,* op. cit., pp. 316-17.
27. Goodwin, *The Pilgrim Republic,* op. cit., p. 378.
28. *Massachusetts Historical Society Collection,* 1st Ser., III (1810), 79-80.
29. George P. Gooch, *Political Thought in England from Bacon to Halifax* (1937; reprinted New York: AMS Press, 1976), p. 143.
30. John Wise, *A Vindication of the Government of New England Churches* (Boston, 1772), pp. 39-40.
31. *Plymouth Colony Records,* I, 166.
32. Ibid., IV, 47.
33. A. D. Thrall and J. S. Mann, *Social England* (London, 1904), IV, 299.
34. Bradford, *Of Plymouth Plantation,* op. cit., p. 317.
35. *Judicial Acts,* p. 136.
36. *Plymouth Colony Records,* I, 111, 113.
37. *The Book of the General Laws and Liberty as Concerning the Inhabitants of Massachusetts* (Cambridge, 1649), preface 1939 edition.
38. *Marshfield Church Records, The Mayflower Descendants,* 1907, II, 38.
39. George D. Langdon, Jr., *Plymouth Colony: A History of New Plymouth, 1620-1691* (New Haven, Conn.: Yale University Press, 1966), pp. 81-82.
40. Robinson, "A Justification for Separation from the Church of England" (1610), p. 433.
41. Edmund S. Morgan, *Visible Saints: The History of a Puritan Idea* (New York: New York University Press, 1963), pp. 43-47.
42. *Plymouth Church Records,* pp. 181-82.
43. Bradford, *Of Plymouth Plantation,* op. cit., p. 370.

44. Darrett B. Rutman, *Husbandmen of Plymouth* (Boston: Beacon Press, 1967), p. 13.

45. Bradford, *Of Plymouth Plantation*, op. cit., p. 352.

For further reference on democratic trends in Plymouth, see Edmund S. Morgan, *Puritan Political Ideas* (Indianapolis: Bobbs-Merrill, 1966); Christopher Hill, *Society and Puritanism in Pre-Revolutionary England* (New York: Shocken Books, 1964), pp. 219ff.

George D. Langdon, Jr. in the *William & Mary Quarterly* (3d Ser., XX, No. 4 [October 1963], 513-26) states: "The Pilgrims did in fact establish a democratic form of government in 1620. By 1623 reports of democracy at Plymouth were drifting across the Atlantic and causing them some concern: so much that in September Bradford thought it politic to write a reassuring letter, stating that it really was not true that women and children could vote in Plymouth." See *American Historical Review*, VIII, 1902-3, 299.

Roland G. Usher in *The Pilgrims and Their History* (New York: Macmillan, 1918) wrote: "There was perhaps only one William Bradford, but quite certainly there was probably never gathered together in one community, before or since, a body of men and women who averaged higher in diligence, in spirituality, and in law-abiding qualities than the Pilgrim fathers and mothers [page 206]."

The Pilgrim Society of Plymouth is sponsoring the publication, under a grant from the National Historical Publication Commission, of the *Plymouth County Common Pleas Records*. Four courts were held each year. The cases reveal much about the economy, the social life, and the morality of the colony.

Two Pilgrim descendants, James Warren and his wife, Mercy Otis Warren, championed the cause of the American Revolution in the Plymouth area. In 1774 James Warren took the celebration of Forefathers Day out of the hands of the local Tories by secretly moving part of Plymouth Rock from the harbor to a spot of honor at the foot of the liberty pole. He cracked the rock in his effort to make a dramatic appeal for the cause of democracy, indicating that the venturesome Pilgrim spirit still prevailed in Plymouth. See Jean Fritz, *Cast for a Revolution* (Boston: Houghton Mifflin, 1972), pp. 126-27.

CHAPTER 7: CHURCH OF THE PEOPLE

1. William Bradford, *Of Plymouth Plantation*, ed. Samuel Eliot Morison (New York: Knopf, 1952).
2. Ibid., pp. 3-7.
3. John Robinson, *Works* (London: John Snow, 1851), II, 367.
4. Ibid., II, 316.
5. Ibid., II, 327.
6. Ibid., II, 336-37; III, 71.
7. Ibid., III, 68.
8. Ibid., III, 33.
9. Ibid., II, 473.
10. Ibid., II, 232.
11. Ibid., II, 473.
12. Ibid., II, 231.
13. John Robinson, Appendix to William Perkins, *Six Principles of Christian Religion* in Wilberforce Eames, *Early New England Catechisms*, proceedings of the American Antiquarian Society, XII (1899), 85.
14. Robinson, *Works*, op. cit., II, 132.
15. Ibid., II, 19.
16. Ibid., II, 398.
17. Henry M. Dexter, *The England and Holland of the*

Pilgrims (Boston: Houghton Mifflin Co., 1909), p. 554.

18. Robinson, *Works*, op. cit., III, 61.
19. Ibid., III, 141.
20. Ibid., II, 363.
21. Ibid., II, 61.
22. Ibid., III, 277.
23. Edmund S. Morgan, *Puritan Political Ideas* (Indianapolis: Bobbs-Merrill, 1966), xxxiv.
24. Robinson, *Works*, op. cit., II, 374-77.
25. Ibid., III, 431.
26. Ibid., II, 42-43.
27. *Plymouth Church Records*, I, 143-80.
28. Robinson, *Works*, op. cit., II, 110-11, 284.
29. Ibid., II, 257-70.
30. Ibid., I, xxx.
31. William Perkins, *Works* (Cambridge, 1603), I, 753.
32. *Plymouth Church Records*, I, 116.
33. John Robinson, "A Justification for Separation from the Church of England" (1610), p. 433.
34. Edward Winslow, *Hypocrisie Unmasked* (London, 1646).
35. John Clarke, *Ill News from New England* (1652) in *Massachusetts Historical Society Collection*, 4th Ser., II, 46.
36. Robinson, *Works*, op. cit., I, 41-42.
37. Bradford, *Of Plymouth Plantation*, op. cit., pp. 224-25.
38. John Cotton, *The Way of the Churches of Christ in New England*, p. 41.
39. Robinson, *Works*, op. cit., I, 139.
40. Virginius Dabney, *Virginia: The New Dominion* (New York: Doubleday, 1971), p. 22.
41. Robinson, *Works*, op. cit., I, 138.
42. *Plymouth Colony Records* (1623-82), p. 113.

43. William Brigham, *The Compact with the Charter and Laws of the Colony of New Plymouth* (Boston: Dutton & Wentworth, 1836), p. 113.

44. Ibid., p. 158.

45. Robinson, *Works*, op. cit., III, 132.

46. Ibid., II, 467.

47. George Bishop, *New England Judged by the Spirit of the Lord* (London, 1667), pp. 131-32.

48. *Plymouth Church Records*, I; *Mayflower Descendant*, V, 214-15; Cotton Family, *Letter Book*, "Of the Visible Church of Christ Under ye Gospel" (Pilgrim Hall, Pilgrim Society, Plymouth), records a church covenant of the early 1730s. Cf. Patrick Collinson, *The Elizabethan Puritan Movement* (Berkeley, Calif.: University of California Press, 1967); Marshall M. Knappen, *Tudor Puritanism: A Chapter in the History of Idealism* (Chicago: University of Chicago Press, 1939); Champlin Burrage, *The Church Covenant Idea: Its Origin and Development* (Philadelphia, 1904); Henry M. Dexter, *The Congregationalism of the Last Three Hundred Years* (New York, 1880) and *Congregationalism as Seen in Its Literature* (Boston, 1880). On the Half-Way Covenant, see David D. Hall, *The Faithful Shepherd: A History of the New England Ministry in the Seventeenth Century* (Chapel Hill, N.C.: University of North Carolina Press, 1972), pp. 21ff., and Williston Walker, *Creeds and Platforms of Congregationalism* (Philadelphia: United Church Press, 1960), p. 417.

In June 1865 the National Council of Congregational Churches met in Boston, with 502 delegates and 16 representatives from Congregational bodies in foreign lands attending. They made a pilgrimage to Plymouth and assembled on June 22 near the site of the first meetinghouse and the resting place of their

Pilgrim forebears. They adopted the Burial Hill Declaration, a pioneer statement on Christian unity:

"In the times that are before us as a nation, times at once of duty and of danger, we rest all our hope in the gospel of the Son of God. It was the grand peculiarity of our Puritan Fathers, that they held this gospel . . . and applied its principles to elevate society, to regulate education, to civilize humanity, to purify law, to reform the Church and the State, and to assert and defend liberty. . . . It was the faith of our fathers that gave us this free land in which we dwell. . . .

"We hold it to be a distinctive excellence of our Congregational system, that it exalts that which is more, above that which is less, important, and by the simplicity of its organization, facilitates, in communities where the population is limited, the union of all true believers in one Christian church; and that the division of such communities into several weak and jealous societies, holding the same common faith, is a sin against the unity of the body of Christ, and at once the shame and the scandal of Christendom.

"We rejoice that, through the influence of our free system of apostolic order, we can hold fellowship with all who acknowledge Christ; and act efficiently in the work of restoring unity to the divided Church, and of bringing back harmony and peace among all 'who love our Lord Jesus Christ in sincerity.'

"Thus recognizing the unity of the Church of Christ in all the world, and knowing that we are but one branch of Christ's people, while adhering to our own peculiar faith and order, we extend to all believers the hand of Christian fellowship, upon the basis of those great fundamental truths in which all Christians should agree.

"Affirming now our belief that those who thus

hold 'one faith, one Lord, one baptism,' together constitute the one Catholic Church, the several households of which, though called by different names,
are the one body of Christ; and that these members
of his body are sacredly bound to keep 'the unity of
the spirit in the bond of peace,' *we declare that we
will cooperate with all who hold these truths.*" (Williston Walker, *Creeds and Platforms of Congregationalism* [Philadelphia: United Church Press, 1960], pp.
563-64.)

For information on later developments in the Con-
gregational Way, see Douglas Horton, *The United
Church of Christ* (New York: Thomas Nelson, Inc.,
1962); Marion L. Starkey, *The Congregational Way*
(New York: Doubleday, 1966); Gaius G. Atkins and
Frederick L. Fagley, *History of American Congrega-
tionalism* (Boston: Pilgrim Press, 1942), Daniel Jen-
kins, *Congregationalism: A Restatement* (New York:
Harper & Bros., 1954); David Dunn and others, *A
History of the Evangelical and Reformed Church*
(Philadelphia: United Church Press, 1961).

The Pilgrim emphasis on tolerance and fellowship
set the Congregationalists in the forefront of efforts
to achieve Christian unity. The International Congre-
gational Union was formed in 1891, embracing the
Congregational Union of England and Wales, the
Congregational Church of the U.S.A., the Reformed
(Huguenot) Church of France, the Church of the
Palatinate in the Rhineland, and Remonstrants of
Holland (followers of Arminius who endeavored to
liberalize Calvinism), and the Covenant Church of
Sweden (which sought to liberalize Lutheranism).
This was one of the early efforts to create an interna-
tional Christian fellowship.

The Christian Church in the United States, with its

emphasis on the autonomous congregation built after the New Testament pattern, united with the Congregational Churches in 1929, creating the Congregational Christian Churches.

In 1957 the Congregational Christian Churches united with the Evangelical and Reformed Church to form the United Church of Christ. John Philip Boehm, a teacher from the Palatinate, came to Pennsylvania in 1720 and founded the Reformed Church, which had close ties with the Dutch Reformed. He was followed by members of the Evangelical Church from Germany and Switzerland. These independent seekers for religious freedom united in 1934 to form the Evangelical and Reformed Church. This union led in time to affiliation with the Congregationalists. Thus was brought to fulfillment the efforts of the Pilgrims in Holland to demonstrate that "we should be one brotherhood of all."

CHAPTER 8: PILGRIM ETHICS

1. William Bradford, *Of Plymouth Plantation*, ed. Samuel Eliot Morison (New York: Knopf, 1952).
2. John Robinson, *Works* (London: John Snow, 1851), I, 34.
3. Ibid., I, 117-18.
4. William Perkins in ibid., III, 191.
5. Ibid., I, 113.
6. Ibid., I, 114-15
7. The Geneva Bible, marginal comment, Acts 17:6.
8. Emmanuel Altham in *Three Visitors to Early Plymouth*, ed. Sidney V. James (Plymouth: Plimoth Plantation, 1963), pp. 11-15.
9. Ibid., p. 29.

10. In *Massachusetts Historical Society Collection*, 2d Ser., V (1822), 183.
11. Bradford, *Of Plymouth Plantation*, op. cit., p. 97.
12. George Haskins, "The Legacy of Plymouth," *Social Education*, Vol. 26, No. 1 (January 1962).
13. *Book of Laws* (1685), p. 47.
14. *Plymouth Colony Records* (1638), I, 38.
15. Ibid., I, 68.
16. Edwin Powers, *Crime and Punishment in Early Massachusetts 1620-92* (Boston: Beacon Press, 1966), p. 181.
17. Thomas J. Wertenbaker, *The Puritan Oligarchy* (New York: Charles Scribner's Sons, 1947), p. 167.
18. George D. Langdon, Jr., *Pilgrim Colony: A History of New Plymouth 1620-1691* (New Haven, Conn.: Yale University Press, 1966), pp. 308-9.
19. Robert Cushman in Alexander Young, *Chronicles of the Pilgrim Fathers* (Boston: Little, Brown & Co., 1841), p. 264.
20. Bradford, *Of Plymouth Plantation*, op. cit., p. 120.
21. Ibid., p. 121.
22. Ibid., p. 174.
23. Ibid., p. 113.
24. William Bradford, *Letter Book* (Massachusetts Mayflower Society, 1901), pp. 58-59.
25. Samuel Eliot Morison, *The Old Colony of New Plymouth* (New York: Knopf, 1956), pp. 152-53.
26. George F. Willison, *Saints and Strangers* (New York: Harcourt, Brace, 1945), p. 261.
27. Morison, *The Old Colony of New Plymouth*, op. cit., p. 130.
28. John C. Miller, *This New Man, the American: The Beginnings of the American People* (New York: McGraw-Hill, 1974), pp. 122ff.
29. Charles and Katherine George, *The Protestant Mind*

of the *English Reformation, 1570-1640* (Princeton, N.J.: Princeton University Press, 1961), p. 160.

30. Bradford, *Of Plymouth Plantation*, op. cit., p. 327.
31. Ibid.
32. Ibid.
33. Cotton Mather, *Magnalia Christi Americana* (London, 1702), II, 305.
34. Edward Arber, *The Story of the Pilgrim Fathers, 1606-1623* (London: Ward & Downey, 1897), p. 44.
35. Bradford, *Of Plymouth Plantation*, op. cit., p. 260.
36. Ibid., p. 170.
37. Nathaniel Morton, *New-Englands Memoriall* (Boston, 1669).
38. Ibid., p. 230.
39. *Mayflower Descendant*, XVIII, 34ff.
40. *Plymouth Colony Deeds*, I and II, 271.
41. Morton, *New-Englands Memoriall*, op. cit.
42. *Plymouth Wills.*
43. Bradford, *Of Plymouth Plantation*, op. cit., pp. 240-46.
44. *Court Orders*, Vol. 904, pp. 56-57.
45. Bernard Bailyn, *The New England Merchants of the Seventeenth Century* (Cambridge, Mass.: Harvard University Press, 1955), pp. 41, 115.
46. *Massachusetts Historical Records*, I, 290; Robert Keayne, *Apologie*, ed. Bernard Bailyn, *William & Mary Quarterly*, 3d Ser., VII (1950), 508ff.
47. Bradford, *Of Plymouth Plantation*, op. cit., p. 234.
48. Morton, *New-Englands Memoriall*, op. cit., p. 68.
49. Bradford, *Of Plymouth Plantation*, op. cit., p. 234.
50. Willison, *Saints and Strangers*, op. cit., pp. 437-53.

For further reference on Pilgrim ethics, see Michael Walzer, *The Revolution of the Saints: A Study in the Origins of Radical Politics* (Cambridge, Mass.: Harvard University Press, 1965), pp. 278ff.; Alan Simpson, *Puritanism in Old and New England* (Chicago: University of Chicago Press, 1955), chap. "The Covenanted Community"; Alice Morse Earle, *The Sabbath in Puritan New England* (New York, 1893).

John E. Pomfret and Floyd M. Shumway, in *Founding the American Colonies, 1583-1660* (New York: Harper & Row, 1970), state that the main purpose of the Pilgrims "was to attain to the Kingdom of Heaven, and while working to earn this reward, they endeavored to lead exemplary Christian lives [p. 129]."

Carl Bridenbaugh, in *Vexed and Troubled Englishmen, 1590-1642* (New York: Oxford University Press, 1968), states: "Between 1620 and 1642 close to 80,000 or 2% of all Englishmen, left Britain. They forsook not only their homes but their homeland in the quest for a better life [p. 395]."

Misinterpretation of Pilgrim ethics is common, as is illustrated by an editorial in *The Councilor* (Shrevesport, La.), Summer 1975: "Socialism is not a new experiment in the United States. Neither is Communism. The Socialist community was tried by the Pilgrims in New England over three hundred years ago. The dream of the Pilgrims didn't work and the Mayflower Compact was a total failure [p. 35]."

The facts are sadly distorted. It was the communal program, demanded by the London Merchant Adventurers, against the desires of the Pilgrims, and bitterly opposed by them, that was a dismal failure. This system of forced labor, without personal profit, was not socialism or communism. It proved an unfair and ineffective business arrangement and was promptly replaced by private enterprise, due to the sound business judgment of the Pilgrims.

CHAPTER 9: NO ONE TURNED AWAY

1. John Robinson, *Works* (London: John Snow, 1851).
2. William Bradford, *Of Plymouth Plantation*, ed. Samuel Eliot Morison (New York: Knopf, 1952), p. 103.
3. Ibid., p. 189.
4. Ibid., p. 192.
5. John Winthrop, *Journal*.
6. Nathaniel Morton, *New-Englands Memoriall* (Boston, 1669), p. 79.
7. Bradford, *Of Plymouth Plantation*, op. cit., pp. 108-11.
8. Ibid., p. 119.
9. Ibid., p. 120.
10. Ibid., p. 138.
11. Ibid., p. 204.
12. Ibid., pp. 204-5.
13. Ibid.
14. Edward Winslow, *New England's Salamander* (London, 1647), *Massachusetts Historical Society Collection*, 3d Ser. (1830), p. 172.
15. Thomas Morton in ibid., pp. 172-73.
16. Bradford, *Of Plymouth Plantation*, op. cit., pp. 273-75.
17. Ibid., pp. 233-35.
18. Ibid., pp. 216-17.
19. Ibid., pp. 378-79.
20. Ibid.
21. J.F. Jameson, ed., *Narratives of New Netherlands, 1609-1664* (New York: Barnes & Noble, 1909), pp. 102-15.
22. Bradford, *Of Plymouth Plantation*, op. cit., pp. 257-60.
23. Ibid.
24. Ibid., p. 280.
25. Ibid., p. 281.
26. Ibid., pp. 282-84.
27. Ibid., p. 290.

28. Ibid.
29. R. G. Thwaites, *Jesuit Relations and Allied Documents* (Cleveland, 1897), XXXVI, 91.

CHAPTER 10: NATIVE NEIGHBORS

1. In *Mourt's Relations*, ed. Dwight Heath (New York: Citadel Press, 1963).
2. Henry S. Burrage, ed., *Early English and French Voyages, 1534-1608* (New York: Barnes & Noble, 1906), p. 391.
3. *Mourt's Relations*, op. cit., pp. 35-37, 52.
4. Ibid., p. 70.
5. Ibid., pp. 77-80.
6. Ibid., pp. 22-23.
7. Ibid., pp. 77ff.
8. Ibid., pp. 80-81.
9. In Alexander Young, *Chronicles of the Pilgrim Fathers* (Boston: Little, Brown & Co., 1841), pp. 258-59.
10. *The New York Times*, November 27, 1970.
11. Virginius Dabney, *Virginia: The New Dominion* (New York: Doubleday, 1971), p. 21.
12. Alden T. Vaughan, *New England Frontier: Puritans and Indians, 1620-1675* (Boston: Little, Brown & Co., 1965), p. 65.
13. William Bradford, *Of Plymouth Plantation*, ed. Samuel Eliot Morison (New York: Knopf, 1952), p. 114.
14. Ibid., pp. 88-89.
15. Edward Winslow, *Good News from New England*; Edward Arber, *The Story of the Pilgrim Fathers, 1606-1623* (London: Ward & Downey, 1897), pp. 350-53.
16. *Massachusetts Historical Society Collection*, 3d Ser. (1834), pp. 72-74, 93-95; Edward Winslow, *The Glorious Progress of the Gospel Among the Indians*

in New England; Roger Williams, *The Complete Works* (New York, 1933), I, 84.

17. Bradford, *Of Plymouth Plantation*, op. cit., p. 21.
18. Winslow, *Good News from New England*.
19. In Bradford, *Of Plymouth Plantation*, op. cit., pp. 374-75.
20. Ibid., p. 271.
21. Ibid.
22. John Winthrop, *Journal*, I, 241.
23. Nathaniel Morton, *New-Englands Memoriall* (Boston, 1669).
24. *Plymouth Colony Records*, II, 41.
25. In Winifred Cockshott, *The Pilgrim Fathers* (New York: G. P. Putnam, 1909), p. 271.
26. *Plymouth Colony Records*, IV, 177-78; V, 31, 152.
27. *Plymouth Court Orders*, p. 161.
28. *Plymouth Colony Records*, I and II, 133.
29. Ibid., III and IV, 21.
30. Bradford, *Of Plymouth Plantation*, op. cit., pp. 294-301.
31. *Plymouth Court Orders*.
32. Bradford, *Of Plymouth Plantation*, op. cit., p. 301.
33. Winslow, *Good News from New England*, op. cit., pp. 489-90.
34. Williams, *The Complete Works*, op. cit., 91-98, 160.
35. Winslow, *The Glorious Progress of the Gospel*, op. cit., p. 75.
36. David Pulsifer, ed., *Acts of the Commissioners of the United Colonies*, pp. 277-79.
37. John Cotton, Jr., *Journal*.
38. George D. Langdon, Jr., *Pilgrim Colony: A History of New Plymouth, 1620-1691* (New Haven, Conn.: Yale University Press, 1966), p. 155.
39. *Plymouth Colony Records*, II, 41.
40. For advocates of the land lust theory of the war, see

James T. Adams, *The Founding of New England*
(Boston, 1921), and George L. Howe, *Mount Hope:
A New England Chronicle* (New York: Viking
Press, 1959). Cf. Alden T. Vaughan, *New England
Frontier: Indians and Puritans* (Boston: Little, Brown
& Co., 1965), p. 214.

41. Winthrop, *Journal*, II, 83-98.
42. *Plymouth Church Records.*
43. Josiah Winslow to John Winthrop, Jr., *Massachusetts
Historical Society Collection*, 5th Ser., No. 1, 428.
44. *Plymouth Church Records*, I, 149-53.
45. Douglas E. Leach, *Flintlock and Tomahawk: New
England in King Philip's War* (New York: W.W.
Norton & Co., 1966), pp. 243-50.
46. Ola E. Winslow, *Master Roger Williams* (New York:
Macmillan, 1957), p. 260.

Thomas Walley, minister of the Barnstable church,
said in 1669 that the colony was full of sick souls:
"Faith is dead and Love is cold. The power of godliness decays, the trumpet sounds, the alarm is given
yet the most sleep on." (Thomas Walley, *Balm in
Gilead to Heal Sions Wounds* [Cambridge, 1669],
p. 9.)

The Plymouth church pledged to "lye in the dust
before God" when John Cotton upbraided the colony,
saying: "We have greatly lost our first love to and
precious esteem of the Gospel and the ordinances of
the Lord Jesus." (*Plymouth Church Records*, I, 45 ff.)

For details on King Philip's War, see Benjamin
Church, *Entertaining Passages Relating to Philip's War*
(Boston, 1716), and William Hubbard, *A Narrative
of the Indian Wars in New England* (Danbury, 1803).
For efforts to help the Indians, see John Eliot, *A Briefe
Narrative of the Progress of the Gospel amongst the
Indians in New England* (London, 1671), and Lloyd

C. Hare, *Thomas Mayhew: Patriarch to the Indians* (New York, 1932).

CHAPTER 11: NO WITCHES IN PLYMOUTH

1. John Robinson, *Works* (London: John Snow, 1851).
2. George F. Kittredge, *Witchcraft in Old and New England* (New York: Russell & Russell, 1958), pp. 331ff.
3. *A Tryal of Witches at the Assizes at Bury St. Edmunds* (London, 1664), p. 41.
4. Cotton Mather, *Wonders of the Invisible World*, 1693.
5. Ibid.; see Kai T. Erikson, *Wayward Puritans, A Study in the Sociology of Deviance* (New York: John Wiley & Sons, 1966), chap. 3, and Sally Smith Booth, *The Witches of Early America* (New York: Hastings House, 1975).
6. In George L. Burr, ed. *Narratives of the Witchcraft Cases, 1648-1706* (New York: Charles Scribner's Sons, 1914; New York: Barnes & Noble, 1959).
7. *Diary of Samuel Sewall*, ed. Harvey Wish (New York: G.P. Putnam, 1967), pp. 140ff.
8. Robert Calef, *More Wonders of the Invisible World* (London, 1700), pp. 387-88.
9. *Massachusetts Historical Society Collection*, 7th Ser., 47, 215.
10. *A Confrontation and Discovery of Witchcraft* (London, 1648).
11. Ola Elizabeth Winslow, *Samuel Sewall of Boston* (New York: Macmillan, 1964), p. 114.
12. Kittredge, *Witchcraft in Old and New England*, op. cit., p. 366.
13. Francis Hutchinson, *Historical Essay on Witchcraft* (1718).
14. *Diary of Samuel Sewall*, op. cit.
15. *Plymouth Colony Records*, III, 205-7, 211.

16. Ibid., p. 211.
17. *Plymouth Judicial Acts*, 1666-67; cf. Edwin Powers, *Crime and Punishment in Early Massachusetts, 1620-92* (Boston: Beacon Press, 1966), p. 535.

CHAPTER 12: MASTER ROGER WILLIAMS

1. Roger Williams, *The Complete Works* (New York, 1933).
2. William Bradford, *Of Plymouth Plantation*, ed. Samuel Eliot Morison (New York: Knopf, 1952), p. 148.
3. Ibid., p. 157.
4. Ibid., pp. 122-23; *Plymouth Church Records* in *Colonial Society of Massachusetts Publication*, XXII, 64.
5. Bradford, *Of Plymouth Plantation*, op. cit., pp. 122-23.
6. In Ola Elizabeth Winslow, *Master Roger Williams* (New York: Macmillan, 1957), p. 97.
7. Bradford, *Of Plymouth Plantation*, op. cit., p. 257.
8. Roger Williams, *The Bloody Tenet Yet More Bloody*, IV, 104-5.
9. Cotton Mather, *Magnalia Christi Americana* (London, 1702), VII, chap. 2.
10. In Bradford, *Of Plymouth Plantation*, op. cit., p. 257.
11. Ibid.
12. In John Goodwin, *The Pilgrim Republic* (Boston: Houghton Mifflin, 1888), pp. 378-80.
13. Nathaniel Morton, *New-Englands Memoriall* (Boston, 1669), p. 152.
14. Winslow, *Master Roger Williams*, op. cit., p. 49.
15. John Winthrop, *Journal*, I, 162-63.
16. In ibid.
17. In Goodwin, *The Pilgrim Republic*, op. cit., p. 368.
18. Bernard Bailyn, *The New England Merchants in the Seventeenth Century* (Cambridge, Mass.: Harvard University Press, 1955).
19. Edward Winslow, *Hypocrisie Unmasked* (London,

1646); cf. Alan Simpson, *Puritanism in Old and New England* (Chicago: University of Chicago Press, 1955).

20. Winslow, *Master Roger Williams*, op. cit., pp. 273-79.
21. *Records of Rhode Island Colony*, I, 28.
22. In Perry Miller, *Roger Williams, His Contribution to the American Tradition* (New York: Atheneum, 1962), pp. 236-39.
23. Ibid., pp. 225-26.
24. *Resolves of General Court of Massachusetts* (1636), chap. II.

   For additional reading on Roger Williams, see Edmund S. Morgan, *Roger Williams, The Church and the State* (New York: Harcourt Brace Jovanovich, 1968); Perry Miller, *Roger Williams, His Contribution to the American Tradition* (New York: Atheneum, 1962); Alan Simpson, "How Democratic Was Roger Williams?", *William & Mary Quarterly*, 3d Ser., XIII (1956), 53-67; John Gannett, *Roger Williams, Witness Beyond Christendom* (New York: Macmillan, 1970).

CHAPTER 13: PASTORS CHARLES CHAUNCY AND JOHN COTTON, JR.

1. In Increase Mather, *Old South Leaflet* (Boston), pp. 19-20.
2. Samuel Eliot Morison, *Three Centuries of Harvard, 1636-1936* (Cambridge, Mass.: Harvard University Press, 1936), p. 322.
3. *New England Historical and Genealogical Register*, X (1856), 253-54.
4. William Bradford, *Of Plymouth Plantation*, ed. Samuel Eliot Morison (New York: Knopf, 1952), pp. 313-14.
5. Ibid.

6. John Winthrop, *Journal*, I, 332.
7. Morison, *Three Centuries of Harvard*, op. cit., p. 314.
8. Samuel Deane, *History of Scituate* (1731), p. 182.
9. C.S.M. XV, 200-07.
10. In David D. Hall, *The Faithful Shepherd: A History of the New England Ministry in the Seventeenth Century* (Chapel Hill, N.C.: University of North Carolina Press, 1972), p. 179; Charles Chauncy, *God's Mercy, shewed to his people* (Cambridge, 1655), pp. 23-24.
11. *Old South Leaflet* 185, 20.
12. In Cotton Mather, *Magnalia Christi Americana* (London, 1702), I, 472.
13. Chauncy, *God's Mercy*, op. cit., pp. 19-20.
14. In Mather, *Magnalia*, op. cit., I.
15. Ibid., III, 136ff.
16. Ibid.
17. Chauncy, *God's Mercy*, op. cit., pp. 19-20.
18. *Massachusetts Archives*, LVIII, 35.
19. *Plymouth Court Records* (1647).
20. *Plymouth Colony Records*, II, 121.
21. Mather in *Old South Leaflet*, p. 185.
22. Ibid., pp. 19-20.
23. Ibid., pp. 172ff.
24. Bradford, *Of Plymouth Plantation*, op. cit., pp. 293, 284.
25. *Plymouth Church Records*, I, 92.
26. *Plymouth Church Records* (1668), I.
27. Edward Winslow, *Hypocrisie Unmasked* (London, 1646), p. 98; Charles Chauncy, *The Plain Doctrine of the Justification of a Sinner in the Sight of God* (London, 1659), a series of twenty-six sermons, theological in content, full of scriptural references along with Hebrew, Greek, and Latin.

CHAPTER 14: THE SERMON

1. John Robinson, *Works* (London: John Snow, 1851).
2. Ibid., II, 373.
3. Ibid., II, 502.
4. Ibid., II, 398.
5. Horton M. Davies, *The Worship of the English Puritans* (Philadelphia: Westminster Press, 1948), p. 258.
6. Douglas Bush, *English Literature in the Earlier Seventeenth Century, 1600-1660* (2d ed. rev.; New York: Oxford University Press, 1962), p. 296.
7. In Thomas Hooker, *Ecclesiastical Polity*, ed. Benjamin Hansbury (1530), II, 759.
8. Robinson, *Works*, op. cit., III, 485.
9. Ibid., II, 374-75.
10. Ibid., III, 290-98, 325-35.
11. Ibid., III, 301.
12. Ibid., II, 246-47.
13. Ibid., II, 249-51.
14. Ibid., II, 334.
15. Ibid.
16. John Winthrop, *Journal* (1908), pp. 92-94.
17. Robinson, *Works*, op. cit., I, 405.
18. Ibid., II, 54-55.
19. *The Remains of Edmund Grindal*, ed. W. Nicholson (Parker Society, 1843), p. 379.
20. *Letters, Speeches, and Proclamations of Charles I*, ed. Sir C. Petrie (1935), p. 200.
21. "English Political Sermons 1603-40," *Huntingdon Library Quarterly*, 1939, III, 1-2.
22. W.F. Adney, *Early Independents* (London: Congregational Union of England and Wales, 1895), p. 29.
23. William Haller, *The Rise of Puritanism* (New York: Columbia University Press, 1938). Cf. Joseph Gaer and Ben Siegel, *The Puritan Heritage: America's Roots*

in the Bible (New York: New American Library, 1964), p. 23; Marshall M. Knappen, *Tudor Puritanism: A Chapter in the History of Idealism* (Chicago: University of Chicago Press, 1939), pp. 200ff.; Darrett B. Rutman, *American Puritanism: Faith and Practice* (Philadelphia: J.B. Lippincott, 1970), pp. 106ff.; Robert M. Bartlett, *The Pilgrim Way* (Philadelphia: United Church Press, 1971), chaps. 3 and 8.

CHAPTER 15: PRAYER

1. William Bradford, *Of Plymouth Plantation*, ed. Samuel Eliot Morison (New York: Knopf, 1952).
2. Ibid., p. 47.
3. Ibid., p. 76.
4. Ibid., p. 61.
5. *Mourt's Relations*, ed. Dwight Heath (New York: Citadel Press, 1963), p. 35.
6. Bradford, *Of Plymouth Plantation*, op. cit., pp. 71-72.
7. *Mourt's Relations*, op. cit., p. 40.
8. Bradford, *Of Plymouth Plantation*, op. cit., p. 130.
9. Edward Winslow, *Good News from New England*; Edward Arber, *The Story of the Pilgrim Fathers, 1606-1623* (London: Ward & Downey, 1897), pp. 377-79.
10. Winslow, *Good News from New England*.
11. *Record of Plymouth Colony Court Orders*, III-IV, 5.
12. In F.J. Powicke, *John Robinson* (London: Hodder & Stoughton, 1920), pp. 52-54.
13. John Robinson, *Works* (London: John Snow, 1851), I, 142.
14. Ibid., III, 21.
15. Ibid., III, 28.
16. Ibid., II, 276.
17. Ibid., II, 254.
18. Ibid., III, 131.
19. Ibid., II, 300-01.

20. Bradford, *Of Plymouth Plantation*, op. cit., p. 328.
21. Nathaniel Morton, *New-Englands Memoriall* (Boston, 1669), p. 334.

    See also Horton M. Davies, *The Worship of the English Puritans* (Philadelphia: Westminster Press, 1948); Gordon S. Wakefield, *Puritan Devotion: Its Place in the Development of Christian Piety* (London: Epworth Press, 1957), pp. 22ff.; Geoffrey F. Nuttall, *Visible Saints: The Congregational Way, 1640-1660* (Oxford: Basil Blackwell, 1957).

CHAPTER 16: MUSIC

1. Edward Winslow, *Hypocrisie Unmasked* (London, 1646).
2. John Calvin, *Sermons*, p. 66.
3. John Calvin, *Institutes*, I, IV.
4. *Puritan Documents relating to the Settlement of the Church of England by the Act of Uniformity of 1662* (London, 1662), p. 24.
5. Horton M. Davies, *The Worship of the English Puritans* (Philadelphia: Westminster Press, 1948), pp. 17ff.
6. Waldo S. Pratt, *The Music of the Pilgrims* (Boston: Oliver Ditson, 1921).
7. In ibid., pp. 8-13.
8. Henry Ainsworth, *The Book of Psalmes: Englished both in Prose and Metre* (Amsterdam, Giles Thorp, 1612), pp. 65, 225, 253, 319.
9. Ibid.
10. Ibid.
11. Ibid.
12. *Bay Psalm Book* (Cambridge, 1640); facsimile reprint, introduction by Wilberforce Eames (New York, 1903).

13. Carl Bridenbaugh, *Vexed and Troubled Englishmen, 1590-1642* (New York: Oxford University Press, 1968), pp. 348ff.
14. Wallace Notestein, *The English People on the Eve of Colonization, 1603-1630* (New York: Harper & Bros., 1954), pp. 111-12.
15. Alfred L. Rowse, *The England of Elizabeth* (New York: Macmillan, 1951), pp. 25-26.
16. Percy A. Scholes, *Puritans and Music in England and New England* (New York: Oxford University Press, 1934).
17. Edward Winslow, *A Brief Narration* in Alexander Young, *Chronicles of the Pilgrim Fathers* (Boston: Little, Brown & Co., 1841).
18. *Diary of Samuel Sewall*, ed. Harvey Wish (New York: G. P. Putnam, 1967).
19. Scholes, *Puritans and Music in England and New England*, op. cit., p. 50.
20. Marshall M. Knappen, *Tudor Puritanism: A Chapter in the History of Idealism* (Chicago: University of Chicago Press, 1939).
21. *Plymouth Court Order*, p. 188.
22. Sidney V. James, ed., *Three Visitors to Early Plymouth* (Plymouth: Plimoth Plantation, 1963).

On music and dancing, cf. Alfred L. Rowse, *The Elizabethan Renaissance: The Life of Society* (New York: Charles Scribner's Sons, 1971), pp. 247-50. William Brewster's interest in music is indicated by the books in his library, such as Richard Alison, *The Psalmes of David in Metre* (1559), Thomas Ravenscroft, *The Whole Book of Psalmes* (1592), Philip Steele, *The Earliest English Music Printing* (to 1660), and psalm books by Ainsworth, Johnson, and Hopkins and Sternhold. *Massachusetts Historical Society Proceedings*, 2d Ser., V, 45, 64, 72.

CHAPTER 17: THE SACRAMENTS

1. Edward Winslow, *Hypocrisie Unmasked* (London, 1646).
2. W.H. Frere and C.C. Douglas, *Puritan Manifestoes* (New York: Burt Franklin Pub., 1907), p. 13.
3. *A Parte of a Register* (London, 1586).
4. John Robinson, *Works* (London: John Snow, 1851), II, 98.
5. In William Bradford, *Of Plymouth Plantation*, ed. Samuel Eliot Morison (New York: Knopf, 1952), p. 353.
6. In ibid., p. 354.
7. Robinson, *Works*, op. cit., II, 418.
8. Ibid., III, 169.
9. Ibid., III, 168.
10. Ibid., II, 334.
11. Ibid., I, 462.
12. Ibid., III, 185; II, 417.
13. Ibid., III, 201; cf. E. Brooks Holifield, *The Covenant Sealed: The Development of Puritan Sacramental Theology in Old and New England* (New Haven, Conn.: Yale University Press, 1974), pp. 65ff.
14. Robinson, *Works*, op. cit., III, 181.
15. Ibid., III, 45.
16. Ibid., III, 46.
17. Bradford, *Of Plymouth Plantation*, op. cit., pp. 224-25.
18. John Winthrop, *Journal*, I, 95.
19. William Bradford, *Dialogue* (Boston, 1870), p. 45.
20. Robinson, *Works*, op. cit., III, 414.
21. John A. Goodwin, *The Pilgrim Republic* (Boston: Houghton Mifflin, 1888), p. 389; *Life and Records of John Howland of Rhode Island*, p. 491.
22. Bradford, *Of Plymouth Plantation*, op. cit., p. 25.
    For further information on the Leyden Pilgrims'

views on baptism, see Robert M. Bartlett, *The Pilgrim Way* (Philadelphia: United Church Press, 1971), pp. 151-57, and B.R. White, *The English Separatist Tradition: From the Marian Martyrs to the Pilgrim Fathers* (New York: Oxford University Press, 1971), pp. 133-41.

The Roman Catholic Church accepted seven sacraments. At one point in the Middle Ages there were twelve.

CHAPTER 18: TIES WITH CALVINISM

1. John Robinson, *Works* (London: John Snow, 1851).
2. Roger Williams, *The Complete Works* (New York, 1933).
3. In W.H. Frere and C.C. Douglas, *Puritan Manifestoes* (New York: Burt Franklin Pub., 1907), p. 45.
4. John Milton, *Works*, ed. F.A. Patterson and others (New York: Somerset Pub., reprint of 1931 ed.), V, 52.
5. Thomas Shepard, *Autobiography* (Boston, 1832), pp. 92-93.
6. William Haller, *The Rise of Puritanism* (New York: Columbia University Press, 1938), pp. 85ff.
7. Samuel Eliot Morison, *The Puritan Pronoas* (New York: New York University Press, 1956), p. 155.
8. B.R. White, *The English Separatist Tradition: From the Marian Martyrs to the Pilgrim Fathers* (New York: Oxford University Press, 1971), p. xiv.
9. In John T. McNeill, *The History and Character of Calvinism* (New York: Oxford University Press, 1954), p. 198.
10. Haller, *The Rise of Puritanism*, op. cit., p. 192.
11. John Calvin's "Reply to the Letter of Cardinal Sadolet to the Senate and People of Geneva" (1535), in *Theo-*

logical Treatises, ed. John K. Reid (Philadelphia: Westminster Press, 1954), p. 228.

12. John Calvin, *Institutes*, I, xiv, 18.
13. Cf. Michael Walzer, *The Revolution of the Saints: A Study in the Origins of Radical Politics* (Cambridge, Mass.: Harvard University Press, 1965), pp. 215ff., 278ff.
14. Robert Cushman in Alexander Young, *Chronicles of the Pilgrim Fathers* (Boston: Little, Brown & Co., 1841), pp. 258ff.
15. Walzer, *The Revolution of the Saints*, op. cit., preface.
16. Paul Baynes, *A Commentarie upon the first chapter of Ephesians* (1643), pp. 114, 83.
17. Robinson, *Works*, op. cit., III, 239.
18. Ibid., III, 39.
19. Ibid., III, 238.
20. Ibid., I, 67.

Leonard J. Trinterud argued in *Church History* (March 1951), pp. 37-55, that Puritanism was indigenous, not alien to England. He stated that the foreign influences taken up by the English Puritans as they sought to give intellectual content to their ideas were not primarily from John Calvin of Geneva but from the Reformers of the Rhineland: Zwingli, Jud, Bullinger, Oecolampadius, Capito, Bucer, Martyr, and other leaders in the Reformation in Zurich, Basel, Strasbourg, and other Rhineland cities. During King Edward's reign there came to England a number of Rhineland leaders like Peter Martyr, Bucer, Tremellius, Fagius, and Drylander. The Marian exile was decisive for the English Reformation since it brought numerous leading ministers and theologians out of England into the Rhineland cities.

Samuel Eliot Morison, in *The Puritan Pronoas* (New

York: New York University Press, 1956), p. 55, stated that the founders of New England were far from being strict Calvinists and that the first New England Calvinist was Jonathan Edwards.

For a full discussion of the Antinomian controversy in the Bay Colony, see David D. Hall, ed., *The Antinomian Controversy, 1636-1638: A Documentary History* (Middletown, Conn.: Wesleyan University Press, 1968).

John T. McNeill, *The History and Character of Calvinism*, op. cit., p. 342, pointed out that the Dutch settlers who followed Henry Hudson to New York were Walloon and Huguenot Calvinists. Worship was conducted by laypersons until 1628, when Jonas Michaelius, a Leyden graduate, organized a church in New Amsterdam. He was preceded by and aided by Comforters of the Sick, who carried on minor pastoral duties similar to deacons. In 1640 it was declared that only the Reformed Church was to be permitted in New Netherlands. A Lutheran minister who came to organize a church was sent back to Holland.

Alan Simpson stated: "The essence of Puritanism is an experience of conversion which separates the Puritan from the mass of mankind and endows him with the privileges and duties of the elect. The root of the matter is always a new birth, which brings with it a conviction of salvation and dedication to warfare against sin." ("The Puritan Tradition," *Puritanism in Old and New England* [Chicago: University of Chicago Press, 1955], pp. 99-114.)

For the story of the Remonstrants, see George O. McCulloch and G.J. Hoenderdall, *Man's Faith and Freedom: The Theological Influence of Jacob Arminius* (Nashville: Abingdon Press, 1962).

CHAPTER 19: PILGRIMS AND PURITANS

1. John Robinson, *Works* (London: John Snow, 1851).
2. *A Parte of a Register* (London, 1586).
3. In Cotton Mather, *Magnalia Christi Americana* (London, 1702), III, 11.
4. In William Bradford, *Of Plymouth Plantation*, ed. Samuel Eliot Morison (New York: Knopf, 1952), pp. 223-24.
5. William Bradford, *Letter Book* (Massachusetts Mayflower Society, 1901).
6. William W. Sweet, *Religion in Colonial America* (New York: Cooper Square Publishers, 1942).
7. Bradford, *Letter Book*, op. cit., pp. 57-58.
8. Ibid., pp. 58-59.
9. Ibid.
10. Ibid., p. 56.
11. John Winthrop, *Journal* in Alexander Young, *Chronicles of the Pilgrim Fathers* (Boston: Little, Brown & Co., 1841), p. 296.
12. Bradford, *Of Plymouth Plantation*, op. cit., p. 236.
13. John Winthrop, *Journal*, I, 51-52.
14. Ibid., I, 55-56, 11.
15. Ibid., I, 128.
16. Bradford, *Letter Book*, op. cit., p. 56.
17. George F. Willison, *Saints and Strangers* (New York: Harcourt, Brace, 1945), p. 272.
18. *Massachusetts Historical Society Collection*, Ser. III, 74.
19. Willison, *Saints and Strangers*, op. cit., p. 272.
20. William Rathband, *A Brief Narration of Some Courses* (1694), pp. 54-55.
21. Edward Winslow, *Hypocrisie Unmasked* (London, 1646), p. 92; *Plymouth Church Records*, I, 123.
22. Winslow, *Hypocrisie Unmasked*, op. cit., p. 92.

23. William Bradford, *Dialogue* in Young, *Chronicles of the Pilgrim Fathers*, op. cit., p. 426.
24. In Perry Miller, *Orthodoxy in Massachusetts, 1630-60* (Cambridge, Mass.: Harvard University Press, 1933), p. 100.
25. John Cotton, *Way of the Congregational Churches Cleared* (London, 1642), p. 82.
26. Ibid., p. 190.
27. Ibid., p. 25.
28. Ibid., p. 195.
29. William Hooke, *New England Sence, of Old England and Ireland Sorrowes* (London, 1695).
30. David D. Hall, *The Faithful Shepherd: A History of the New England Ministry in the Seventeenth Century* (Chapel Hill, N.C.: University of North Carolina Press, 1972), p. 81.
31. Larzer Ziff, *The Career of John Cotton* (Princeton, N.J.: Princeton University Press, 1962), p. 203.
32. Cotton, *Way of the Congregational Churches Cleared*, op. cit., p. 8.
33. Richard Mather, *Church Government and Covenant Discussed* (London, 1643), p. 82.
34. William Haller, *The Rise of Puritanism* (New York: Columbia University Press, 1938), p. 189.
35. Williston Walker, *Creeds and Platforms of Congregationalism* (Philadelphia: United Church Press, 1960), p. 185.
36. John A. Rickard, *History of England* (New York: Barnes & Noble, 1953), chap. VI; George D. Langdon, Jr., *Pilgrim Colony: A History of New Plymouth, 1620-1691* (New Haven, Conn.: Yale University Press, 1966), chaps. 16 and 17.

For the founding of the Bay Colony, see Samuel Eliot Morison, *The Oxford History of the American People* (New York: Oxford University Press, 1965),

p. 65, and John E. Pomfret and Floyd M. Shumway, *Founding the American Colonies, 1583-1660* (New York: Harper & Row, 1970), pp. 161ff.

See Larzer Ziff, *The Career of John Cotton*, op. cit., p. 190, for Richard Mather's statement on Congregationalism in New England.

Indifference to the facts of the Pilgrim-Puritan story has been widespread. Perry Miller wrote in 1961: "All around me, in the 1920s, I was being shown by the pundits and philosophers whom I respected, that 'Puritanism' was the source of everything that had proved wrong, frustrating, inhibiting, crippling in American culture. I recall that my stubborn decision to write upon Puritanism was reenforced by my sense that it was an unfathomable subject. My obstinacy was further strengthened when one of my instructors told me that the subject was exhausted, that nothing more was to be discovered, and that I ought to devote my youthful energies to some subject more relevant to the twentieth century." (*The New England Mind: The Seventeenth Century* [Cambridge, Mass.: Harvard University Press, 1961], preface.)

The general, prevailing ignorance of the Pilgrim Story is illustrated by the account of the first meeting of the Old Colony Club in Plymouth in 1770 to commemorate the landing of the Pilgrims. Toasts were made "to pious ancestors": Carver, Morton, Standish, Massasoit, and Cushman, but the names of Brewster, Bradford, Winslow, Fuller, Alden, Willet, Collier, Howland, and Warren were not even mentioned. See *Massachusetts Historical Society Collection*, 2d Ser., III, 400-401.

Index